CAMBRIDGE COMPANIONS TO LITERATURE

CAMBRIDGE COMPANIONS TO CULTURE

THE CAMBRIDGE COMPANION TO

CHARLES DICKENS

EDITED BY

JOHN O. JORDAN

CAMBRIDGE
UNIVERSITY PRESS

PUBLISHED BY THE PRESS SYNDICATE OF THE UNIVERSITY OF CAMBRIDGE
The Pitt Building, Trumpington Street, Cambridge, United Kingdom

CAMBRIDGE UNIVERSITY PRESS
The Edinburgh Building, Cambridge CB2 2RU, UK
40 West 20th Street, New York, NY 10011-4211, USA
10 Stamford Road, Oakleigh, VIC 3166, Australia
Ruiz de Alarcón 13, 28014 Madrid, Spain
Dock House, The Waterfront, Cape Town 8001, South Africa

http://www.cambridge.org

First published 2001

Printed in the United Kingdom at the University Press, Cambridge

Typeface Adobe Sabon 10/13pt   *System* QuarkXPress™   [SE]

A catalogue record for this book is available from the British Library

Library of Congress Cataloguing in Publication data

The Cambridge companion to Charles Dickens / edited by John O. Jordan.
p.   cm. – (Cambridge companions to literature)
Includes bibliographical references (p. 224) and index.
ISBN 0 521 66016 5 – ISBN 0 521 66964 2 (pb.)
1. Dickens, Charles, 1812–1870 – Criticism and interpretation.   2. Dickens, Charles,
1812–1870 – Handbooks, manuals, etc.   I. Jordan, John O.   II. Series.

PR4588.C26   2001
823'.8 – dc21   00-065162

ISBN 0 521 66016 5 hardback
ISBN 0 521 66964 2 paperback

CONTENTS

CONTENTS

ILLUSTRATIONS

NOTES ON CONTRIBUTORS

MURRAY BAUMGARTEN, Founding Director of the Dickens Project, and Editor-in-Chief of the Strouse Carlyle Edition, has written widely about Victorian literature and culture, as well as modern Jewish and Holocaust writing.

NICOLA BRADBURY is Lecturer in English at the University of Reading. Her books include *Henry James: The later novels*, *Charles Dickens's Great Expectations*, and the Penguin Classics edition of *Bleak House*.

BRIAN CHEADLE is Honorary Professorial Research Fellow at the University of the Witwatersrand, Johannesburg. He has published on *Great Expectations* and *Bleak House* in *Dickens Studies Annual* and is the author of "Despatched to the Periphery: the Changing Play of Centre and Periphery in Dickens's Work," in Anny Sadrin's collection *Dickens, Europe, and the New Worlds*.

KATE FLINT is Professor of English at Rutgers University, and author of *The Woman Reader 1837–1914* and *The Victorians and the Visual Imagination*, as well as numerous articles on Victorian and contemporary literature and cultural history. She is currently working on the place of the Americas in the Victorian cultural imagination.

JOHN GLAVIN is Professor of English at Georgetown University. He is the author of *After Dickens: Reading, Performance and Adaptation* and has published articles and book chapters on nineteenth- and twentieth-century British literature and culture. He is also a playwright. His plays have been performed by the Philadelphia Company and the Contemporary Arts Theatre Company.

JOHN O. JORDAN is Professor of English and Chair of the Department of Literature at the University of California, Santa Cruz. He has written numerous articles on Dickens and Victorian literature and is the coeditor of two collections of essays on Victorian topics. Since 1985 he has served as Director of the Dickens Project, a multi-campus research consortium headquartered at UC Santa Cruz.

JOSS MARSH is Associate Professor of Victorian Studies at Indiana University, Bloomington, and the author of *Word Crimes: Blasphemy, Culture, and Literature in Nineteenth-Century England*, as well as articles on Dickens, celebrity and silent film, Victorian tourism, film design, and adaptation. She has written on film for a variety of publications – from academic journals to rock magazines – since 1982, and is currently at work on a book called *Dickens/Cinema*.

J. HILLIS MILLER is UCI Distinguished Professor of English and Comparative Literature at the University of California, Irvine. He is the author of *Charles Dickens: The World of His Novels*, as well as a number of other essays about Dickens. In addition he has published many books and articles on nineteenth- and twentienth-century literature and literary theory. His most recent books are *Reading Narrative* and *Black Holes*.

ROBERT NEWSOM is Professor of English at the University of California, Irvine. His writings on Dickens include *Dickens on the Romantic Side of Familiar Things*, several contributions to *The Oxford Reader's Companion to Charles Dickens*, and, most recently, *Charles Dickens Revisited*, as well as essays and reviews. He has also written about the problem of fictionality in *A Likely Story: Probability and Play in Fiction* and is currently working on a book about Dickens and Bentham.

ROBERT L. PATTEN is Lynette S. Autrey Professor in Humanities at Rice University and editor of *SEL Studies in English Literature 1500–1900*. He has published books and articles on Charles Dickens, George Cruikshank, and nineteenth-century British book history.

HILARY SCHOR is Professor of English at the University of Southern California. She is the author of *Scheherezade in the Marketplace: Elizabeth Gaskell and the Victorian Novel*, and *Dickens and the Daughter of the House*, as well as articles on Victorian literature and culture. Her current projects include a study of women, realism, and the law, and a new edition of *Hard Times* for the Bedford series of Cultural editions.

GRAHAME SMITH is Professor of English Studies at the University of Stirling. His major publications on Dickens include *Dickens, Money and Society*, *The Novel and Society: Defoe to George Eliot*, and *Charles Dickens: A Literary Life*. He has also published articles and book chapters on aspects of film adaptation, an interest that will come to fruition in

Dickens and Film, Film and Dickens, forthcoming from Manchester University Press.

RICHARD L. STEIN teaches at the University of Oregon. His books include *The Ritual of Interpretation: The Fine Arts as Literature in Ruskin, Rossetti, and Pater* and *Victoria's Year: English Literature and Culture, 1837–1838*. He is currently finishing a book on Victorian visual culture.

GARRETT STEWART is James O. Freedman Professor of Letters at the University of Iowa and the author of several books on Victorian fiction, including *Dickens and the Trials of Imagination* and *Dear Reader: The Conscripted Audience in Nineteenth-Century British Fiction*. His most recent book is *Between Film and Screen: Modernism's Photo Synthesis*.

CATHERINE WATERS is Senior Lecturer in English at the University of New England (NSW, Australia). Her first book, *Dickens and the Politics of the Family*, was published in 1997. She is currently working on a study of the discourse of the commodity in *Household Words*.

NOTES ON REFERENCES AND EDITIONS

So many editions of Dickens's works are in use that the most useful citations are simply parenthetical references to chapter numbers (e.g., *BH* 35) or book and chapter numbers in the case of *Hard Times*, *Little Dorrit*, *A Tale of Two Cities*, and *Our Mutual Friend* (e.g., *OMF* 2.5). Title and chapter numbers are not included where the context makes them clear.

The best modern editions of Dickens's works are generally those of the Clarendon edition of the novels, published by Oxford University Press. These also appear (without textual notes) in the more recent volumes in the Oxford World's Classics editions. The Norton Critical editions of *Oliver Twist*, *Hard Times*, *Bleak House*, *David Copperfield*, and *Great Expectations* are excellent, and the Penguin editions are usually the next best, though these are being challenged by a new series of Everymans and volumes published by Bedford/St. Martin's and Broadview that, like Norton Criticals, include much supplementary material. In quoting from the novels, contributors to this volume have relied principally on Clarendons, Norton Criticals, and Penguins. Quotations from the minor works have been taken from the New Oxford Illustrated Dickens (Oxford University Press, 1947–58).

For letters, we have used the now authoritative Pilgrim edition where possible, citing by date (British format, as in Pilgrim). Quotations from Forster's *Life of Charles Dickens* are cited by book and chapter.

ABBREVIATIONS

ACC	*A Christmas Carol*
AYR	*All the Year Round*
BH	*Bleak House*
BR	*Barnaby Rudge*
DC	*David Copperfield*
DS	*Dombey and Son*
GE	*Great Expectations*
HT	*Hard Times*
HW	*Household Words*
LD	*Little Dorrit*
MC	*Martin Chuzzlewit*
MED	*The Mystery of Edwin Drood*
NN	*Nicholas Nickleby*
OCS	*The Old Curiosity Shop*
OMF	*Our Mutual Friend*
OT	*Oliver Twist*
PP	*The Pickwick Papers*
SB	*Sketches by Boz*
TTC	*A Tale of Two Cities*
Forster	*The Life of Charles Dickens*
Pilgrim	*The Letters of Charles Dickens*. The Pilgrim edition. Madeline House, Graham Storey, Kathleen Tillotson, et al. (eds.). Clarendon Press, 1965 to present. Currently in 10 volumes. References are to volume and page.

1812 Born in Portsmouth (7 February) to John and Elizabeth Dickens.

1817 Family moves to Chatham, near Rochester in Kent.

1821 Dickens begins education at William Giles's School. Writes the tragedy, *Misnar, the Sultan of India*.

1822 John Dickens transferred to London (summer). Family moves to Camden Town.

1824 John Dickens imprisoned for debt in the Marshalsea Prison (20 February–28 May). The young Charles Dickens is sent to work at Warren's Blacking Factory (late January/early February–June).

1825 Attends Wellington House Academy.

1827 Family evicted for non-payment of rates (March). Dickens leaves school and becomes a clerk at Ellis & Blackmore, solicitors.

1828–29 Learns shorthand and works as a freelance reporter at Doctors' Commons.

1830 Falls in love with Maria Beadnell.

1831–34 Works as a parliamentary reporter.

1832 Considers a career in acting but fails, on account of illness, to keep his appointment for an audition at Covent Garden Theatre.

1833 Publishes first story, "A Dinner at Poplar Walk," in *The Monthly Magazine*.

1834 Becomes reporter for *The Morning Chronicle*. Meets Catherine Hogarth (August). Publishes stories in various periodicals.

1836 Collects previously published stories into his first book, *Sketches by Boz* (First Series, 8 February). Marries Catherine Hogarth (2 April). Serialization of *Pickwick Papers* (April 1836–November 1837). *The Strange Gentleman* produced at the St. James's Theatre (29 September) followed by *The Village Coquettes* (22 December). *Sketches by Boz*, Second Series published (17 December). Resigns from *The Morning Chronicle* to assume editorship of *Bentley's Miscellany*.

1837	First number of *Bentley's Miscellany* (1 January). The first of his ten children is born (6 January). Moves to 48 Doughty Street (April). Death of Mary Hogarth (7 May). First visit to Europe (July). *Oliver Twist* serialized in *Bentley's* (February 1837–April 1839).
1838	Edits and publishes *Memoirs of Joseph Grimaldi*. *Nicholas Nickleby* serialized (April 1838–October 1839).
1839	Resigns editorship of *Bentley's Miscellany* (31 January).
1840	*Sketches of Young Couples* (10 February). *Old Curiosity Shop* serialized in *Master Humphrey's Clock* (25 April 1840–6 February 1841).
1841	*Barnaby Rudge* serialized in *Master Humphrey's Clock* (13 February–27 November).
1842	Visit to America (January–June). *American Notes* published (19 October).
1843	*Martin Chuzzlewit* serialized (January 1843–July 1844). *A Christmas Carol* published (19 December).
1844	Lives one year in Italy with his family (from July). *The Chimes* published (16 December).
1845	Returns to London (June). Directs and acts in Jonson's *Every Man in His Humour*. *The Cricket on the Hearth* published (20 December). Begins composition of the autobiographical fragment (c. 1845–48).
1846	Edits *The Daily News* (21 January–9 February) and lives part of the year in Switzerland and Paris. *Pictures from Italy* published (18 May). *Dombey and Son* serialized (October 1846–April 1848).
1848	*The Haunted Man* published (19 December).
1849	*David Copperfield* serialized (May 1849–November 1850).
1850	Founds and edits the weekly journal *Household Words* (until May 1859).
1851	Dickens family moves to Tavistock House (November).
1852	*Bleak House* serialized (March 1852–September 1853).
1854	*Hard Times* serialized in *Household Words* (1 April–12 August).
1855	Meets Maria Beadnell (now Mrs. Winter) again. Lives in Paris (October 1855–April 1856). *Little Dorrit* serialized (December 1855–June 1857).
1856	Purchases Gad's Hill Place, near Rochester in Kent.
1857	Directs and acts in Wilkie Collins's *The Frozen Deep*. Meets Ellen Ternan.
1858	Gives his first public readings for profit (29 April–22 July). Legal separation from Catherine (May). First provincial reading tour (2 August–13 November).

1859 Founds and edits *All the Year Round*. *A Tale of Two Cities* serialized in the new weekly journal (30 April–26 November).

1860 *Great Expectations* serialized in *All the Year Round* (1 December–3 August 1861).

1864 *Our Mutual Friend* serialized (May 1864–November 1865).

1865 Staplehurst train wreck (9 June). Dickens sustains minor injuries and long-lasting trauma.

1867 American reading tour (November 1867–April 1868).

1870 Twelve farewell readings in London (January). Received by Queen Victoria (9 March). Begins serializing *The Mystery of Edwin Drood* (April). Dies on 9 June at Gad's Hill of a cerebral hemorrhage.

PREFACE

Dickens is unusual if not unique among canonical English-language authors in remaining at once a vital focus of academic research and a major figure in popular culture. Only Shakespeare, Mark Twain, and perhaps Jane Austen can compare with him in terms of their ability to hold the attention of both a scholarly and a general audience. The range of Dickens's appeal throughout the English-speaking world can be measured not only by his regular presence on school reading lists and in university courses, but by the frequency with which his novels continue to be adapted for the stage, for television, and for feature-length films. In Britain, where his image has appeared on postage stamps and on the ten-pound note, Dickens has become a staple of the national culture, a commodity available for export as well as for internal circulation. In North America, where hardly a day goes by without some Dickens reference appearing in the local or national press, *A Christmas Carol* has attained virtually the status of myth and elicits parodies, piracies, and annual theatrical performances with increasing frequency. Extending Paul Davis's apt phrase about the *Carol*, one might say that Dickens has become a "culture-text" for the world at large.

Meanwhile, Dickens's reputation in the academy continues to rise.[1] No longer dismissed as a mere comic entertainer, he is widely recognized as the preeminent novelist of the Victorian age and a major figure in world literature. Recent criticism has come to value not only the journalistic and documentary side of his work, but the very qualities of excess – sprawling melodramatic plots, larger-than-life characters, verbal extravagance – that earlier critics had identified as signs of artistic weakness. His novels provide a fertile testing ground for new theories and methodologies. They attract the attention of scholars coming from a wide variety of critical approaches: feminist, new historicist, psychoanalytic, and deconstructionist, as well as from more traditional historical and formalist perspectives.

The Cambridge Companion to Charles Dickens takes cognizance of the diverse audiences to which Dickens appeals and of the different approaches that his novels have attracted in recent decades. Its fourteen chapters aim not so much at making Dickens more accessible – he needs little help in that regard – as at providing contexts that will enhance the understanding and appreciation of his major novels. The volume opens with an account of Dickens's life and times that seeks less to rehearse well-known and widely accessible facts than to reflect on what it means to write the biography of Dickens in a time of poststructuralist theory, when the very idea of authorship has been called radically into question. The five essays that follow address major works of fiction in the Dickens canon from *Sketches by Boz* to *Our Mutual Friend*. Subsequent chapters take up important Dickensian themes: childhood, the city, and the family. Two further chapters examine aspects of Dickens's novelistic practice, his distinctive use of language and the formal organization and structure of his novels. Three final chapters consider Dickens in relation to other artistic modes and media: illustration, theatre, and film. Each chapter contains a list of suggested further reading. A selected bibliography, focused on major studies and on more recent work, brings the volume to a close.

Inevitably, as in any collection of this kind, much is left out. The immensity of Dickens's literary production, the extent of his influence, and the variety of his involvement in the issues of his age make comprehensive treatment impossible. The reader will find no discussion of Dickens's journalism, for example, no consideration of his travel writings or short fiction, including the Christmas books, and no assessment of his role as a social reformer. Rather, the emphasis throughout has been on Dickens the novelist and on providing fresh ways of looking at his major works of fiction.

The contributors to this volume live and teach in a number of countries and are actively engaged in the ongoing process of revising critical opinion of Dickens and his work. They bring to bear diverse scholarly and critical traditions – American, British, and Continental. The volume takes advantage of the rich heritage of Dickens studies that has accumulated since the 1940s and, in particular, situates itself in relation to the critical movements and debates of the past two decades. It also profits from the important scholarly and editorial work that has given us the Clarendon editions of Dickens's novels and the Pilgrim edition of his *Letters*.

In preparing this volume I have benefited from the advice and assistance of many people. Chief among them has been my research assistant, Jon Varese, himself a knowledgeable and dedicated Dickensian. Others to whom I am indebted for generous help at various stages in the project include Barbara Lee, Joss Marsh, Robert Newsom, Robert L. Patten, JoAnna Rottke, Richard L. Stein, and, at Cambridge University Press, Josie Dixon and Linda Bree. For their cooperation and timeliness in meeting deadlines as well as for numerous other courtesies I am grateful to all of my contributors. My wife Jane continues to tolerate my long immersion in matters Dickensian. To her I owe the greatest debt of all.

JOHN O. JORDAN

NOTES

1 For a useful survey of Dickens's critical reception since the nineteenth century, see the "Introduction" to Steven Connor's collection of essays, *Charles Dickens*, ed. Steven Connor (Longman, 1996), pp. 1–33.

I

GRAHAME SMITH

The life and times of Charles Dickens

What does it mean to write the life and times of a major writer in the era of poststructuralist literary theory? What it doesn't mean, of course, is to contrast the current situation with some pretheoretical paradise in which the exercise would have been unproblematic. The fact is that the *study* of literature is by definition theoretical; it is simply that the terms of the debate differ between then and now. An example of how one method challenges another can be seen by glancing at the impact of new, or practical criticism, on two of the favorite kinds of Dickens studies from earlier in the century. Prototype studies attempted to identify the "real" human beings behind Dickens's characters, while topographical studies sought to identify the "real" places which formed the inspiration for the settings of Dickens's novels. New criticism, which flourished as a movement in the 1950s and 1960s, sought to remove literary texts from the historical arena through a concentration on their structure and language, and so was committed to a rejection of this implied equation of art and reality. This approach was superseded by new kinds of theory which problematized, among other matters, the existence of an external reality without the experience of the observer as subject and suggested that the author was now dead, as a challenge to the traditional role of the artist as creator of fictional worlds which mirrored both external reality and the writer's personal life. But whatever the differences between new criticism and poststructuralist literary theory, they do have one thing in common in their stress on the primacy of language. Contemporary theory has, of course, taken this position further by way of the concept of textuality, the notion that the individual and the world, as well as the literary artifact, are *written*; that is, are inscriptions of those ideological formations which are the distinguishing features of major historical epochs.

There are signs that the more extreme versions of these positions are beginning to loosen their grip on the academic study of literature. The movement known as new historicism has provided renewed opportunities for history in the search for cultural, as well as specifically literary, understanding, and it is even possible that the author is struggling back into life, although in different forms from those that *he* enjoyed in his heyday as creative genius. However, it would reduce cultural enquiry to a trivial game of swings and roundabouts to suggest that it is now possible simply to return to older versions of a life and times. Poststructuralist literary theory seems certain to have a legacy, and among its most important discoveries is its stress on the centrality of writing in the construction of the self and the world, as well as literary texts.

A glance at the first major biography of Dickens, published only a few years after his death in 1870, by his life-long friend, John Forster, may illustrate the relevance of contemporary theory to this discussion. Forster was a highly intelligent professional biographer and his work has the inwardness with Dickens that comes not merely from their intimacy, but also from his shared position as a fellow Victorian. Even this privileged access is subject to reservations, however. For one thing, Forster chose to ignore material, such as Dickens's relationship with the young actress Ellen Ternan, which he thought would damage Dickens's reputation, and also be hurtful to living people. But a more fundamental reservation arises when we grasp how much of the biography was orchestrated by Dickens himself, in that Forster's sources are mainly letters written to him by Dickens and reports of their conversations together. This dependence is strengthened by our knowledge that Dickens wished Forster to be his biographer, a challenge that Forster embraced.

It is obviously possible to feel superior toward these apparent limitations, especially in light of the massive Clarendon British Academy edition of Dickens's letters which is currently in the process of appearing. Vivid and amusing, they provide us with what amounts to an autobiography, but like all autobiographies it is partial and to some extent self-regarding. Nonetheless, countless critics, scholars, and biographers rely on these letters as evidence of Dickens's life with little acknowledgement of this partiality and bias. The life and times attempted here will, then, be written in recognition of the extent to which Dickens's life is a textual construct, much of it created by the writer himself. The method will be thematic, examining major aspects of his life and times, and the ways in which these might relate to the work, although a simplistic reduction of the novels as explicable in terms of the life, or vice versa, will be avoided as much as possible. Many would argue that Dickens's stylistic innovations are radical; in keeping with this view, a radical account will be offered of his personal life and the ways in which it relates to the life of his times.

An appropriate starting point is one of Dickens's best-known writings outside the novels, the so-called "Autobiographical Fragment" written for Forster in 1847, which recounts his incarceration in Warren's Blacking Factory, a shoe-polish warehouse, at the age of twelve for probably a year. Incarceration is a loaded word, with its connotations of imprisonment, and the primacy of the experience has been challenged in recent years while its writing has been seen to indulge in a self-dramatizing sentimentality. There is no doubt that the Fragment, precipitated by a stray word of Forster's, is carefully crafted, presenting its boy hero's suffering in a series of pathetic vignettes which, designedly or otherwise, maximize the stresses and potential dangers of the episode on a child who is seen as sensitive, imaginative, and highly intelligent.

However, the story needs to be contextualized within a wider narrative if it is to be fully appreciated. Dickens's family background is richly representative of the social and class tensions which had existed for many generations in English society and intensified in the Victorian period as part of the general movement toward reform. His grandparents, on his father's side, were servants of a superior kind in being butler and housekeeper in an aristocratic family, and thus holding positions of power and authority, which were as likely to claim the respect of their masters as the awe of their inferiors. (The position of Mrs. Rouncewell in Sir Leicester Dedlock's household in *Bleak House* is a good indication of the esteem in which such upper servants could be held.) This settled prosperity, and access to aristocratic influence, were the springboard for an upward social mobility on the part of Dickens's father, John, who was a clerk in the Navy Pay Office, retiring in 1825 on grounds of ill health. Clerkships were important positions in the evolving world of nineteenth-century bureaucracy, and John Dickens moved through a number of promotions which afforded him, by the standards of the day, an excellent salary and secure pension. The available evidence suggests that Dickens's father was an able, attractive, and hard-working man but liable to a prodigality difficult to separate from a generous response to the pleasures of life and an admirable desire to move up the social scale. Its results were, however, disastrous in the short term. In 1819 he borrowed £200, then a very large sum, the starting point for a gradual descent into debt signaled by frequent changes of address. John Dickens was transferred to London, for a second time, in 1822; Dickens was not sent to school; and his father was overwhelmed by financial difficulties which led to his imprisonment for debt in the Marshalsea Prison. Shortly before this, Dickens began work at Warren's Blacking, presumably as an aid to the family finances.

How should this be interpreted for clues to Dickens's inner life, and its possible connections with his work? His own view of the Blacking Factory episode has been dismissed by some recent critics as the self-indulgent whining of a poor little rich boy whose fate was much better than that of hundreds of thousands of child laborers in the period. But this is to discount the expectations of a twelve-year-old brought up in a comfortable lower-middle-class home in which he was made much of and his talents admired. He can hardly have set his sights on university, which in the England of the day would almost certainly have meant Oxford or Cambridge, but he must have expected to remain at school until about sixteen, followed by entry to the law, a clerkship, or some other respectable calling. The reality was his removal from school, in 1822, which he clearly chafed under, and then a job which he was surely right to see as demeaning and stultifying to his talents, even if some find excessive his revelations of "the secret agony of my soul as I sunk into this companionship . . . of the shame I felt in my position . . . of the misery it was to my young heart" (Forster, 1.2). What cannot be doubted, however, is that this was an experience "which at intervals haunted him and made him miserable even to that hour" (Forster, 1.2) in which he was writing. Equally understandable is Dickens's belief that in wandering alone and unprotected through the streets of a wild and violent city he might well have become " . . . a little robber or a vagabond" (Forster, 1.2).

But there are positives, one of them being the repeated kindnesses shown to him by his fellow workers, especially the interestingly named Bob Fagin, which may suggest a link from the life to the work. Dickens worked the Fragment into the early, autobiographical passages of *David Copperfield* (1849–50) and the runaway David marks the conclusion of his early deprivations by a prayer: "I prayed that I might not be houseless any more, and never might forget the houseless" (13). Even if we accept that Dickens succumbed to a sentimental idealization of his personal life, in the work his suffering was objectified into generous indignation and righteous anger at the fate of the helpless, the poor, and the unprotected. Having glimpsed dispossession fueled Dickens's concern for the dispossessed for the whole of his writing life. And the very intensity of this concern may relate to his famous repression of this period. Dickens's claim to have told no one of Warren's is debatable (one of his sons claimed that it was known to his wife), but it is certain that it was a closely guarded, and rankling, secret. However, personal repression did not prevent the experience from flowing into his work, in however subterranean a way, as we can see from a glance at *Bleak House* (1852–53). The fate of Jo, endlessly moved on, and the dangers faced by vulnerable little girls such as Charley, move the novel to superbly controlled irony and anger. More profound is the study of a young woman, Esther Summerson, who is as much an abused child as the others despite her more comfortable material surroundings. Esther represses the trauma of her upbringing in the interests of a positive engagement with life, an effort which exacts its penalties in her dreams and in an inner life whose stresses are hinted at, although masked by Esther herself. This is only one of a number of anticipations of Freud which have their roots in Dickens's own meditated experience.

The intensity of living through the imprisonment of a beloved and respectable family seems also to have made an indelible impression which, again, was objectified in action as well as in creativity. Just as Dickens campaigned for the poor in his philanthropic activity, his journalism, and his speeches, as well as the fiction, so his evident obsession with prisons, visiting them at every available opportunity, was transformed into a rationally humane concern for penal reform expressed in a similar range of activities. Imaginatively, his work is haunted by the "taint of prison and crime" which pervades *Great Expectations* (1860–61, 32). The genial humour of his first novel, *Pickwick Papers* (1836–37), modulates into the darkness of Mr. Pickwick's imprisonment for refusing to pay the damages awarded against him for supposed breach of promise. Prisons are broken into, and their inmates released, most notably in *Barnaby Rudge* (1841) and *A Tale of Two Cities* (1859). And what many regard as one of Dickens's greatest novels, *Little Dorrit* (1855–57), is permeated by prisons, real and imaginary, its structure and the texture of its writing inescapably implicated up to, and including, its vision of "the prison of this lower world" (1.30).

One of Dickens's best-known statements concerning the Blacking Factory period arose at his moment of release from it: "I do not write resentfully or angrily: for I know how all these things have worked together to make me what I am: but I never afterwards forgot, I never shall forget, I never can forget, that my mother was warm for my being sent back" (Forster, 1.2). This leads into a network of relationships within the life, and between the life and the work, that can be pursued in a number of ways. Dickens's mother has been written into history largely on the basis of this and similar statements, and through her identification with the absurdly scatterbrained figure of the hero's mother in *Nicholas Nickleby* (1838–39). What is frequently ignored in this reductionism is that Elizabeth Dickens gave the small Charles his basic educational grounding at home, including in Latin. In addition, his mother was described by an accurate-sounding observer as a woman who possessed "an extraordinary sense of the ludicrous, and her power of imitation was something quite astonishing . . . as also considerable dramatic talent."[1] If true, this would suggest a fruitful influence for any writer, one unacknowledged by Dickens himself and pretty much ignored by those writing on him.

What we are examining in Dickens's biography is, clearly, the transmutation of the life into myth. One way of reading Dickens is as a representative

Victorian figure, the self-made man, and it is certainly the case that he made himself over a number of times in the early part of his life. He makes the claim for himself in the Warren's Blacking period that, despite the suffering involved, "I kept my own counsel, and I did my work. I knew from the first that, if I could not do my work as well as any of the rest, I could not hold myself above slight and contempt" (Forster, 1.2). This determination to do what had to be done hardens into the drive for success revealed by his determination to master the "savage stenographic mystery" (*DC* 43) of Gurney's shorthand system while in his second job, as a solicitor's clerk. This enables him to leave and become a freelance shorthand reporter at Doctors' Commons, an obscure part of the current legal system in England. He then moves to *The Mirror of Parliament*, a publication devoted to recording the proceedings of the House of Commons. It is widely accepted, although at least some of the evidence is Dickens's own, that he became a crack parliamentary reporter noted for his speed and accuracy. He moved between a number of periodicals at this stage – he was still only twenty – and in 1834 became a reporter for the *Morning Chronicle*, where he remained until 1836, leaving behind him "the reputation of being the best and most rapid reporter ever known!" (to Wilkie Collins, 6 June 1856, Pilgrim 8.131).

During this period Dickens wrote many of the brilliant little vignettes, collected as *Sketches by Boz* (First Series 1836), and then resigned from the paper because the success of the serialization of *The Pickwick Papers* opened the way to his career as a professional writer. This is an amazing series of achievements, and Dickens obviously enjoyed the sense that they were due to his own unaided efforts, struggles in which his parents had little part to play. However, allowing for their possession of the usual human failings, it seems clear that his mother and father were talented and energetic people who had provided a loving, supportive environment in the pre-Warren's period. But the Blacking Factory was a watershed in Dickens's feelings about them, and in his general attitude to the world, which helps to explain the extent to which the novels are on the side of youth, and the generally disparaging view they adopt of mothers and fathers. It is hard to find examples of normally happy families in his work, and *Bleak House* again provides a particularly vivid example of his exploration of domesticity. The Pardiggles are the nearest approach to the ordinary, although not without their own touches of the bizarre. The Smallweeds, on the other hand, are a brood monstrous in their greed and miserliness. Those who seem marked out for parenthood by their vigorous warmth – Mr. Jarndyce, Boythorn, and George – are singularly childless, although Jarndyce does at least acquire a surrogate family. And it is noteworthy that Caddy Jellyby's touchingly happy marriage to her Prince produces a severely disabled baby. But the fictions' rendering of the deficiencies of parents is far from the petty revenge of a disappointed adult. As with other aspects of his personal experience, this is objectified and transformed by Dickens into a comprehensive artistic vision of a parentless, above all a fatherless, world. The societies depicted in *Bleak House*, *Little Dorrit*, *Great Expectations*, and *Our Mutual Friend* signally fail to provide for their poorest members. Personal experience – the fear of becoming "a little robber or a vagabond" – is transmuted into metaphor, the depiction of worlds which ignore the most basic of fatherly roles in the traditional scheme of things, that of provider, an example of the radicalism that will be discussed in more detail later.

It is no accident that the avowedly autobiographical *David Copperfield* depicts a relationship between child and mother which is both edenic and open to a psychoanalytic reading. The text could hardly be more cunningly orchestrated for these purposes. The father is dead, the evil second father, Mr. Murdstone, is not yet on the scene, and the tiny David has two "mothers"! One is the bustling, stout, commonsensically affectionate servant, Peggotty, the other the sensationally glamorous and helpless Clara. It is impossible to exaggerate the charm, delicacy, and exquisite comedy of this early section of the book, all of which suggest an element of control guiding Dickens's ability to tap into depths of feeling which must have some relation to his mother, either as part of a lost paradise or in the dramatization of a relationship he longed for but never had. Yet again, there is a foreshadowing of Freud. This, then, is the first of a number of relationships with women central to Dickens's life and work. Those to be singled out are his first love, Maria Beadnell; two sisters-in-law, Mary and Georgina Hogarth; his wife, Catherine; and Ellen Ternan.

Dickens met Maria in 1830, when he was eighteen, and was in love with her for three or four years. It is obvious, given the intensity of his nature, that this was a serious relationship for him. Maria, and her feelings, are much harder to make out, lost as she is not merely in the mists of time, but in the role of heartless manipulator so firmly inscribed for her by Dickens himself. Her interest for us lies in her reappearance, more than twenty years after he broke off their relationship in 1833. Two days after his forty-third birthday, on 9 February 1855, Dickens received a letter from Maria, now Mrs. Winter, which initiated a correspondence remarkable for the strength of its feeling, on Dickens's part, and not without comic overtones. It provides yet another example of a psychological pattern already analyzed in relation to Warren's Blacking and *David Copperfield*: repression followed by a passionate outburst of feeling, artistically controlled in the depiction of David's relationship with his mother, more nakedly raw in the Autobiographical Fragment, although shaped even there into an overarching narrative reinforced by vividly realized episodes. Dickens's letters to his former sweetheart follow a rapidly increasing intimacy, from Mrs. Winter to Maria, with an abrupt return to the more formal address once they had met. In its recall from the depths of his memory the episode provoked an almost alarming degree of emotion in Dickens. He clearly expected, at some level, that the Mrs. Winter of now would be the Maria of yesterday and the visual evidence of his fatuity brought his dreams (whatever, precisely, they were) and the potential relationship to an abrupt, if not unkindly managed, conclusion. Artistry takes over, yet again, although with a possible hint of revenge on this occasion as Mrs. Winter was unfortunate enough to make her reentry at about the time he was meditating on a new novel. She thus makes her appearance as Flora Finching in *Little Dorrit*, the youthful sweetheart of Arthur Clennam whose looks, twenty years later, provide such an unflattering series of contrasts: "Flora, whom he had left a lily, had become a peony; but that was not much. Flora, who had seemed enchanting in all she said and thought, was diffuse and silly. That was much. Flora, who had been spoiled and artless long ago, was determined to be spoilt and artless now. That was a fatal blow" (1.13).

One can only flinch at what Maria Winter made of all this when she read the novel, as one supposes she must have done, but what does it tell us about Dickens? The contrast between abandonment to feeling, followed by iron control, is remarkable. And yet his letters suggest that his withdrawal from intimacy was managed with a degree of tact as well as unyielding firmness. In the fiction also, the picture of Flora is not simply cruelly comic. She is kindly as well as fatuous, and is genuinely helpful in providing employment for the impoverished Little Dorrit. But, such is the unsparing complexity of great art, Flora cannot resist indulging in a kind of torment of Little Dorrit, who is in love with Clennam, by constantly reminding her of her own past relationship with him.

Another woman of major importance in Dickens's life, his sister-in-law Mary Hogarth, was at least spared the invidious comparisons of age by dying at seventeen. Examination of Mary plunges us into a number of problems, some arising out of Victorian social habits that may seem strange to us, others that demand psychoanalytic probing. Dickens married Catherine Hogarth in April 1836, and their first child was born ten months later, in January 1837. Mary joined the new family in February for a month's holiday, and from then until her early death became part of the household, moving into their first permanent London home, in Doughty Street, in April 1837, and dying there suddenly and unexpectedly on 7 May. The modern emphasis on privacy makes such arrangements appear odd, but they were perfectly usual for the Victorians. Large extended families demanded some sharing of responsibilities, especially toward unmarried daughters, and it would have seemed obvious that a sister who had acquired a home of her own should be willing to share it; the easy acceptance of such arrangements should raise no contemporary eyebrows. What is less easy to explain is the intensity of Dickens's feelings for Mary, especially once she was dead. But if interpretation is unavoidable here, so is judgment, and it is imperative to insist that whatever else was going on, Dickens was not "in love" with Mary at the expense of her sister. On the other hand, we have to note that he was unable to complete his monthly installments of *Pickwick Papers* and *Oliver Twist* for June. (Such were the pressures of his early career that he was forced to write parts of both novels concurrently.) We know that Dickens wished to be buried in the same grave as Mary, and was distraught when it was occupied by her brother, George, who died aged twenty in 1841. She occupied an important place in his dreams until February 1838, and then returned in a dream of extraordinary vividness in 1844, while he was living in Italy. And he does not fail to note the eleventh anniversary of her death in a letter to Forster of 1848.

It is, of course, impossible to say who or what the "real" Mary Hogarth was, so many years after her untimely death. She seems to have been a charming young person, lively, intelligent, and attractive. In Dickens's life and work, however, she appears as a kind of palimpsest, an initially almost blank document memorialized and inscribed by a combination of his desires and the images of femininity presented by Victorian society. It is probably the case that she died in Dickens's arms, but from that dramatic moment on she was consigned to the realm of reflection, rather than independent selfhood, as a mirror in which Dickens could see one of his ideal versions of the womanly. Implicit in the praise of the purity heaped on her by her adoring brother-in-law is the fact of sexual inexperience, an absence which became a significant presence in Dickens's fictional representations of young women. And it is hardly possible to doubt that Rose Maylie, the young aunt of Oliver Twist in the novel he was writing at the time of her death, is not some kind of tribute to Mary. Unfortunately, Rose is one of the most vacuous characters he ever created. This is not the place to pursue Dickens's attempts to confront the depiction of youthful femininity in artistically successful terms. The most that can be done is to point to the interesting levels of complexity achieved with Esther Summerson in *Bleak House* and the eponymous heroine of *Little Dorrit*, both of whom suggest that Dickens was able to work through and modify this troubling area of response, in art if not in life.

Patterns seem to repeat themselves in Dickens's experience, as well as in his work, a fact revealed by the role of another sister-in-law, Georgina Hogarth, who became an important and permanent member of the family circle from the age of fifteen. Again, there is nothing particularly odd, in Victorian terms, about this arrangement. Georgina seems to have been a friend and helper to Dickens, his wife, and the children. She no doubt eased the burden of suffering at the death of an infant, Dora, in 1851, and she seems to have assisted in tasks such as helping with the arrangements for the family's often complicated holidays, a regular feature of their domestic routine.

But the amazing moment in her life with Dickens arose in 1858 with his separation from Catherine after twenty-two years of marriage. In May 1858 Catherine left the family home accompanied by only one of her children; the rest remained with their father, and Georgina elected to stay on, apparently as a mother-surrogate or housekeeper. She was thirty-one years old and could hardly have done anything more damaging to her prospects of marriage. As an intensely famous public figure whose work had been associated in the public mind with what we would now call family values, Dickens's break-up of his domestic life caused rumours to abound, leading him to publish denials of the whispering campaign against him in his own weekly magazine, *Household Words*. One of the more scurrilous suggestions was that he and Georgina were conducting an affair, a relationship that would have been considered incestuous given the Victorian prohibition on marrying a deceased wife's sister.

What, then, motivated these surprising decisions? It is hard to decipher what lay behind Georgina's apparent betrayal of a beloved sister. Clearly she loved Dickens, although it seems unlikely that she was in love with him. She may well have felt genuine concern for a family of "motherless" children, but it is equally plausible that the lively and intelligent Georgina enjoyed her proximity to the most famous writer of the day and the excitements that accompanied this position. But what does the arrangement tell us about Dickens? Only a combination of passionately intense self-belief and a radical contempt for Victorian social mores could have enabled him to carry off such a bizarrely unconventional ménage. He seems to have respected as well as loved Georgina, turning to her for advice and appreciating her assistance in the smooth running of the household upon which he insisted. He was apparently disturbed from time to time that his monopolization was endangering her marriage prospects, but a deeper response is indicated by his joking reference to her in conversation as "the virgin". This seems to have caused no offense to anyone, including Georgina herself, but does suggest another expression of the complex of feelings released by the death of Mary. Here, however, we are in the realm not of the helplessly girlish Rose but, rather, the angelic and yet domestically competent Agnes Wickfield of *David Copperfield*.

It may seem odd that this attempt to recreate a sense of Dickens's personal life through the women who occupied important places within it should have placed such emphasis on her sisters rather than the wife herself. It is, of course, partly what was unusual in the relationships with Mary and Georgina that gives them interest. But at another level, the apparently central relationship is the more difficult to recover as Catherine seems to have been the victim as much of erasure as of inscription. From the moment that Dickens decided that she had to disappear from his life – he never saw her again after the separation and she was not present at her daughter, Kate's, wedding in 1860 – he rewrote her character, personality, and their life together in terms that have been almost wholly accepted by biographers. Catherine's appearance on the stage of Dickens's life is, then, at best shadowy and at worst that of an emotionally frigid incompetent constructed by him as justification for actions that would seem cruel in any period and near damning in the Victorian era. We are dealing here, it goes without saying, with one of the towering geniuses of western culture, a writer whose creative processes exerted a sometimes dominating influence on his personal and social life; how far that excuses the rejection of conventional morality is a large issue. But what seems clear from the tone, and forms of address, of his own letters to her is that Dickens found in his wife a desirable, engaging, and responsive companion for many years, although any remaining rapport was shattered at the moment in August 1857 when Ellen Ternan entered his life.

This is one of the most engrossing, if mysterious, phases of Dickens's personal odyssey; however, it is important to remember at this point that we are seeking to explore not merely his life but also his times. In fact, this is a moment when the division between life and times becomes a false dichotomy. In other words, the crisis engendered by the appearance of Ellen Ternan is not simply part of a sentimental melodrama of desire, or the most boringly predictable of crises, that of mid-life. Dickens may have been forty-five in 1857, looking and perhaps feeling much older, while Ellen was eighteen. But the intensity of his response to her, and rejection of Catherine, can be fully understood only in the context of Dickens's public life and his involvement in the events of his epoch.

How, then, did Dickens relate to the social and political world of the nineteenth century and how can we see this playing its part in these determining actions of his life? It is, of course, impossible to offer an "objective" account of the main events of Victorian history in Dickens's lifetime. Many would now agree that history of any kind can only be written from a specific viewpoint; in any event, what follows will be an attempt to glimpse the outlines of Victorian politics and social history from Dickens's own perspective. The best starting point might be the three dominating passions of his political life: education, penal and legal reform, sanitation and public health. Dickens's judgment of his society's performance in these fields was colored by an essential feature of his character and success in life, the extent to which his achievements were built on the foundations not merely of literary genius but on the energy and efficiency with which he conducted his career as a professional writer, what has been called a literary producer.[2] We have seen already that Dickens was liable to depreciate the possible contributions of his parents to his self-made success. Even if only to that extent, it thus becomes possible to see him as representative of the middle-class energies released by, among other forces, the Industrial Revolution. Dickens gloried in his status as a professional writer, supported by the patronage of his readers, and a clue to his general hostility toward public life in his period is his belief that he was a professional in a country run by amateurs. Such a stance explains one thread of contemporary hostility toward him, the conviction that he was an undereducated upstart whose satirical attacks via, for example, the Court of Chancery and the Circumlocution Office, were the jibes of an ignorant outsider.

What Dickens saw himself as up against is suggested by a House of Commons speech in 1846 by the young Benjamin Disraeli, who is often credited with real insight into the life of his times as novelist as well as politician. Disraeli suggested that there is "a balance between the two great branches of national industry . . . and we should give a preponderance to the agricultural branch."[3] He was defending the past here as well as the status quo, and also the material interests of aristocratic landowners. In doing so, he failed to understand the changes precipitated by the Industrial Revolution and the new social order demanded by the move toward industrial production, life in cities, and middle-class entrepreneurship, an error of lasting importance to the national health of the United Kingdom. A glance at *Hard Times* is enough to show that Dickens's attitude toward industrialization is far from idealized, although a balancing perspective is provided by the presentation of the ironmaster, Mr. Rouncewell, in *Bleak House*. In this context, it is worth noting that, before the First Reform Bill of 1832, Birmingham, Manchester, Leeds, and Sheffield had not a single Member of Parliament between them, and that into the twentieth century the House of Commons was still dominated by the interests of the aristocratic land-owning class.

Specific examples of the amateurism that Dickens railed against in the novels, as well as in his journalism, public speaking, and philanthropic activity, come readily to mind. Until the year after he died, appointments to the Civil Service were made on the recommendation of a Member of Parliament or peer, and when entry was opened by public examination in 1871, the

Foreign Office was excluded because of internal opposition. This was the seed-bed of such literary ideas as the division of government between the Coodles and Doodles in *Bleak House*, with the latter eventually coming to the national rescue: "At last Sir Thomas Doodle has not only condescended to come in, but has done it handsomely, bringing in with him all his nephews, all his male cousins, and all his brothers-in-law. So there is hope for the old ship yet" (40). Equally relevant is the domination in *Little Dorrit* of the Circumlocution Office by the Tite Barnacles, an aspect of their battening on the ship of state, from Lord Decimus Tite Barnacle himself down, through the sprightly young Barnacle, Ferdinand, to the lower depths of the idiot Barnacle Junior, Clarence. The great radical journalist, William Cobbett, frequently referred to what he saw as the corruptions of aristocratic patronage as "The System," and Dickens agreed in regarding much of the social and political structure of his time as a vast amateurish racket in which, for example, the "one great principle of the English law, is to make business for itself" (*BH* 39). Again, we know that the sleazy farce which is the Circumlocution Office was prompted by Dickens's anger and disgust at the conduct of the Crimean War in which thousands of soldiers died of privation and sickness because of bureaucratic bungling and inefficiency. This is the world in which, until the reforms of the army instituted in the late 1860s and early 1870s, commissions could be bought and sold with no regard whatever to the professional competence of those involved. And just as with the Foreign Office's opposition to competitive examinations, there was resistance at the highest levels to the setting-up of a permanent General Staff and persistence in the use of muzzle-loading, as opposed to breech-loading, cannon, reforms which had previously been accepted by the armies of Prussia and France.

The conflict between professionalism and amateurism was, for Dickens, a struggle between the forces of life and death, and goes a long way to explain his relative indifference to the Reform Acts of 1832 and 1867. For him, neither was significant enough to change the class-based power structure of Victorian society. If this seems a limited and even philistine view it is worth remembering of the second Act that, although it doubled the electorate, which now included industrial workers living in towns, it excluded agricultural laborers and miners living in villages, as well as all women, and it still failed to incorporate the secret ballot, one of the major planks of radical reform throughout the nineteenth century. From an ideological position other than Dickens's, the Victorian era can be, and is, seen as one of the great reforming epochs of British history. But for Dickens reform came with agonizing slowness – always against huge opposition and often qualified – or not at all. Victorian society was driven, to a large extent, by the principle of *laissez-faire* (governmental non-interference in the actions of individuals), a doctrine regarded by many as God-given, and so was a world in which services were provided to the well-to-do by private utilities, and to the poor by benevolence and Christian charity. Against this background, government intervention in education, perhaps the most passionately held of all Dickens's causes, was minimal until the Education Act of 1870, and even that failed to make school attendance compulsory. The muddle and piecemeal development of the legal system since medieval times was not fully dealt with until the Judicature Act of 1873. And the worst problems of public health and sanitation were not remedied until the Public Health Act of 1875, although numerous attempts had been made previously in, for example, the Act of 1848, which failed because it lacked powers of compulsion.

One group in Victorian society which shared Dickens's commitment to efficiency and professionalism was the Utilitarians or Philosophical Radicals, whose immensely influential challenges to the status quo were put into practice by the commitment and energy of figures such as Edwin Chadwick. Dickens was happy to cooperate with Chadwick in areas of mutual concern such as public health, but the movement as a whole was anathema to him since it was as strongly committed to *laissez-faire* as it was to efficiency. One of its most famous reforms was the Poor Law Amendment Act (the New Poor Law) of 1834, pilloried by Dickens in *Oliver Twist* for the inhumanity of its underlying motivation, which was to make entrance to the workhouse as unattractive an option for the poor as possible. This led to the tyrannizing over the helpless by public officials (the beadle, a minor parish functionary, remained one of Dickens's life-long *bêtes noires*), the provision of food just above the level of deprivation, and the separation of children from parents, and of married couples even when they were long past childbearing.

The fusion of Dickens's public and private worlds is revealed in a letter of 1861 in which he contrasts the uproar made by bishops over theological disputes and their silence "when the poor law broke down in the frost and the people . . . were starving to death. The world moves very slowly, after all, and I sometimes feel as grim as – Richard Wardour sitting on the chest in the midst of it" (to Mrs. Nash, 5 March 1861, Pilgrim 9.389). Richard Wardour was the character he played in Wilkie Collins's play, *The Frozen Deep*, the first occasion on which he met Ellen Ternan. We can see at this point a complete fusion between the life and the times which make up the substance of Dickens's biography. His rage and disappointment at a society which seemed to him willing to tolerate ignorance, poverty, and suffering indefinitely is mirrored in what he saw as the failure of his marriage. But if he had failed, in his own eyes, to achieve the kinds of social change he had struggled for, he could at least effect changes in his personal life, as the rejection of Catherine in favour of a kind of renewal with Ellen shows. The reading of Dickens offered here is, then, of a man radical in his personal as well as his social life who, rightly or wrongly, felt himself driven to desperate measures by desperate times.

NOTES

1 Michael Allen, *Charles Dickens' Childhood* (Macmillan, 1988), p. 58.
2 See Grahame Smith, *Charles Dickens: A Literary Life* (Macmillan, 1996).
3 Norman Low, *Mastering Modern British History* (Macmillan, 1998), p. 95.

FURTHER READING

Ackroyd, Peter. *Dickens*. HarperCollins, 1990.
Allen, Michael. *Charles Dickens' Childhood*. Macmillan, 1988.
Ingham, Patricia. *Dickens, Women and Language*. Harvester/Wheatsheaf, 1992.
Slater, Michael. *Dickens and Women*. Stanford University Press, 1983.
Smith, Grahame *Charles Dickens: A Literary Life*. Macmillan, 1996.
Tomalin, Claire. *The Invisible Woman: The Story of Nelly Ternan and Charles Dickens*. Viking, 1990.
Welsh, Alexander. *From Copyright to Copperfield: The Identity of Dickens*. Harvard University Press, 1987.

2

ROBERT L. PATTEN

From *Sketches* to *Nickleby*

In 1847 Dickens was a world-famous author raking in profits from serial novels and Christmas books. At that time he wrote several versions of his earlier life, attempting to explain to himself and his vast public how he had transformed himself from an ill-educated boy sent to work at the age of twelve in a shoe-blacking factory into the toast of European letters. The inauguration of a cheap edition of his novels provided an opportunity to write new prefaces accounting for each work's origin. For *Pickwick Papers*, his second title (1836–37) and first novel, he disclosed the beginning of his vocation as writer. William Hall, formerly a bookseller and in 1836 the partner of Edward Chapman in a modest publishing firm, arrived at Dickens's rooms in Furnival's Inn on 10 February 1836 with a proposal for the young author, known for his street sketches and tales published under the pseudonym "Boz." It was to supply letterpress accompanying etched illustrations by the comic artist Robert Seymour, some of which had already been prepared to illustrate the story Seymour had in mind.

In Hall, Dickens reported, he recognized

> the person from whose hands I had bought, two or three years previously . . . my first copy of the [*Monthly Magazine*] in which my first effusion – dropped stealthily one evening at twilight, with fear and trembling, into a dark letter-box, in a dark office, up a dark court [Johnson's Court] in Fleet Street – appeared in all the glory of print; on which occasion by-the-bye – how well I recollect it! – I walked down to Westminster Hall, and turned into it for half-an-hour, because my eyes were so dimmed with joy and pride, that they could not bear the street, and were not fit to be seen there. I told my visitor of the coincidence, which we both hailed as a good omen; and so fell to business.[1]

On the surface this would seem to be a familiar plot: poor aspiring writer submits a piece to a magazine, and when later on he meets someone connected to that first publication who brings a proposal for a new venture, he senses "a good omen" and signs a contract that leads within months to fame and, a decade later, fortune. But on closer examination the narrative shimmers with half-concealed alternatives hovering below the surface. Although the magazine to which the twenty-two-year-old Dickens submitted his story did not pay contributors, he went on, after this first successful application, publishing in it anonymously for another fifteen months, during which period Dickens was so desperately poor he could not afford to marry. Why give away stories? On the other hand, these stories received about forty complimentary notices, whereas the extensive range of paid journalism and fiction Dickens published over the next two years never was reviewed anywhere.[2] Furthermore, "appearing in all the glory of print" would seem to be cause for celebration, but Dickens confesses that seeing his writing published reduced him to tears; he hid from the street whose activities he would pry into in subsequent sketches, almost as if he were ashamed for being known as a writer. These seem mixed, even contradictory, responses, especially when presented as the definitive start of a literary career. But they are consistent with the self-fashioning of an author who publishes anonymously and pseudonymously, striving to be at once a professional author, writing for pay, and a gentleman and amateur, working for the love of it.

When Dickens began life on his own account (the title of a chapter in the autobiographical novel *David Copperfield*), he didn't exactly know what he wanted to become. He only knew what he wanted to be: "famous and caressed and happy," as he put it in an autobiographical fragment also composed around 1847 (Forster, 1.2). Dickens's childhood alternated between times when he did a star turn in the parlor before his parents' friends and months – years, they seemed – when his education was neglected or he was sent to work while his parents and siblings lived in debtors' prison. One early love affair, with Maria Beadnell, daughter of a banker, had withered because, though as suitor he was lively, agreeable, and clever in composing party rhymes, his background and prospects made him unsuitable. As office boy in a succession of lawyers' chambers, he was not much more promising. He mimicked customers and denizens of the neighborhood and attended popular entertainments – everything from Shakespeare to circuses – most evenings. Yet he kept himself apart from the shabby debaucheries he witnessed and maintained a neat, "military" appearance that was his way of distancing himself from his Marshalsea past.

Cleverness, energy, high jinks, and a tendency to extremes of emotion are characteristic of adolescents; Dickens did not turn 21 until 7 February 1833. One passing ambition was to go onto the stage of the public theatres he frequented after work. The impersonations achieved by dress, costume, gesture, and speech, the rapid-fire jokes and plot development, the dramatized, essentialized moral and spiritual conflicts – all appealed to the young

Dickens. But something kept him from pursuing an acting career: he caught a cold the night before his audition, missed it, and never rescheduled it.

Another outlet for this as yet undirected energy and talent was reporting. When Dickens left the law at sixteen, he taught himself shorthand and perfected his skill in taking down speeches until he was the most accurate and speedy stenographer in Parliament. This, like acting, was a way of ventriloquizing others' words. The rhetoric of civic discourse permeated Dickens's imagination, while the histrionics of parliamentary debate fitfully aroused his critical and humorous faculties. In 1828 Dickens commenced as a freelance shorthand writer at the Consistory Court of Doctors' Commons (a site memorably represented in *David Copperfield*); three years later, he advanced to a job transcribing parliamentary debates for his maternal uncle's paper, *The Mirror of Parliament*, just when politicians were agitated over impending electoral reform. Many of Dickens's colleagues in the gallery were destined for careers in the law, but the profession never particularly appealed to him, though from time to time into the mid-1840s he would think about entering it.

In 1834, through the influence of a friend, Dickens obtained a position at the liberal, Whig-owned *Morning Chronicle*, second only to *The Times* in circulation. The editor, John Black, sent him out to cover events throughout Britain; the cub reporter relished the coach races home to beat competitors into print. In October of that year Dickens began contributing theatre reviews and sketches, first to the daily *Morning Chronicle*, and from January 1835 also to the tri-weekly off-shoot, the *Evening Chronicle*, edited by Dickens's future father-in-law George Hogarth.

Those pieces about urban middle-class life, sometimes acutely observed, sometimes brash, and sometimes trite, brought in cash, but at twenty-two Dickens was still not clear what direction to pursue or whether he should publicize his own name. He signed his *Chronicle* sketches and tales "Boz," borrowing a nickname from a younger brother. Its peculiar character attracted attention; some thought it meant that the writer was a Boswell for the middling classes. Within two years Dickens had, in fact, made quite a reputation as "Boz." He sold stories to other journals under that pseudonym, and a young publisher, John Macrone, proposed collecting the papers, adding illustrations by the veteran London caricaturist George Cruikshank, and republishing them. But while *Sketches by Boz* were being revised and prepared for the press in the winter of 1835–36, Dickens wrote twelve more journalistic pieces published in *Bell's Life in London* under the pseudonym of "Tibbs." Although these papers, no longer by "Tibbs," were eventually swept up into the February 1836 two-volume *Sketches by Boz* or the one-volume December 1836 supplement, at some level Dickens was not yet, at the age of twenty-four, fully invested in a single literary projection, Boz.

Nor was he committed to a particular genre. He speaks, during these formative years, of having a novel planned or partly written, which later on he thinks of cutting up into journalistic snippets. In 1836 and 1837, in addition to writing two novels, Dickens composes (1) a pamphlet attacking Sabbatarianism, *Sunday Under Three Heads*, illustrated by Hablot Knight Browne and written by "Timothy Sparks"; (2) a farce in two acts, *The Strange Gentleman*, adapted from one of the *Sketches by Boz*; (3) an "operatic burletta," *The Village Coquettes*, with music by his sister Fanny's friend John Pyke Hullah; (4) a one-act burletta, *Is She His Wife? or Something Singular*, written "long before I was Boz" but premiered in March 1837 by John Pritt Harley, star of the previous pieces; (5) fourteen new "Sketches by Boz"; (6) revisions of many of his previous sketches for the collected volume publication; (7) a dozen miscellaneous papers and reviews, and (8) a children's book he abandons.

Thus in February 1836, at the age of twenty-four, Dickens might have picked one of several careers: newspaper journalism, leading perhaps to a position as editor, editorialist, and political spokesperson, possibly even as MP for a London constituency; theatre, in which he would write, act, direct, or produce plays and musical entertainments; or more general writing, of kinds, subjects, and genres not yet clear. As it turned out, Dickens continued in both journalism and theatre. In the 1840s he edited a newspaper for a few months and in the 1850s and 1860s he edited two periodicals running for twenty years. In those same decades he staged amateur theatricals, wrote plays, and gave readings from his fiction. But the writing of fiction received a decisive impetus from William Hall's invitation to contribute letterpress to Robert Seymour's illustrations about the mishaps of Cockney sportsmen.

What Seymour, Chapman, and Hall envisaged was a monthly publication featuring four etchings by the artist along with text written to match. Dickens, from the moment the proposal was offered, knew he wanted to go in a different direction – toward connected incidents and fiction, not a succession of illustrated comic anecdotes. His relations with Seymour were strained, in large part because the artist was unhappy about many things in his life including the direction his "junior" partner wanted to take the collaboration. When Seymour committed suicide before the second monthly number was published, and his successor proved inept at etching plates, Dickens took charge. All the energy that had characterized his madcap races to beat *The Times* in delivering copy about provincial elections, all the directorial verve he threw into amateur theatricals, all the management he exhibited in instructing his future wife, Catherine Hogarth, how to behave ("I perceive you have not yet subdued one part of your disposition," (18 December 1835, Pilgrim 1.109–10), became focused on this failing venture, the monthly part-serial entitled *The Pickwick Papers*. And Dickens succeeded. He hired an illustrator (Hablot Knight Browne, known as "Phiz") capable of producing effective images consonant with Dickens's improvised, developing story and characters; he expanded the number of pages of letterpress from twenty-four to thirty-two and reduced the number of pictures from four to two, changes that shifted costs and primacy from illustrator to author; and he convinced the publishers to continue the venture until it caught on with the public.

It did catch on. The last number sold 40,000 copies. It was a "double" number of sixty-four pages, comprising the wind-up of the story, four illustrations including a frontispiece and a vignette title, a Preface, a Table of Contents, and a List of Illustrations, so the whole twenty numbers could be bound up as a book. Chapman and Hall had stumbled on a gold mine. Dickens was capable of turning out effervescent copy on a regular basis; the publishers could invest in a single thirty-two-page publication, sell it, and reinvest the proceeds, so their capital turned over and multiplied manyfold in the course of publishing a single title. No wonder they were keen to secure from Dickens a contract for another book in the same format.

But Dickens was not exclusively bound to one firm. John Macrone was desperate to repeat his success by commissioning a new novel from Dickens in three volumes ([9] May 1836) and by reissuing the *Sketches* in monthly parts. Dickens was not about to have materials which had already appeared at least twice recycled as if they were another *Pickwick*. To forestall Macrone, Dickens persuaded Chapman and Hall (17 June 1837) to buy the copyrights he had signed over to Macrone; then, since somebody was likely to profit from the success of *Pickwick*, they could publish the *Sketches* in shilling monthly numbers on their own account. But this arrangement put the young author more in the hands of his *Pickwick* publishers, at a time when the expense of maintaining his family forced him to work ever harder just to keep solvent.

Meanwhile, another enterprising publisher, Richard Bentley, eager to bind Dickens to future publications for his firm, negotiated a contract (22 August 1836) for two further novels by Dickens, each to be published in the conventional three-volume format. He then snapped up Dickens and his *Sketches* illustrator, George Cruikshank, to edit and illustrate respectively a new half-crown monthly magazine, *Bentley's Miscellany*, starting in January 1837 (Agreement, 4 November 1836). In addition to editing, Dickens contracted to provide "an original article of his own writing, every monthly Number, to consist of about a sheet of 16 pages." By January 1837 Dickens was disastrously overcommitted – a burletta in the offing, the *Pickwick* installments due monthly, the *Miscellany* to edit, his monthly budget of writing for Bentley to complete, a three-volume novel, *Gabriel Vardon, the Locksmith of London*, promised to Macrone, and two novels for Bentley looming in the not-too-distant future. He had, at least, dropped his job as a *Chronicle* journalist. But, despite the statement in the Prologue to the first issue of *Bentley's* that it would "have nothing to do with politics," Dickens thought perhaps he could continue his journalistic strain in the new periodical. Accordingly, he wrote a humorous tale about the Mayor of Mudfog, a provincial town near London, for the January issue, and began a story satirizing the New Poor Law as it affected the management of the Mudfog workhouse for the February number.

That was a wholly unanticipated development. Bentley thought he had bought "Boz," a humorist, not a journalist attacking the governing class. But on the strength of his previous sketches and the buoyant installments of *Pickwick*, Boz was irresistibly attractive to the market. Grumbling all the way to the bank, Bentley allowed Boz's searing indictment of Utilitarian charity to continue with a second installment of *Oliver Twist* in the March *Miscellany*. And then Dickens, metamorphosing as a writer, editor, and man of letters with unprecedented rapidity, began making demands of his publisher that would eventually free him from journeyman drudgery and allow the pulsating creative powers to flow unchecked. Dickens wanted more money (17 March 1837), *Oliver Twist* to fulfill his obligation to write sixteen pages per month and to constitute the first three-volume novel (28 September 1837), *Barnaby Rudge* (the renamed *Gabriel Vardon*) to follow on the same terms (22 September 1838), and more control over his copyrights and the *Miscellany*. At the end of two years of almost continuous negotiation between author and publisher, Dickens achieved all his ends. He got clear of the journal, got *Oliver Twist* accepted as his monthly installment *and* the first of the two novels, and eventually even bought out the obligation to furnish a second novel on the same terms to Bentley.

Those protracted negotiations mark not only the transformation of Boz into Charles Dickens but also the confirmation of Dickens's vocational choice as a writer, principally of fiction very profitably circulated in installment formats. Whereas Dickens had published previously under pseudonyms, when Bentley brought out the three-volume *Oliver Twist* in November 1838 Dickens requested that the original "Boz" title page be replaced with one attributing the work to Charles Dickens. He was by then willing, and able, to take credit in his own right for his writing, and he was learning how to make his name a kind of trademark for quality, compassion, humor, and prodigious invention. He was well on the way to becoming a phenomenon, a celebrity and a talent of such magnitude that he could only be called "the Inimitable."

Pickwick did not finish until November 1837, by which date Dickens had written nine installments of *Oliver*. *Oliver* was completed in time for November 1838 volume publication, though it ran on as a serial in the *Miscellany* through April 1839. But Dickens had obligations to Chapman and Hall as well. So he started another monthly parts novel, *Nicholas Nickleby*, in April 1838; it continued until October 1839. Even these over-lapping fictions did not soak up all of Dickens's energy. As a favor to Bentley when they were still on good terms, in 1838 Dickens dictated to his father revisions to the autograph manuscript of the *Memoirs of Grimaldi*. Joey Grimaldi was a famous pantomime clown Dickens had seen as a boy, and whose life, from poverty to hard-earned fame, seems oddly consonant with Dickens's own trajectory. He also contributed a story to, and nominally edited, a three-volume charitable publication, *The Pic Nic Papers*, for the benefit of the widow and children of his first publisher, John Macrone. And secretly – because he was contracted to Bentley not to write for any other publisher – he wrote the Preface and facetious notes for George Cruikshank's rendering of a popular pub song, *The Loving Ballad of Lord Bateman* (1839). These ventures indicate that Dickens was not yet, despite his enor-mous success with serial fiction, set in a single mode of writing. Journalism and editing continued to be options – as they were in the succeeding decades as well.

What did Dickens find to write about? While all four of his first long works have things in common, they also draw on different sources in Dickens's cultural heritage. The *Sketches* derive in part from a tradition of graphic representations of urban scenes. The explosive growth of London during and after the Napoleonic wars and the thousands of workers who immigrated to the metropolis in search of jobs and a new identity produced a kind of dizzying dislocation for old and new inhabitants. Streets were torn down and rebuilt, fields converted to tenements, rivers bridged over, and shops opened and closed, seemingly overnight. Finding one's way around in this city of transformations was difficult enough; understanding the babble of tongues and the semiotics of signs – printed ones, but the equally impor-tant signs of clothing and behavior – required expert guidance. Artists and writers offered their expertise, portraying the "types" that by their charac-teristic garments, locations, speech, and habits identified them as typical – that is, simultaneously unique and representative. Dickens's early street sketches combined close though often emotionally distanced readings of the lives of the urban middle classes with the "types" familiar to him from popular theatre and comic versions of police reports. Many of the stories are rehashings of old fare, enacted by stock figures such as scheming maidens, bumbling wooers, dyspeptic bachelors, henpecked husbands, and suffering mothers. Pressure converted the ordinary, however, into something different, and better. Dickens in time learned to write *through* the stereotypes; he pushed himself to attempt a range of voices and effects, from farcical to horrific. His own, and his age's, unsettled response to the extraordinary changes taking place around them enabled a medley of impressions and attitudes to represent the spirit of the age.

Other condiments spiced the dish. The American writer Washington Irving had published a *Sketch Book* (1820) largely comprised of his experiences as a visitor in England; Dickens much admired it. He also admired, and in ways emulated, the sketches of character and essays on moral reflection contained in the great eighteenth-century periodicals: *The Tatler*, *The Spectator*, *The Bee*. The artist William Hogarth had in the mid-eighteenth century produced series of pictures on modern moral subjects. These were widely distributed through copies often accompanied by commentary explaining the narrative and morality, and were a source of inspiration for all Dickens's early fiction; a reviewer of *Pickwick* called Dickens "the literary Hogarth of the day."[3]

Hogarth was given credit by Henry Fielding, often identified as the "father" of the novel, for having done in pictures what Fielding wanted to accomplish in prose, to write comic moral narratives. To point a moral, a narrative needs closure; but another aspect of the "sketch" was its evanescence, its incompleteness, its refusal to do more than gesture at the multiplicity of phenomena comprising modern life. Some of Dickens's sketches enunciate a moral, more or less heavy-handedly, while others simply register a scene or the passing parade. And despite the sometimes good-natured, sometimes dour humor of the pieces, they are generally structured around a declension: shops, marriages, expeditions, speculations, turn out more often than not to deteriorate. Two of the more deliberately affecting narratives concern death: the first, "A Visit to Newgate," concludes by imagining the "last night on earth" of a condemned man, a subject Dickens reinscribed in Fagin's final hours; the second, "The Black Veil," describes the frantic, unavailing efforts of a mother to resuscitate her son, a hanged felon.

Seymour's notion of an illustrated serial about Cockney sportsmen skewed declensions in the direction of bathos – toward send-ups of pretentious urbanites who try to emulate the activities of country gentry. Dickens knew nothing about hunting and shooting, having been raised in naval towns and in London. He borrowed heavily from preceding comic writers, such as Robert Surtees and Thomas Hood, from Cervantes, Le Sage, and the eighteenth-century picaresque novelists, and from the theatre, for his initial depiction of the Pickwickians; the *Athenaeum* in December 1836 provided additional ingredients in Dickens's recipe: "two pounds of Smollett, three ounces of Sterne, a handful of Hook, and a dash of a grammatical Pierce Egan." Dickens initially wrote in a style both parodying and, because it was fluent and easy to produce, extemporizing upon parliamentary rhetoric. But even though the subject, format, characters, and situations for the first numbers were stereotypical, there was something about Hall's appearance in Furnival's Inn, about the contract for a serial that would pay Dickens enough to marry, and about the freshness of a new project rather than yet another installment of the Boz sketches, that at a fundamental level seemed like a new beginning.

Pickwick is about beginning; critics have likened it to a solar myth of regeneration or transcendence, with Mr. Pickwick's rotund, ever youthful corpus rising each morning like the sun. Its "beginnings again" are very powerful and very frequently repeated. In Dickens's own day, and for the next generation of Dickensians – notably G. K. Chesterton – the mythic creative powers of the benevolent, foolish amateur scientist and his cynical, good-hearted, knowledgeable sidekick Sam Weller produced "something nobler than a novel . . . [it] emit[s] that sense of everlasting youth – a sense as of the gods gone wandering in England."[4] *Pickwick* is a quintessential "road" narrative: the Pickwickians travel across the countryside getting into, and out of, scrapes, finding temporary havens that often, by their own ineptitude, they break up, and emerging at the book's conclusion changed in circumstance, undoubtedly, but little changed in character.

The Edwardians and Bloomsbury could not stand Dickens, especially the early Dickens. His sentimentality, uncontrolled and sometimes ungrammatical prosings, stagy plots, and impossible heroines repelled authors from Oscar Wilde to Aldous Huxley. Some redress of balance emerged after Edmund Wilson's seminal 1940 reading of Dickens: in this version, the works – especially the darker, later novels – were to be regarded seriously because of the author's manic-depressive personality.[5] The alternating lights and darks of his imagination – the benevolent Pickwick, for instance, invented alongside the malevolent Fagin in *Oliver Twist* – were for Wilson manifestations of a cripplingly divided personality, out of which both Dickens's taste for melodramatic contrasts and the failures of his marriage and his happiness devolved. Then British scholars began to reexamine the thesis that Dickens was a bad, careless, unstructured writer pandering to debased popular taste and compelled to overwrite because of his excessive ambition for social status and wealth. After the 1950s, efforts were made to rehabilitate the early works. Their thematic and imagistic coherence was elaborated; Dickens's painstaking (and unremunerative) revisions were tracked; his metaphoric fecundity and his social conscience were reappraised.

The theatre rescued Dickens's first novels from neglect far more than universities did. David Lean's 1948 masterpiece, *Oliver Twist*, lopped off a number of the weaker elements in Dickens's cobbled-together plot and left viewers with an indelible image of Fagin (played by Alec Guinness) threatening the body and soul of Oliver. This relationship was converted into a less Manichean, more comic and high-spirited one in Lionel Bart's musical, *Oliver!* (1960). The Royal Shakespeare Company, on its uppers in the 1970s with huge expenses and slender resources, pulled off an enormous coup with David Edgar's inspired two-part, nine-hour adaptation of *Nicholas Nickleby* (1980). This production reveled in all those parts of Dickens reprobated by Bloomsbury: the theatricality of the second-rate Crummles troupe, the sentimentality of Nicholas's care for the crippled Smike, and the ill-assorted mixture of comedy, tragedy, farce, and romance. Thus, by tapping back into the improvisatory, performative, and melodramatic roots of Dickens's early fictions, the late twentieth century rediscovered their vitality.

Reconsideration on other levels has also reclaimed these early works. The novels are characterized by an acute regressivity: their trajectories all point toward some kind of recovered, idyllic childhood free of the temptations and complications of adult sexuality. The powerful fairy-tale plot of recovering an imagined presexual home is more than irresponsible wish-fulfillment, however; it taps, as recent critics have noted, fundamental constituents of our making sense and finding comfort in the world. Dickens's women have come under sustained reexamination by feminist critics and Dickens's biographers; as a result, much more complicated stories are now told about the cultural, economic, educational, moral, and sexual functions performed by mothers, wives, mistresses, daughters, and sisters. And the picaresque tradition that so deeply scored Dickens's youthful imagination has been revalued, not as an inartistic succession of unrelated tales but as one of the primary ways stories are made. The picaresque imagination, which features provisional solutions to immediate challenges in a universe without absolutes, and the melodramatic imagination, which strongly embeds fundamental, emotionally rendered notions of good and evil within sharply contrasting characters who act out our deepest fears and desires, combine, despite their apparently contradictory natures, to produce in Dickens's early work a fecund, turbulent transformative world.

All of Dickens's experiences and concerns, from parliamentary reporting to child abuse to theatre, enter the text of *Nickleby*, where the chemistry of Dickens's wizard imagination transmutes the dull, shabby, and one-dimensional into a boisterous picaresque pantomime. *Nickleby* is the culmination of Dickens's early career. He began writing in mid-February 1838, intending the new serial to be another blow against cruelty to children in the "radicalish" vein mined by *Oliver Twist*. To that end, Dickens and Browne visited Yorkshire schools at the dead coldest point of winter, the beginning of February. He was, Forster discloses, "bent upon destroying" the cheap schools clustered around Barnard Castle that prominently advertised "no vacations" (2.4). These were depositories for unwanted and illegitimate children, as well as for the offspring of parents deluded by the schoolmasters' lying advertisements. During this visit Dickens met the "originals" of Squeers and John Browdie and conceived the story of Smike from the inscription on a gravestone.

Dickens's initial impulse centered around homes – figured as economic as well as domestic centers – and their breaking-up. The Nicklebys are exiled from their Devonshire farm because of their improvident father's ruinous speculations and early death – circumstances certainly imaginable and to some extent experienced by Dickens on account of his own father's improvidence. The challenge of establishing a new home "where," Nicholas tells Smike, "those I love are gathered together" (35), combines the traditional marriage plot with the plot of the *Bildungsroman* (novel of development). But it also, and from the beginning, involves for Dickens issues raised by the middle of *Oliver Twist*: What kind of home might there be for innocent children? Could there be a home uncontaminated by profligacy yet still nurturing and, unlike the Maylie and Brownlow households, also fertile? Is there a kind of benevolent violence that will protect rather than destroy the young, such as Nancy tries to exercise on behalf of Oliver at the cost of her life? Is home compatible with any kind of business? In mixing together these themes and narratives, Dickens "writes through" the conventions he inherited and opens his novel out into unexplored territory.

There is another influence operating on the imaginative inception of *Nickleby*. On 25 January 1838, just five days before setting out for Yorkshire, Dickens attended the opening of William Macready's new production of *King Lear* at Covent Garden. Four years earlier Macready had produced the play using Nahum Tate's sentimentalized redaction in which the Fool's role is eliminated, Cordelia lives, and Lear regains his crown. This time Macready "restored" the "original" text. Forster was too ill to attend the opening, so Dickens supplied his friend with material for the review Forster published in the *Examiner* on 28 January. A number of things about this production could have steeped in Dickens's mind over the next month: the cold, bleak setting; "the attachment and fidelity of the poor *Fool* to the houseless, broken-hearted King" (Forster's phrase); and the combination of fury and love, well characterized by Forster in his 27 October 1849 review of Macready's revival of *Lear*: "The tenderness, the rage, the madness, the remorse and sorrow, all come of one another and are linked together in a chain. Only of such tenderness, could come such rage."[6] Such insights may account for many features of Nicholas's character: his "breaking up" of Dotheboys Hall, his spirited defense of his sister's honor against Sir Mulberry Hawk, his pummeling of Squeers. These are effective, if violent, actions taken to defend the unprotected, and arise out of Nicholas's combination of fierce self-regard and genuine caring.

Another transformation of material that Dickens's exposure to Yorkshire schools and *Lear* may have effected is the rewriting of the traditional "buddy" relationship between two travelers. The Samuels – Pickwick and Weller – inscribe Don Quixote and Sancho Panza within a preindustrial England. With Nicholas and Smike, the relationship alters in the direction of Lear and his Fool: Nicholas is the houseless head of his family (more extensive and in need of more protection than he knows or, finally, can provide), and Smike enacts a loving loyalty to his protector so intense it contributes to his death. The other factor in this mix is Cordelia, who dies for her father's cause. While in the Macready production Cordelia and the Fool were not a doubled role, played by a single actress, the blurring of distinction between the two characters and their fates in Shakespeare's play can be observed as well in Smike. Furthermore, Dickens continued in subsequent novels to rescript the Lear–Cordelia relationship.

At the time Dickens was thinking about beginning *Nickleby*, he was fervently interested in Macready's management of Covent Garden, partly because the impresario might stage Thomas Noon Talfourd's new play. To Talfourd Dickens dedicated *Pickwick* in October 1838; to Macready Dickens dedicated *Nickleby* in September 1839. Talfourd was a champion of the rights of authors because he had introduced into Parliament a bill extending the period of copyright; Macready was the reformer of the stage. But though Macready was more faithful to "legitimate" drama than to pantomimes, farces, and burlettas, he was still an actor of histrionic gesture and a director inclined to melodramatic stagings.

Exactly how to write through theatrical claptrap to the spiritual and moral principles underlying melodrama's stock figures and black–white contrasts was a vexing issue for Dickens. In *Oliver Twist*, the narrator both exploits and apologizes for the juxtaposition of tragedy and comedy "in as regular alternation, as the layers of red and white in a side of streaky bacon" (17). Moreover, ever since the advent of Jingle in the first number of *Pickwick*, Dickens had been wrestling with the indeterminacy of character. Jingle, Job Trotter, even Nancy, can assume any number of guises, can by costume and speech perform many characters. How does one know, perform, or write, genuine character, "inner" selfhood, as it was understood to exist within bourgeois and Christian cultures in the nineteenth century?

A second strain, therefore, of Macready's influence on *Nickleby* is the incorporation of theatricality. Dickens may have visited Portsmouth in September 1838 and spied an old playbill advertising a performance by T. D. Davenport (1792–1851) and his daughter Jean (1829–1903). Almost certainly Dickens did not anticipate the Crummles company and the "Infant Phenomenon" (based on the Davenports) earlier in the novel's composition. However, the high-spirited comic episodes involving Nicholas and Smike in the Portsmouth theatre furthered Dickens's novelistic investigation into the complex relationships between person and impersonation. This relationship was never simple: overplaying a scene might be just as "genuine" as underplaying, or not playing at all, and the Kenwigses overcome by their tribulations are not the less genuine for their histrionics than Ralph is in his rigid, but finally unsupportable, emotional and conversational self-control. Outright artifice can express reality. Adding the Crummleses to Dickens's ingredients furthered his writing *through* conventions to something more potent. When Smike says to Nicholas as they flee from Yorkshire, "I will be your faithful hard-working servant . . . I only want to be near you" (13), language, character, and relationship clarify. Both the picaresque and the melodramatic are invoked and transcended, as in *Lear*.

Another aspect of early Victorian drama and the fairy-tale was sudden transformation – in pantomime, of "real" characters into "stage" ones of Harlequin and Columbine and Clown, and in the fairy-tales Dickens loved, of neglected children into ones blessed with loving families and higher class status. The typical pantomime plot, which Dickens varied in several ways in *Nickleby*, has a greedy father who insists that his daughter marry, not the worthy but poor young man, but an unworthy rich old dotard (a Pantaloon); a Benevolent Spirit intervenes in the Harlequinade, transforming everyone, and the youngsters live happily ever after. John Bowen has written about the "peculiarly ambivalent transformational energies" of *Nickleby*.[7] These energies are manifested in everything from the mantua-making Mantalinis to the sudden reversals of the plot. But there are a lot of strange figures orchestrating the changes. What the novel lacks, from the opening chapter, are parents willing to acknowledge and care for their children, to supervise them during the period of transformation from infancy to adulthood. While Mrs. Nickleby has the right plot (marriage and confirmed middle-class status for her children and herself) constantly on her lips and in what passes for her mind, she is incapable of effecting transformations for her offspring, querulous about her own changes and responsibilities, and only at the end willing to exchange the marriage plot with the madman next door for a parenting plot on behalf of Nicholas and Kate. Fathers are notably missing from the lives of their children, either through death or deliberate policy.

In their stead, uncles or pseudo-uncles negotiate the space where the protected family within the house must meet and interact with the outside world.[8] What uncles, ambiguously, must do is to put the family into circulation within the economy. Ralph performs these transformations in ways that violate the boundaries between private sanctity and public exposure: he wants to sell out Nicholas and to cash in on Kate by selling her to lecherous spendthrifts. Many other avuncular figures preside over species of transformations: Mr. Lillyvick, of himself and his relations; Mr. Crummles, impresario of his family/theatrical company; and, doubled as fairy-godfathers, the Cheeryble brothers, who transform the fortunes of Nicholas, Madeline Bray, Kate, and their nephew Frank. What seem to be working themselves out in this novel are complex issues about how a boy becomes father and how relationships of affection and loyalty that bind a family together stand over against the financial dealings that characterize business.

As in the previous novels, Dickens gifts the generous-handed and -hearted with the power not only to effect beneficial transformations of their wards but also to succeed in business without resorting to any business-like practices. The closest the novel can come in allowing Nicholas to succeed as a wage-earner in the "real" world is to have him earn his keep as author and actor, one who entertains and is paid for providing wholesome pleasure. But "shame" attends performance; Nicholas plays under an assumed name and quickly exits the company. Once he is apprenticed to the Cheerybles, he is assured of coming again to home and family at last; but the harsh realities of commercial affairs, represented by the buying and selling of children, servants, partners, and strangers, is not allowed to contaminate the world of Cheeryble, Linkinwater, and company. Indeed, as John Glavin has observed, Dickens figures Nicholas keeping the firm's "books"; the Cheerybles function for Nicholas as Chapman and Hall did for Dickens, providing the wished-for godparent who purposes and effects the son's well-being.[9]

There is one other figure in the novel who works for a living (though no payment ever passes through her hands): Miss La Creevy. In some ways she is a focus for Dickens's anxieties about professional authorship. A miniaturist, she paints portraits, not of people exactly as they are, but of them as they wish to be or of persons imaged as presenting a type – naval officer or lady. Her reproductions come close to those of actors who portray a character by performing according to standard conventions and artifices rather than by submerging the actor's personality into the character's. Furthermore, the artist reads character and fortune in physical features and employs art to express fate. Miss La Creevy's portraits are like characters in a story, rendered visible by visual means. So, too, are Browne's illustrations, which marry the presentation of characters to their narrative functions within the

1 Portrait of Charles Dickens, engraved from the painting by Daniel Maclise, *Nicholas Nickleby*, numbers 19 and 20, 1839.

story. People are not just people in Browne's etchings, but people interacting with others, within a setting that is often itself symbolic or filled with emblematic, commenting accessories. Thus Miss La Creevy's portraits are like early Victorian drama, Browne's illustrations, and Dickens's narrative – presentations of characters understood in terms of their physical appearance and action within the social world.

Selling such a product, one that "reads" or "interprets" or "tells" about the world, seems to escape the otherwise general opprobrium that *Nickleby* heaps on commercial enterprises, from the United Metropolitan Improved Hot Muffin and Crumpet Baking and Punctual Delivery Company to Dotheboys Hall to Ralph Nickleby's usury and Brooker's blackmail. It may be exculpatory rationalization, but Dickens sets forth such artistic activity as somehow less complicit in using others as objects than, for instance, the utilitarian "philosophers" who manage workhouses in *Oliver Twist*. Dickens's verbal portraits of characters and Browne's visual images "sold" the monthly parts. Moreover, other artists muscled in on the action: Thomas Onwhyn, under the pseudonym of "Peter Palette," supplied "extra illustrations" from installment 4 onward of portraits (ten in all) and scenes (thirty), while Kenny Meadows issued a suite of twenty-four engravings in 1839 under the title *Heads from Nicholas Nickleby drawn by Miss La Creevy*.

The crowning "portrait," however, is the one Chapman and Hall commissioned of Dickens from his young Irish friend, Daniel Maclise. This was engraved by William Finden and offered as frontispiece in the final double number, October 1838. It supplies a full-length view of Dickens, with a meditative expression on his youthful countenance, seated by his writing desk, his hand touching a manuscript, surrounded by a setting bespeaking modest but comfortable middle-class status – something that in fact Dickens could provide the Nicklebys but could not yet guarantee for his own family through his writer's income. The iconography of Maclise's portrait became *the* canonical way of representing the bourgeois writer for the next decade.

But whatever modesty the picture presents is qualified by where it is presented. Readers might reasonably expect that the frontispiece to a novel entitled, on the monthly number wrappers, *The Life and Adventures of Nicholas Nickleby containing a Faithful Account of the Fortunes, Misfortunes, Uprisings, Downfallings, and Complete Career of the Nickleby Family* would be of said Nicholas Nickleby, especially as the continuation of the wrapper title, "edited by Boz," implies that Nicholas is the author of his own adventures. But when the final installment was published, and thereafter when buyers ripped off the wrapper and had their installments bound in proper order with the frontispiece facing a vignette title page which shortened the book's name to *The Life and Adventures of Nicholas Nickleby*, several things happened. The text was no longer implicitly attributed to Nickleby, as edited by Boz, but to "Charles Dickens." And the frontispiece depicts, not the expected portrait of the titular hero, but Charles Dickens (figure 1). Moreover, the frontispiece is not only a picture, but also a text; inscribed below the portrait in an etched facsimile of Dickens's handwriting are the words "Faithfully yours, Charles Dickens." The "faithful" that once described the telling ("a Faithful Account") now describes the relationship between the author *in propria persona* and his readers: "Faithfully yours." To what is Dickens as author being faithful? To the life of Nicholas Nickleby, which he once pretended to "edit" as "Boz"? To the reader, who imagines that the purchase of this work of art (portrait frontispiece and serial fiction) establishes a connection of trust between buyer and author? To the conventions of the "periodical essayist," like Henry Mackenzie, to whom Dickens pays tribute in the *Nickleby* Preface for delivering himself to his readers "with the freedom of intimacy and the cordiality of friendship"? To some pervasively secular ideal of "faith," "uncovering, demonstrating, and making operative the essential moral universe in a post-sacred era," as Peter Brooks defines the principle of melodrama?[10] To the arts of portraiture and story-telling? Or is the closing and signature the conventional termination of correspondence written by a gentleman (or a businessman?), ensuring trust between writer and recipient?

Perhaps all these implications of the *Nickleby* portrait and subtended inscription jostle for preeminence, depending on what context they are placed within. In the largest of contexts, this frontispiece marks the apogee of the first phase of Dickens's vocational career. As anonymous, Boz, Tibbs, Timothy Sparks, or Charles Dickens, he had composed three volumes of sketches, three novels, three plays, a pamphlet, and nearly fifty newspaper reports and reviews of theatre and books, and edited the *Memoirs of Grimaldi*, Cruikshank's *Lord Bateman*, and *Bentley's Miscellany*. At the age of twenty-six Dickens had published around 1,500,000 words. He had made himself a name, and that name was author.

NOTES

1 Charles Dickens, "Preface to the Cheap [1847] Edition," *The Pickwick Papers*, ed. James Kinsley (Clarendon Press, 1986), p. 884.
2 Kathryn Chittick, *Dickens and the 1830s* (Cambridge University Press, 1990), p. 48.
3 *Bell's Life in London*, 12 June 1836.
4 G. K. Chesterton, *Charles Dickens* (Methuen, 1906), p. 79.
5 Edmund Wilson, "Dickens: the Two Scrooges," *The Wound and the Bow* (Oxford University Press, 1941).
6 Quoted in *"The Amusements of the People" and Other Papers: Reports, Essays,*

and Reviews, 1834–51, the Dent Uniform Edition of Dickens' Journalism, vol. II, ed. Michael Slater (Ohio State University Press, 1996), p. 171.

7 John Bowen, *Other Dickens: Pickwick to Chuzzlewit* (Oxford University Press, 2000), p. 109.

8 Helena Michie, "The Avuncular and Beyond: Family (Melo)drama in *Nicholas Nickleby*," in *Dickens Refigured: Bodies, Desires and Other Histories*, ed. John Schad (Manchester University Press, 1996), pp. 80–97.

9 John Glavin, *After Dickens: Reading, Adaptation, and Performance* (Cambridge University Press, 1999).

10 Peter Brooks, *The Melodramatic Imagination* (Yale University Press, 1976), p. 15.

FURTHER READING

Butt, John and Kathleen Tillotson. *Dickens at Work*. Methuen, 1957.

Cohen, Jane R. *Charles Dickens and His Original Illustrators*. Ohio State University Press, 1980.

Kincaid, James. *Dickens and the Rhetoric of Laughter*. Clarendon Press, 1971.

Marcus, Steven. *Dickens: From Pickwick to Dombey*. Chatto and Windus, 1965.

Miller, J. Hillis. *Charles Dickens: The World of His Novels*. Harvard University Press, 1958.

Patten, Robert L. *Charles Dickens and His Publishers*. Clarendon Press, 1978.

Schor, Hilary. *Dickens and the Daughter of the House*. Cambridge University Press, 1999.

Slater, Michael. *Dickens and Women*. Stanford University Press, 1983.

Steig, Michael. *Dickens and Phiz*. Indiana University Press, 1978.

Welsh, Alexander. *From Copyright to Copperfield: The Identity of Dickens*. Harvard University Press, 1987.

3

KATE FLINT

The middle novels: *Chuzzlewit, Dombey,* and *Copperfield*

There is a conspicuous restlessness about the novels which Charles Dickens conceived in the 1840s: *Martin Chuzzlewit* (1843–44), *Dombey and Son* (1846–48), and *David Copperfield* (1849–50). In part, their mobility is geographical: travelers voyage and return from England to the Continent, the United States, Australia, and India. England is a commercial hub: at the center of trading networks and a growing colonial power. Internally, conceptions of spatiality shift as a result of new modes of travel. The coaches of *Martin Chuzzlewit* are replaced by the railways which slice through urban and rural environments in *Dombey and Son*, effecting shifting points of view. And travel, these novels make clear, has everything to do with offering different perspectives. The shifts of location are one of the means by which the reader's attention is continually redirected, especially in the first two novels. In these, different groupings of characters are interwoven, juxtaposed, brought into implicit conversation with one another in a way which amplifies the novels' central conceptual concerns with selfishness, with forms of value, with families, with desire, and with self-realization. If the third of the novels, *David Copperfield*, differs from the other two in being unified by one central narrative voice, its own sense of motion is given not just by the successive stages through which David passes on "the road of life" (64), but by the continual oscillation of time between the present of the narration, and the recollections – sometimes sharp, sometimes dream-like and hazy – which haunt the writer, causing him to lose "the clear arrangement of time and distance" (57).

What Dickens starts to explore in a sustained fashion in his fiction of the 1840s is the dialogue between consciousness and world, and the incessant interaction between the conscious and the unconscious mind. It is in this sense that travel is not just important in its own, thematic right, but as a metaphor for individual growth, or for experiencing estrangement; as a quest for understanding, or as a process for learning and exchanging human sympathy. Mr. Micawber, in *David Copperfield*, is the embodiment of outrageous optimism, and this spills over into his vision of how easy it will be for his family to send letters home as they voyage out to Australia. But he is made the vehicle for a more serious point: the relation of geographical space to the mind: "'The ocean, in these times, is a perfect fleet of ships; and we can hardly fail to encounter many, in running over. It is merely crossing,' said Mr. Micawber, trifling with his eye-glass, 'merely crossing. The distance is quite imaginary'"(57). The imaginative resonances of distance and of home, both in terms of domestic relationships and in relation to the development of national identity, are fundamental to these novels.

During the 1840s, Dickens's own life was a peripatetic one. His travels to America and Canada in 1842 not only provided the material for *American Notes*, and the setting for lengthy sections of *Martin Chuzzlewit*, but caused shifts in the novelist's self-perception. In America, not just his writing, but his persona, was publicly commented on and critiqued. He found himself a cultural commodity, and its circulation had passed out of his control. This may well have been a factor in consolidating his interest in the theme of disjunctions and discrepancies between public and private selves. The intensified sense of national identification resulting from this trip was a factor in his assumption of the role of influential commentator on a whole range of public issues, both within and outside his fiction. In 1844, with *Chuzzlewit* and *A Christmas Carol* completed, Dickens's need for a change of scene, and a breather from constant literary production – combined with economic pressure – led him to take his household through France to Italy. He returned briefly to England at the end of the year to publish *The Chimes*, arriving home with his family in June 1845.

Pictures from Italy (1846), with its phantasmagoria of foreign scenes dissolving into one another, was not the only result of this trip. European scenes erupt into the predominantly English settings of both *Dombey and Son* and *David Copperfield*. Travel, for Dickens, was both flight and quest: in both cases, internal and external restlessness fuse. Tellingly, the impulse to move onward, running away from oneself yet finding that self, and the past, to be always with one, is, in the first of these novels, projected onto the greedy, ambitious, villainous Carker: "commotion, discord, hurry, darkness, and confusion in his mind, and all around him . . . a fevered vision of things past and present all confounded together; of his life and journey blended into one" (55). He uses his feverish journey as an excuse to postpone thought, yet is "always tormented with thinking to no purpose." Ultimately, this traveling, seeking a rest which will not come, is claustrophobic, turning the self in upon itself, leading to self-destruction. Reading *David Copperfield*, after this, it is impossible not to find a parallel in David's experience, as he moves through Europe in the blur of consciousness that follows the death of

Dora, his first wife; passing on, "from city to city, seeking I know not what, and trying to leave I know not what behind" (58). The vocabulary of dreaming that Dickens has David employ is disconcertingly close both to Carker's nightmarish state of mind, and to his own repeated use of the language of dream and vision in *Pictures from Italy*. Dickens's writings of the 1840s displace their characters' anxieties about the degree of control they have over their own lives onto metaphors of motion. It is tempting to link this, at however unconscious a level, to Dickens's own driven energies. These were reflected not just in travel (the family again lived abroad, in Lausanne and Paris, between June 1846 and March 1847) but in the range of commitments he undertook, from the brief editorship of the *Daily News* in 1846, to the establishment, with Angela Burdett-Coutts, of Urania Cottage, for women who were, or were in danger of becoming, prostitutes. In 1850, he launched his own weekly journal, *Household Words*. The eclectic mixture of articles and imaginative writing which this contained invites the reader to jump from domestic social problems to aspects of life in other countries, thus demonstrating that Dickens's restlessness was much more than a personal psychological trait. It can be seen as a response to modernity, and to the multiplicity of choices that a rapidly changing world brings with it.

Mobility encompasses even more than moving from one place, one subject to another. It is a facet of style. Dickens unsettles his readers from the start of *Martin Chuzzlewit*, refusing to give us any stable position from which to read. He opens with a mock-pedantic satire on aristocratic genealogy – a peculiarly oblique beginning, which understandably failed to grip his original readership – and moves to a suspiciously gushing eulogy on the virtues of the Pecksniff family. Hyperbole, in this novel, is, disconcertingly, both a means of attack and of sentimental endorsement, especially when describing the domestic idylls of Tom Pinch and his sister Ruth, or the courtship of Ruth and John Westlock. The novel pivots around the despicable trait of hypocrisy and the benevolent possibilities of deception, and Dickens's own shifts of tone provide further instances of disguise, encouraging the reader to become an active interpreter, assessing the grounds of our own judgment.

John Forster recounts how Dickens deliberately set out in this novel, rather after the manner of Henry Fielding, to display "the number and variety of humours and vices that have their root in selfishness" (Forster, 4.1). As was to be the case in *Dombey and Son*, too, these center on the proper use of money, and the effects and potential corruption of wealth, or the expectation of wealth. The plot outline is simple enough, with the older Martin Chuzzlewit anxiously guarding the fate not just of his finances, but of his cherished young companion, Mary; his grandson, also called Martin, is made to prove himself a worthy suitor and inheritor through undergoing a number of trials – particularly his dismal sojourn in America – which teach him not just fortitude but, all-importantly, altruism. Alongside this romance plot, Pecksniff's obsessive egoism, his own repulsively lascivious pursuit of Mary, and his daughters' tragi-comic search for husbands, become entangled with further levels of deception, both personal and financial. Martin Chuzzlewit senior performs dotage and decrepitude, the better to draw out and eventually expose Pecksniff's appalling attitudes, and Pecksniff's younger daughter, Merry, marries the abusive Jonas Chuzzlewit – not just one of the many birds of prey who circle around the Chuzzlewit family fortunes, but someone who becomes "caged, and barred, and trapped" (38) in the fraudulent dealings of the Anglo-Bengalee Disinterested Loan and Life Assurance Company.

The success of this company relies on public gullibility. Its weapon is style, both linguistic and aesthetic. The solidity of its self-description, the tones of its self-advertisement, appear to vouch for its worth. "It is too common with all of us, but it is especially in the nature of a mean mind," warns the narrative voice, "to be overawed by fine clothes and fine furniture" (27), and Jonas is no exception, completely taken in, like the company's clients, by a reception room crammed with pictures, with copies from the antique in alabaster and marble, china vases and lofty mirrors – "costly toys of every sort in negligent abundance" (28). But Dickens refuses to make the rhetorical surface of *Martin Chuzzlewit* any less opaque for his own reader. Early in the novel, he describes the contents of the booksellers' windows in the market town of Salisbury, and the promise that their display holds out to the imaginative literary traveller: here "were the dainty frontispiece and the trim vignette, pointing like handposts on the outskirts of great cities to the rich stock of incident beyond" (5). A promising signpost is one thing, though, and making the journey another. Dickens deliberately misroutes the reader in an act of narrative deception which he was to repeat with the figure of Mr. Boffin in *Our Mutual Friend* (1865), making us believe in the decline into helpless vulnerability of the elder Martin. But it is the reader who is ultimately shown up as truly vulnerable. If *Martin Chuzzlewit* teaches one lesson, it is not so much about the more obvious pitfalls of selfishness but about the dangers of being too trusting, too confident in one's own interpretative powers.

Interpretation involves both observation and communication, and this is a novel filled with allusions to these activities, and to their varying degrees of reliability and legitimacy. The titles of American newspapers – the *Sewer*, the *Stabber*, the *Family Spy*, the *Private Listener*, the *Peeper*, *Plunderer*, and *Keyhole Reporter* – form part of Dickens's satiric armory against American hypocrisy, giving the lie to that society's proclaimed democratic openness.

But spying and overhearing and detective work are no less endemic to his own plotting: he, and the reader, utilize the very mediums which are also condemned, thus, again, confusing the reader's confidence in being able to arrive at clear-cut judgments as to whether to condone or condemn specific activities. This repetitious interpretive indeterminacy is figured in more literal terms in the text through the ways in which channels of communication are often frustrated or perverted. There is, for example, a good deal of letter-writing in *Martin Chuzzlewit*, but no guarantee that epistles will reach those for whom they are intended. At the London boarding house run by Mrs. Todgers, where Mr. Pecksniff and his family stay when visiting the metropolis, one of the other lodgers, with the inexplicably outlandish name of Tamaroo, "was a perfect Tomb for messages and small parcels; and when dispatched to the Post Office with letters, had been frequently seen endeavouring to insinuate them into casual chinks in private doors, under the delusion that any door with a hole in it would answer the purpose" (32). The reference to the Post Office is, in itself, a sign of modernity. Rowland Hill's penny post was introduced in 1840, and hence this serves as a further pointer to the way in which, in this novel, Dickens invests social change with anxieties concerning legibility on the one hand, and the vulnerability of openness on the other. When the narrator comments on Tom's simplicity, and its "contemptible" trustingness (39), it is not easy to determine the tone except inasmuch as it is both deeply affectionate, and highly regretful that such qualities are ultimately impractical, even dangerous ones in these times. Similarly, in *David Copperfield*, the young and gullible David finds himself continually taken advantage of by those ostensibly serving him, something which not only highlights how much he has to learn, but establishes a distance of spectatorship between reader and naive subject. Such a distance would seem to consolidate the reader's position of knowingness, but, as we have seen, the assumption of a trusting position is also one of which we would do well to beware.

This need to be continually on one's guard is a necessary response, it would seem, to the rapidly shifting ways of life, and the consequent illegibility and arbitrariness of social signifiers, which Dickens and his readership were learning to negotiate. "Change begets change," comments the narrator in chapter 18.

> Nothing propagates so fast. If a man habituated to a narrow circle of cares and pleasure, out of which he seldom travels, step beyond it, though for ever so brief a space, his departure from the monotonous scene on which he has been an actor of importance, would seem to be the signal for instant confusion. As if, in the gap he had left, the wedge of change was driven to the head, rending what was a solid mass to fragments, things cemented and held together by the

usages of years, burst asunder in as many weeks. The mine which Time has slowly dug beneath familiar objects is sprung in an instant; and what was rock before becomes but sand and dust.

Dickens here offers a startlingly compact version of the violence which may be performed by the passage of time, collapsing apparently stable edifices. Buildings, or, more precisely the practice of architecture, play an important role in the novel, and architectural metaphors, like the castles in the air which the young Martin builds regarding his future, cluster round the characters. Houses, however, prove to be sites of unease, often housing temporary residents, belying the sense of permanence ostensibly offered by bricks and mortar.

Nor are they impermeable fortresses against the pressures of modern society. It can be helpful here to borrow Walter Benjamin's concept of "porosity" – the phrase he used in the 1925 essay on Naples which he wrote with Asja Lacis – in order to intimate how the life of the street and the life inside dwelling-places, public and private zones, dissolve into one another.[1] This is applicable in *Martin Chuzzlewit* both literally, in the way in which the pigs, toads, damp, and vegetable rottenness invade the settlers' huts in the swampy city of Eden, and more figuratively, in the ways in which houses and rooms are used to figure their inhabitants' characters. One of the novel's most striking features is the way in which Dickens uses images of enclosure and apertures to signify the workings of human consciousness, collapsing the boundaries between material and mental space.

This porosity of the psychological and the topographical can be located both in occasional analogy, and in more sustained treatments. Thus we are early told, apropos of the uneasy Pecksniffian domestic arrangements, that "in the quiet hours of the night, one house shuts in as many incoherent and incongruous fancies as a madman's head" (5); later, Dickens describes a room in a Liverpool tavern as having "more corners in it than the brain of an obstinate man" (35). More notably, the treatment of Jonas Chuzzlewit's state of mind, however, as he moves toward and away from the murder of his business associate Montague Tigg, provides a prolonged demonstration of Dickens's fascination with the blurred ground between the inner and the outer self: his acknowledgment, which continues spasmodically in the portrayal of Mr. Dombey and then resurfaces repeatedly in David Copperfield's narration, of the uncontrollable force wielded by what we now term the unconscious. The deepening evening darkness blends with the less definable "dark shade emanating from within" Jonas (46). Although he thought he had left his bloody, murderous secret behind him in the wood where he kills Tigg, it refuses to stay there, but moves with him, haunting his room back in London. This room, which he had left locked, pretending to be in it, while away on his homicidal mission, obsesses him, and becomes, moreover, the imprisoning chamber of his own mind, investing him with "its mysterious terrors," so that "he became in a manner his own ghost and phantom, and was at once the haunting spirit and the haunted man" (47).

Jonas Chuzzlewit's haunted self is both an example of Dickens's developing interest in the inescapable mark made by the past on every individual, and an acknowledgment of the shaping power of subjectivity. Jonas's tortured mental restlessness is the obverse of the security which the midwife Mrs. Gamp takes in her person and in her surroundings: her apartment "was not a spacious one, but, to a contented mind, a closet is a palace" (49). Home, in other words, is more a state of mind than an actual physical location. "Though home," proclaims the narrator in a context that is patriotic as well as domestic, "is a name, a word, it is a strong one; stronger than magician ever spoke, or spirit answered to" (35). What actually constitutes "home" is a constant preoccupation in Dickens's writing during this period.

All three of the novels possess a highly contradictory dynamic: a pull, on the one hand, toward domestic contentment, and the emotional succour and safety that a true home might offer, yet, on the other, a powerful imaginative involvement with the abuse, the manipulation, and the cruelty that homes can contain. The Dombey home is no exception. Dickens comes close to caricature in the earlier chapters of the novel which portray Mr. Dombey as a man obsessed with his firm, with trade, and with a damaging conflation of his "house" – in the sense of his business – and his home. If *Martin Chuzzlewit* aimed to illuminate the working of a range of humors, this novel more deliberately focuses on the sin of pride. For Dombey, pride's chief embodiment, his son Paul's prime importance is to foster this business's sense of solidity and continuity, and the death of the boy, who seems doomed from the start of the novel not just by his sickliness but by his preternatural solemnity in asking pointed questions about what money can do, is not so much the occasion for personal grief as for acute frustration at the failure of Dombey's commercially oriented plans. Mr. Dombey sees his daughter, Florence, as providing no substitute, despite her worryingly masochistic, self-abnegating devotion toward a paternal figure who offers no response of affection. As the caricature breaks down, offering a more complex depiction of a man trapped in his pride, dampening down any "mutterings of an awakened feeling in his breast" and showing himself to be, "in his pride, a heap of inconsistency, and misery, and self-inflicted torment" (40), Dickens explores the damaging effects of imposing, whether deliberately or through reiterated thought and action, emotional stasis upon oneself.

Dombey's taking of a second wife is, effectively, the purchase of a potential breeding partner. It is also linked to the domestic dynamic I identified earlier, because counterpointed with Dickens's ostensible praise of harmonious home life is his lively interest in strong, often angry women – like Edith Dombey or, in *David Copperfield*, Rosa Dartle. The articulate outbursts of these women illuminate the economic as well as the emotional structures underpinning personal relations. Edith was under no illusions about the degrading financial deal involved in marrying Dombey: "knowing that my marriage would at least prevent the hawking of me up and down; I suffered myself to be sold as infamously as any woman with a halter around her neck is sold in any market-place" (54). Her passion and resentment fire up not just in relation to him, but in response to Carker – his "parasite and tool," as she terms him – with whom she runs away. This flight is not, however, to commit adultery, but to punish the arrogance of them both, men who, in their different ways, thought they could own and subdue her. What looks transgressive in the eyes of the world is one of the few options open to her through which she can act autonomously and exert a vengeful – but not unsympathetically presented – agency. She refuses to remain as property: the subject of purchase, sale, and exchange.

For much of *Dombey and Son*, the perfect home is a projection of the imagination. When Dombey's gloomy house is being prepared by workmen to welcome his new bride, Florence listens to their voices as they depart in the evenings, and "pictured to herself the cheerful homes to which they were returning, and the children who were waiting for them, and was glad to think that they were merry and well pleased to go" (30). This picturing goes beyond her speculating about the lives of the family in the house opposite: it tells us that Florence does not fall into the same mind-set as her father, seeing working people as cogs in a commercial machine or items on a balance sheet. By a similar token, costly, or even well-chosen and comfortable furnishings do not make a home, as Mr. Carker the Manager's tasteful habitation shows, particularly when juxtaposed with the sparse interior of his brother and sister's suburban house – a house which, nonetheless, is a repository of honesty and devotion. Significantly, the most comforting domestic space is not inhabited by a conventional family, but is the parlor of the Wooden Midshipman, the store selling ships' instruments where Walter Gay lives with his Uncle Sol, and which provides a necessary refuge for Florence when she flees there after her father strikes her, to find everything about her "as convenient and orderly, if not as handsome, as in the terrible dream she had once called Home" (49). Like the converted boat which houses Peggotty's unorthodox family in *David Copperfield*, the Midshipman's associations with the sea help make a deliberately potent figurative connection between meteorological and emotional storms, and the need of a stable and loving center if one is to have any chance of weathering either. Moreover, in *Dombey and Son*, the choice of a commercial establishment to signify such a center – especially one which must learn to relinquish some of its superficially attractive but economically fatal archaism if it is to succeed in modern society – is an essential one. It signifies that while Dickens attacks some of the worst effects of a soul-destroying preoccupation with money, he is hardly anti-capitalist, or anti-imperialist.

The prose luxuriates in its descriptions of imported Indian goods at the opening of chapter 4, before moving with equal enthusiasm to delineate the stock-in-trade of the Wooden Midshipman. Yet the enthusiasm for mercantile expansiveness is informed by a moral conscience, albeit a subdued one. For if there is an overt condemnation of slavery in both *American Notes* and *Martin Chuzzlewit*, so, too, does the practice supply a hidden history in this novel. Walter Gay, for example, is despatched to Barbados: a location instantly reminding one of some of the tainted sources of Dombey's wealth, and also deepening the resonance of the earlier outburst of complaint by the prickly Susan – Florence's maid – that she's "a black slave and a mulotter" (5). The residue of guilt left by slavery is momentarily displaced onto the position of servants within Dombey's household: unexplored, it leaves an uneasy question mark hanging over the nature of class relations in the 1840s, suggesting that the difference between the legal ownership of people and their economic subordination may not be completely clear-cut in its effects. But the desire to make a symbolic break between the destinations of the past and of the future is apparent in the direction taken by Walter. Florence accompanies him in his position as supercargo (the officer on a merchant ship in charge of its stock and its sale and purchase) on their marriage voyage, and their destination is not the West Indies, but China.

What is made material in this wedding trip, moreover, is the integration of work and domesticity that Mr. Dombey so resolutely denies. Dickens's description of the waves which the pair listen to on their honeymoon links back to the language in which he had Paul speak of the way he felt his ebbing life being pulled to join his dead mother. In suggesting that love is a quality which can join past, present, and infinity – "not bounded by the confines of this world, or by the end of time, but ranging still, beyond the sea, beyond the sky, to the invisible country far away!" (57) – Dickens connects temporal with topographical voyaging, albeit with such exaggerated sentimentality that it conveys desire more palpably than it promises actual achievement. It is, this time, the reader's own imagination that is being appealed to, together with a desire to believe in forgiveness, reconciliation, repentance – the final emotions shown by a thoughtful, elderly Mr. Dombey, devoted to Paul and Florence, his grandchildren.

The repetition of these names intimates, on the one hand, a wish to recuperate the past. Yet it also serves to lock the next generation into a self-enclosed world of those whose fates are crafted by the novelist into a form of moralistic romance. Within such a plot, Walter can return from what seemed to be a watery grave. But in the novel, named individuals are set against the anonymous, restless crowds who are swallowed up by the ever-expanding, hungry capital city. Harriet Carker watches with compassion the footsore and weary people who are drawn into its vortex:

> Day after day, such travellers crept past, but always, as she thought, in one direction – always toward the town. Swallowed up in one phase or other of its immensity, toward which they seemed impelled by a desperate fascination, they never returned. Food for the hospitals, the churchyards, the prisons, the river, fever, madness, vice, and death, – they passed on to the monster, roaring in the distance, and were lost. (33)

Theirs is a future with no happy endings; no scope for the integration of private and public existences; no chance of economic success. The fates of Dickens's named characters, in this and his other novels, promise a kind of moral justice in operation, a pattern behind the "hundred thousand shapes and substances of incompleteness, wildly mingled out of their places" (6) that constituted not just the bricks and mortar and excavations of the changing shape of the city, but of the lives that were being accommodated to, or overpowed by, the urban conditions of the mid-1840s. Work and home alike may be ideally animated by a spirit of loving altruism which promises an emotional as well as (by more obscure means) an economically secure future. Dickens's dominant plot lines, however, are uneasily set against the possibility that for many, there is no discernible impetus toward any promising future at all.

This same sense of a nameless, restless population – the loss of aim and direction that accompanies familial and financial deprivation – is found in *David Copperfield*, in the hordes of tramps that David encounters on the Dover road. But despite his own geographical and social mobility in this novel, and the actual voyages undertaken by others which remind one that Britain's urban growth is tied in with the country's growth as a colonial power – from Peggotty's emigration to those who sail to and from India – this text's crucial movements are backward and forward in time.

Ostensibly, *David Copperfield* is a *Bildungsroman.* Dickens's favorite among his novels, it traces the development of David from childhood through his widowed mother's remarriage – leaving him with a memory of a "happy old home, which was like a dream I could never dream again" (8); school – Mr. Creakle's establishment, like that of Dr. Blimber in *Dombey and*

Son, forms part of Dickens's attack on unimaginative, forcing-house methods of education; his mother's death; his brief employment at a wine trader's (the reference to Murdstone and Grinby supplying ships trading in the West as well as the East Indies again uncomfortably suggests connections with slavery); his salvation at the practical hands of his aunt Betsy Trotwood; more education and employment in a law office; a first marriage based on sentiment; and – following Dora's death – a second and far more promising match with Agnes. This last comes as no surprise to the reader: David drops heavy hints as to his blindness to her quiet, practical, loving virtues from the first time he meets her. Shadowing this domestic progress is a less developed, but even more autobiographically infused trajectory as David works first as a recorder of parliamentary business, and then as an increasingly successful novelist. This career is kept almost entirely hidden, however. As Mary Poovey has put it, drawing attention to the porosity between personal and professional themes that runs through this novel as well as its predecessors: "Like a good housekeeper, the good writer works invisibly, quietly, without calling attention to his labor; both master dirt and misery by putting things in their proper places; both create a sphere to which one can retreat – a literal or imaginative hearth where anxiety and competition subside."[2]

That, at any rate, is the ideal. But *David Copperfield* shows how impossible this equilibrium may be to achieve. Dickens's Christmas Book for 1848 was called *The Haunted Man*, and like Jonas Chuzzlewit's inability to shake off the memory of his murderous deed, so David's past haunts his narrative. Some of those aspects of his history and identity with which he is least comfortable may readily be seen as having been distributed around other characters. Thus Steerforth is a surrogate to David's own sexual desire, especially that desire which was stimulated by the figure of Emily Peggotty. In suffering the loss of the object of his male adulation to first moral and figurative shipwreck, and then to a literal storm at sea, it is as though David's own transgressive promptings have been punished. The creepily unctuous Uriah Heep, with his clammy hands – and his own unacceptable designs on Agnes – acts as a viscerally repulsive embodiment of David's own social ambitions and capacity for hard work. (He never stops to consider, overtly, that as a boy washing empty bottles, he was for a time considerably more "'umble" even than Uriah). Even Mr. Micawber's cheerful and habitually unfounded optimism is related to David's capacity for wishful thinking as well as, in the long run, to his ability for fiction writing.

But even if these characters may be read, in part, as the willed expulsion of parts of David's self, parts which he tacitly represents as having necessarily been mastered, less definable aspects of his former life are far harder to control, and at intervals break into the trajectory he describes, disrupting its linear sense. Thus, for example, the decaying floors at Murdstone and Grinby, and the squeaking and scuffling of the rats there, "are things, not of many years ago, in my mind, but of the present instant" (11). While sometimes the phantoms of the past are invoked with a flourish, moving in dim procession across David's mind as he writes, "accompanying the shadow of myself" (43), and in the process acting as pointers to periods that he wishes to present as particularly painful to recollect, at other moments the temporal disturbance is more subtle. What might *seem* to be a memory is in fact reality. Looking back to the period when he lodged in the Wickfield house, he writes as though Agnes is exceptionally vivid in his recollection: "I see her, with her modest, orderly, placid manner, and I hear her beautiful calm voice, as I write these words" (16). Only a retrospective reading reveals that this refers to a literal present as much as it does to a recalled image.

David Copperfield is curiously ambivalent about the past. On the one hand, it is a repository of value, especially of a domestic kind. Age and experience have certainly given David's aunt, Betsey Trotwood, a feistiness and a wisdom which combine to make her one of the strongest, most independent-minded of all Dickens's fictional women characters. Despite her idiosyncrasies, she exemplifies sound judgment, common sense, and social compassion, knowing when to speak out, and when to bide her time. As a model of female resilience, she shows up Dora as the delicate and unprepared hot-house plant that she is: cultivated to attract men but completely incapable of household management; recognizing her deficiencies but unable to remedy them, Dora represents Dickens's attack on a showy and shallow conception of womanhood as ornament that is fostered by aspects of contemporary, consumer-led society. Such a conception is as damaging to women themselves as it is to the men they captivate. And, in falling for Dora, David (called after his father) is himself locked into a cycle of repetition: Betsey Trotwood, not troubling to spare the boy's feelings about his mother, comments that his father "was always running after wax dolls from his cradle" (13). By contrast, part of the homely glow given off by the angelic Agnes comes from the patina of the past which surrounds her. When she is first introduced, she seems at one with the house in which she grew up, which carries an "air of retirement and cleanliness," its oak beams and diamond panes framing her, as she appears with an aura of sanctity which never leaves her, seeming like a figure in a stained-glass window (15). Agnes, and her patient loyalty to David, which even extends toward Dora, is set up to represent the stability and endurance of true domestic love, posited as a sustaining and redemptive force in a shifting and precarious modern world.

But if the generalized provincial English past, and the traditional values Dickens wishes to see it as bearing, is overtly and positively invoked through

Agnes, it nonetheless fails to carry the weight in the novel that is borne by the pressure of the more immediate past upon David. Betsey Trotwood may say, with her customary practicality, that "It's in vain . . . to recall the past, unless it works some influence upon the brain" (23), but David does not seem able to help himself. When he is on the Yarmouth beach during the great storm, "something within me, faintly answering to the storm without, tossed up the depths of my memory, and made a tumult in them" (55), and although specifically this prepares us for the reappearance of Steerforth, it is also suggestive of the more general, unbidden operation of David's past upon his conscious self.

David Copperfield is a novel permeated with loss, with regret, with guilt. The passing of time and David's capacity for misery are foreshadowed in the image from the opening paragraph – "It was remarked that the clock began to strike, and I began to cry, simultaneously" (1) – and the narrative is continually pointing forward to the treachery and the sorrow, which lie ahead for the reader. When first seeing Emily running on the jetty at Yarmouth, David speculates whether "there was any merciful attraction of her into danger," and whether it would have been better had the waters closed over her head there and then (3); when he first encounters Steerforth, "no veiled future dimly glanced upon him in the moonbeams" (6). Although the narrator frequently adopts an earnest tone designed to convince the reader of his sincerity as he presents a journey toward self-knowledge – "I search my breast, and I commit its secrets, if I know them, without any reservation to this paper" (44) – this very attempt to get the reader on his side is part of one further act of narrative displacement, or at least cooptation, on David's part. He brings us very close to the mental processes of telling his story, but these involve exposure, in temporarily veiled terms, to the memories which haunt him. To wish for something awful to happen, because we have been set up to expect it, and it hence forms the subject of our anticipation, is a device which implicates the reader in the pervasive atmosphere of guilt. Our desire demands disaster, and this impetus is just as strong, for the reader of *David Copperfield*, as any pull toward the neatly staged, happy tying-up of narrative loose ends which is what we are ostensibly given.

Guilt is but one manifestation of how the past haunts and affects the pressure of the past on the present, albeit one to which Dickens kept returning in the novels discussed in this chapter. Its recurrent presence in this fiction may be seen as a sign of the times. Guilt, wrote Freud in *Civilization and its Discontents* (1930), is "the most important problem in the development of civilization . . . the price we pay for our advance in civilization is a loss of happiness through the heightening of the sense of guilt."[3] More broadly, its capacity to surge, unbidden, into the mind of characters offers just one instance of Dickens's preoccupation with restlessness, whether mental or physical – so far as the two states may be separated from one another.

To dwell on this restlessness as a trait of Dickens's writing during this period leads us in several directions. It is a feature of his style, something which may in part be attributed to the demands of serial publication, and his perceived need to entertain and retain a variety of audiences simultaneously, but which also represents an exuberant excitement at the animating power of language. This verbal *jouissance* may, in turn, like his personal, physical restlessness, be subjected to psychobiographic interpretation. But it is also, and perhaps predominantly, linked to his role as a social commentator. It was a cliché at the time – and has remained one ever since – to refer to the 1840s as a time of growth and change, a process culminating in the Great Exhibition of 1851. The familiarity of the concept is important, however, since Dickens was continually attuned to popular preoccupations, feeding off, and in turn supplying, the period's uncertainty about the direction the future might take, about shifts in values. His popularity may in part be attributed to his capacity to oscillate between defamiliarization and confirmation of commonly held ways of seeing.

Whether one investigates Dickens's mobility at a biographical or at a broader, social level, one thing emerges: the continual drive and desire on the part of the individual to achieve some kind of equilibrium with society, coupled with the impossibility of ever achieving this. Although his fiction may express the desire for a place of rest and refuge, no amount of neat plotting and emotionally reassuring conclusions can provide it. For as Dickens demonstrates, neither society, nor the mind of the individual, passing between present and past, between volition and the uncontrollable, is ever static.

NOTES

1 Walter Benjamin and Asja Lacis, "Naples," in Walter Benjamin, *Reflections* (Harcourt, 1978), pp. 165–66.
2 Mary Poovey, "*David Copperfield* and the Professional Writer," *Uneven Developments: The Ideological Work of Gender in Mid-Victorian England* (University of Chicago Press, 1988), p. 122.
3 Sigmund Freud, *Civilization and its Discontents* (1930), *Civilization, Society and Religion*, the Pelican Freud Library, vol. XII, ed. Albert Dickson (Penguin Books, 1985), p. 327.

FURTHER READING

Connor, Steven. "Babel Unbuilding: the Anti-archi-rhetoric of *Martin Chuzzlewit*." In *Dickens Refigured: Bodies, Desires and Other Histories*, edited by John Schad. Manchester University Press, 1996, pp. 178–99.

Jordan, John O. "The Social Subtext of *David Copperfield.*" *Dickens Studies Annual* 14 (1985), 61–92.

Marcus, Steven. *Dickens: From Pickwick to Dombey.* Chatto and Windus, 1965.

Moglen, Helene. "Theorizing Fiction/Fictionalizing Theory: the Case of *Dombey and Son.*" *Victorian Studies* 35 (1992), 159–84.

Nunokawa, Jeff. "For Your Eyes Only: Private Property and the Oriental Body in *Dombey and Son.*" In *Macropolitics of Nineteenth-Century Literature: Nationalism, Exoticism, Imperialism,* edited by Jonathan Arac and Harriet Ritvo. University of Pennsylvania Press, 1991, pp. 138–58.

Perera, Suvendrini. "Wholesale, Retail and for Exportation: Empire and the Family Business in *Dombey and Son.*" *Victorian Studies* 33 (1990), 603–20.

Schwarzbach, F. S. "*Martin Chuzzlewit*: Architecture and Accommodation," and "*Dombey and Son*: the World Metropolis." *Dickens and the City.* Athlone Press, 1979, pp. 80–113.

Vanden Bossche, Chris R. "Cookery, not Rookery: Family and Class in *David Copperfield.*" *Dickens Studies Annual* 15 (1986), 87–109.

Van Ghent, Dorothy. "The Dickens World: a View from Todgers's." *Sewanee Review* 58 (1950), 419–38.

Welsh, Alexander. *From Copyright to Copperfield: The Identity of Dickens.* Harvard University Press, 1987.

4

J. HILLIS MILLER

Moments of decision in *Bleak House*

"The Lawyers have twisted it into such a state of bedevilment that the original merits of the case have long disappeared from the face of the earth. It's about a Will, and the trusts under a Will – or it was, once. It's about nothing but Costs, now. We are always appearing, and disappearing, and swearing, and interrogating, and filing, and cross-filing, and arguing, and sealing, and motioning, and referring, and reporting, and revolving about the Lord Chancellor and all his satellites, and equitably waltzing ourselves off to dusty death, about Costs. That's the great question. All the rest, by some extraordinary means, has melted away." (*BH* 8)

I renewed my resolutions, and prayed to be strengthened in them . . . (*BH* 36)

This essay attempts to understand the purport of these two citations in their contexts. In an essay published in 1971 as the introduction to the Penguin edition of *Bleak House* and reprinted a number of times since then, I argued that *Bleak House* is a document about the interpretation of documents.[1] Now I have been asked to turn back to this novel to see what I make of it today. This essay is in response to that demand. I rejoice in the chance to do that. *Bleak House* is a wonderful novel, almost inexhaustibly rich, perhaps even unfathomably so.

Nor have other scholars and critics failed to respond to the demand this splendid novel makes for the generation of more words about its words. Since my essay of 1971 was published, a large number of further essays and books have been written on *Bleak House*. These essays have added greatly to my understanding of *Bleak House* and to our collective understanding. They have tended to match the development of new methodologies and theoretical perspectives in literary study since then. *Bleak House* has been approached from Foucauldian, new historicist, feminist, cultural-studies, postcolonial, psychoanalytic (both Freudian and Lacanian), law- and literature-based, reader-response, and good old-fashioned intellectual historical perspectives.[2] These categories are gross lumpings. They indicate, nevertheless, something of the overlapping panorama of literary studies today as they have generated new essays on *Bleak House*. Many, though by no means all, of these essays have tended to stress the external conditions in Victorian culture that might help the reader understand *Bleak House*, as opposed to the intrinsic or rhetorical reading that I practiced in 1971 and still practice. New stresses on materiality and on the body displace to some degree older approaches focusing on subjectivity and, especially, on language. One can understand the appeal of these new topics. Language-based approaches lead to such distressing "aporias" and seem to conduct the critic further and further away from common sense. Matter and the body seem unambiguously there, not subject to "deconstruction" except by perverse fanatics. Moreover, materiality and the body seem a good perspective from which to approach the questions of race, class, and gender that predominate now. Unfortunately for these hopeful projects, materiality and the body are ancient philosophical categories that are just as problematic and just as prone to lead to aporias if investigated rigorously as are language and the psyche.[3]

The two approaches, extrinsic and intrinsic, certainly complement one another. One should not, however, pretend that they are easily reconcilable. My stress on what is idiosyncratic or singular about *Bleak House* would implicitly challenge any claim that this or any other novel can be satisfactorily accounted for in terms of its cultural context, or of the psychobiography of its author, or even in terms of other work by its author. The reader needs to know as much as possible about the context. That circumambience is enormous, virtually limitless. It is complex and highly overdetermined. These recent essays help immensely to comprehend it.

In the end, however, the reader, informed by all that outside knowledge, needs to return to the text and to attend with passionate intensity to all its minutiae. In the case of *Bleak House* these minutiae are quite amazing, for example the zany speeches and pantomimic behavior of Grandfather Smallweed, or the admirable wackiness of Guppy's proposal to Esther, that absurdly mixes legal and sentimental terminology, or the violent speech of Boythorn, or the legalese of Conversation Kenge, or the unctuous discourse of the Reverend Chadband, or the furtive speech of Richard Carstone's lawyer, the odious Vholes, and so on through the whole gallery of Dickensian eccentrics, each with his or her distinctive way of speaking.

The self-performing speeches of this swarm of idosyncratic secondary characters make up a large part of *Bleak House*. No one but the "inimitable Boz," as Dickens called himself, could have invented these characters or their ways of speaking. The genius is in the detail. This is one reason why a responsible reading of *Bleak House* is obliged to make citations, long or short, bits and pieces torn from the whole to demonstrate one feature or another of Dickens's extraordinary linguistic exuberance. I am by no means so naive, however, as to believe that any reading, however "intrinsic," can be without methodological and ideological presuppositions. Every strong reading is, and should be, interested. It should be performed in view of some good it hopes to accomplish.

Though I do not wish to unsay or forswear that essay of 1971, nevertheless I think I missed in that reading something essential. This something was staring me in the face. I ought to have seen it, just as Inspector Bucket ought to have been able to figure out sooner that he has been duped by Lady Dedlock, that she has changed clothes with the brickmaker's wife and is headed back toward Tom-all-Alone's in London. All those documents in *Bleak House*, like innumerable oral locutions in the novel, and like the novel itself, are not just "constative" texts to be interpreted for what they mean, for their truth or falsity. They are speech acts, felicitous or infelicitous performatives. They are ways of doing things with words, or of trying to do something with words. Moreover, those speech acts tend to register decisions.

Bleak House is punctuated by moments of decision that form turning points or breaks in the action. After each decision everything is different, for that person at least, for those around him or her, and to some degree for the whole vast contradictory "system" that is English society as Dickens sees it. These peripeteias could all be rephrased in a locution taking the form "I hereby decide to do so and so." Here it is useful to recall J. L. Austin's definition in *How to Do Things with Words* of the speech act he calls a "performative." A performative utterance, he says, is one in which "to *say* something is to *do* something; or in which *by* saying or *in* saying something we are doing something."[4] To say "I promise" is to promise, not to make a statement that can be judged to be true or false. *Bleak House* is full of such locutions.

In *Bleak House*, as in most good mystery stories, of which this is one of the best and earliest in the modern European tradition, decisive secret events have preceded the action of the novel when the reader picks it up at the beginning. The forward movement of the novel gradually uncovers those secrets hidden in the past, in what might be called an apocalypse (in the literal sense of "unveiling"). In this case there are two secrets. Both were precipitated by instants of decision registered in speech acts. One was the implicit or explicit saying yes to Captain Hawdon by Lady Dedlock, before her marriage to Sir Leicester Dedlock, when she was Honoria Barbary. The result was the conception and birth of her illegitimate daughter, Esther Summerson. The other originating moment of decision was the will or rather wills signed by Jarndyce who unintentionally initiated the case of Jarndyce and Jarndyce when his will was contested after his death. A will is a paradigmatic example of a written performative. By signing, while being of sound mind and before witnesses, a document properly prepared by a lawyer, the one who makes a will uses language to make something happen after his or her own death, assuming everything is in order and the property is his or hers to bequeath. "I give and bequeath my watch to my brother" is among the first examples of a performative locution in *How to Do Things with Words* (Austin, p. 5).

If two moments of decision recorded in performative documents, the Jarndyce wills and Lady Dedlock's letters, precede the action of the novel and are its presupposition, the novel itself is full of speech acts, both written and spoken. The two most important sets of these correspond to the two plots, the Lady Dedlock and Esther Summerson plot, on the one hand, and the Jarndyce and Jarndyce plot along with its analogues, on the other. Two kinds of performatives are exemplified in these two plots: the private and secret for the first plot, the public and institutionalized for the second plot.

The "cause" of Jarndyce and Jarndyce, as it drags on interminably in Chancery, consists, after all, of innumerable written speech acts: briefs, affadavits, and so on, as listed in my first epigraph, from John Jarndyce's explanation of the case. These come about no doubt at the express command of the court, just as Josef K's first appearance before the Examining Magistrate in Kafka's *The Trial* is demanded by a phone call. Each of the present participles in Jarndyce's speech names a specific kind of performative used by the law, one that is repeated over and over in a perpetually iterated present action that does not go anywhere. Each form of speech act could be the subject of a specific analysis along the lines Austin set out in *How to Do Things with Words*. It could be discussed for its terms, forms, and requirements for "felicity" or efficacy. An interrogation is not the same thing as a motion, nor is a reference the same as a report. All, however, are public, legal, institutionalized performatives. They are models of the sort of speech act Austin identifies as "felicitous" if it is executed by the right people in the right situation. The right people are those authorized to enunciate them or to sign papers inscribing them in written words. Such speech acts are felicitous because they successfully bring about what they say. To recall one of Austin's examples, a captain aboard his ship is authorized to marry people on the ship, but not on land, whereas the purser may not marry anyone anywhere. When the captain on board his ship says, "I pronounce you man and wife," the couple is married. The legal speech acts in *Bleak House* seem to be like that.

What is peculiar about such performatives in *Bleak House*, however, is that though they are entirely legal according to Equity's rules of procedure, their use is not to settle the case and administer justice but to keep the case going and to go on making the lawyers richer and richer by doing so. They use the Court of Chancery to obstruct justice. They use the law of Equity to be inequitable. As Conversation Kenge, one of those lawyers who has battened on the case, boasts of Jarndyce and Jarndyce, it is "in itself a monument of Chancery practice. In which (I would say) every difficulty, every contingency, every masterly fiction, every form of procedure known in that court, is represented over and over again" (3).

The performatives that keep Jarndyce and Jarndyce continuing interminably until it is all used up in costs are echoed in a large number of similar speech acts in analogous stories or situations in the novel. The cases in Chancery of Miss Flite and of Gridley parallel the case of Jarndyce and Jarndyce. All three are ways of "waltzing . . . off to dusty death." All three are apocalyptic in the sense that their endpoint is death in a final moment of revelation. Miss Flite "expects a Judgment, on the Day of Judgment." Her speech is full of echoes of the book of *Revelation*. Gridley dies before his case is settled. Richard Carstone is killed by the news that Jarndyce and Jarndyce has been consumed in costs. Tom Jarndyce, John Jarndyce's great-uncle and the original owner of Bleak House, blew out his brains one day in despair over the case of Jarndyce and Jarndyce. John Jarndyce has saved himself and put Bleak House back in order only by having no hopes that the case will be settled and by having as little to do with it as possible.

A whole series of marriages and deaths, all legally attested, to continue my repertoire of speech acts in the novel, punctuate *Bleak House*. Boythorn engages with boistrous hyperbolic zest in interminable lawsuits against Sir Leicester Dedlock over a disputed right of way. Skimpole is always running up bills that he cannot pay and then getting arrested when he does not pay those debts. Trooper George, like Captain Hawdon before him, owes money on a bill at usurious interest to Grandfather Smallweed. He is arrested, imprisoned, and then his case is "remanded" (52) when he is under suspicion of having murdered Tulkinghorn. The abstract philanthropy of Mrs. Jellyby, Mrs. Pardiggle, and Mr. Quayle is carried on chiefly by way of performative documents in the shape of testimonials and subscriptions. These performatives are entirely inefficacious, except in costing the subscribers money and causing mischief. Of Mr. Quayle, for example, it is said, "All objects were alike to him, but he was always particularly ready for anything in the way of a testimonial to any one" (15). Captain Hawdon's handwriting is recognized on a legal document he has copied for Snagsby. Like Melville's Bartleby the Scrivener, Hawdon's business is to copy legal forms that have as their goal to do something with words, and could do so only if many copies were made by hand, since all the lawyers and their various clients each needed a copy, as my epigraph indicates. His employer, the law stationer Snagsby, is seen at one point preparing "an Indenture of several skins" (47). An indenture is the binding of an apprentice to a master crafts-man or professional for a period of years. Richard Carstone is futilely bound over to a succession of potential careers: medicine, the law, the army. These are more or less the whole gamut, except for the church, of those professions in which a "gentleman" could in that society engage himself.

There are yet other overt performatives in the novel. Guppy's language, even in the most private situations, is steeped in legal terms, as in the scene in which he reneges on his proposal to Esther, after she has been disfigured by disease. Guppy, absurdly, gets Esther to swear in proper legal terms, as if they were in a courtroom, that there has never been any proposal of mar-riage from him (38). Tulkinghorn speaks of the tacit arrangement he has made with Lady Dedlock – not to reveal her secret if she does not change the situation in any way – as an "agreement." He tells her the agreement is broken, like a dishonored contract, and that he will now reveal all. This happens when she acts to free her maid Rosa from the contamination that will spread to her (Rosa) if and when Lady Dedlock's guilt is revealed. Bucket, to give a final example, has an odd way of speaking constatives in such a way that they become performatives, as when he orders Snagsby not to tell of their visit to the slums by stating Snagsby's ability to keep a secret as a fact: "what I like in you, is, that you're a man it's of no use pumping, that's what *you* are" (22). In this case to state something is to bring it about.

The two plots are brought in closest physical proximity in the way Krook's rag-and-bottle shop houses not only Miss Flite, driven mad by her involve-ment in Chancery, but also Captain Hawdon, Lady Dedlock's lover. When Esther visits Miss Flite she passes without knowing it within a yard or two of her father in his sordid rented lodging there. Among all the other junk and trash piled up from the past in Krook's shop, including old clothes, hanks of human hair, and innumerable old law documents, legal bags, and wornout judges' and lawyers' wigs, are hidden both the latest will old Jarndyce made that would perhaps have cleared up the case once and for all, and, ultimately, Lady Dedlock's letters, hidden, after Krook steals them, on a shelf next to the bed of Krook's cat, Lady Jane, and produced by Bucket as evidence of Lady Dedlock's past.

Dickens stresses the material, bodily base of all writing. Law documents, for example, are, the reader is often reminded, written on sheepskin (the name of one of Miss Flite's birds). Lady Dedlock's letters are written on paper, the "little bundle" that Bucket at a crucial moment "produces from a mysterious part of his coat" (54). The second Jarndyce will is passed from Grandfather Smallweed to John Jarndyce via Bucket. It is "a stained discoloured paper, which was much singed upon the outside, and a little burnt at the edges, as if it had long ago been thrown upon a fire; and hastily snatched off again" (62). The past weighs on the present not in some intangible way but as the accumulating mountains of dirt, inscribed paper, refuse, junk, waste, and excrement that are piling up all around and that fill the streets with what Dickens somewhat euphemistically calls "mud." Memorable descriptions of London's filth punctuate the novel. These include not only the celebrated opening pages and Lady's Dedlock's two visits to the pauper graveyard, the second time to die there, but a view of Tom-all-Alone's as seen through Mr. Snagsby's eyes. This matches any description in Engels or in Mayhew or in the Sanitary Reform documents as a rendition of what London slums in the Victorian period were like (22). The basic or ultimate form of materiality, for Dickens, something we are all ultimately to become, is not so much excrement as dead bodies. *Bleak House* is strewn with dead bodies. Dickens stresses their repulsive materiality as being subject to decomposition.

Everywhere one turns in *Bleak House* one finds people who are preparing or signing documents, making promises, swearing oaths to do so and so, bearing witness, certifying that a dead body is really dead, promising to love, honor, and obey until death do us part, making agreements, and so on. For Dickens the everyday tissue of family, social, and political life is woven of innumerable speech acts, performatives small or large, private or public, oral or written, voiced or silent. These momentary breaks, interruptions, or veerings change the whole social system, in however small a degree. Everything is different thereafter. Once the reader begins looking for examples, they may be found on almost every page. Seek and ye shall find, someone might say. Of course we carry on social intercourse through speech acts of one sort or another. What is remarkable about *Bleak House*, however, are the number of these Dickens explicitly registers in the interchanges among his imaginary characters, his sensitive and scrupulous attention to them, and his discrimination among the various kinds.

What can one say of Dickens's (or the novel's) evaluation of such public, rule-bound, and socially sanctioned performatives? On the one hand, they are efficacious as ways of doings things with words. In that sense they are felicitous performatives. On the other hand what they do, for the most part (putting aside the happy marriages), is either to perpetuate injustice or to keep society frozen in the "perpetual stoppage" that will come to an end only at death or on the Day of Judgment. "The one great principle of the English law," says the narrator apropos of Mr. Vholes, "is, to make business for itself" (39). Making the most business for itself means postponing judgment indefinitely through performative documents. This is true even though these documents have as their ostensible function accomplishing justice and settling the cases equitably. Rather than being ways of doing things with words, they are examples of how not to do it, of "How Not to Do Anything with Words," or of "How to Use Words to Avoid Doing Anything." The paragraph after the one I have quoted as an epigraph brilliantly expresses the way speech acts may be used in an endless lateral round or relay, with one performative always generating another. This interminable chain postpones indefinitely ever doing anything material to decide the case or to come to any conclusion:

> "All through the deplorable cause, everything that everybody in it, except one man, knows already, is referred to that only one man who don't know it, to find out – all through the deplorable cause, everybody must have copies, over and over again, of everything that has accumulated about it in the way of cartloads of papers (or must pay for them without having them, which is the usual course, for nobody wants them); and must go down the middle and up again, through such an infernal country-dance of costs and fees and nonsense and corruption, as was never dreamed of in the wildest visions of a Witch's Sabbath. Equity sends questions to Law, Law sends questions back to Equity; Law finds it can't do this, Equity finds it can't do that; neither can so much as say it can't do anything, without this solicitor instructing and this counsel appearing for A, and that solicitor instructing and that counsel appearing for B; and so on through the whole alphabet, like the history of the Apple Pie. And thus, through years and years, and lives and lives, everything goes on, constantly beginning over and over again, and nothing ever ends. And we can't get out of the suit on any terms, for we are made parties to it, and *must* be parties to it, whether we like it or not." (8)

Bleak House is a massive demonstration, contra J. L. Austin's hope that he might be able to establish the conditions for felicitous and just performatives, of Dickens's almost total lack of confidence that the legal system and all its speech acts, along with almost all other publicly sanctioned and attested speech acts, can ever bring justice or do good in the world. Dickens detests lawyers, the legal system, and most legally operative speech acts. He has no confidence in the benign power of the written word in its official, public, legalized form. Lawyers' performatives are, for him, the most infelicitous felicities that could be imagined. They are a pollution of the body politic, like their symbolic analogue in the corrupt humors bred in Krook by his overconsumption of gin.

The performative utterances associated with the Lady Dedlock/Esther Summerson plot are quite different from those associated with the cause of

Jarndyce and Jarndyce and its analogues. Lady Dedlock's giving of herself to Captain Hawdon was registered in private love letters to him and no doubt in private speech. Her decision to flee Chesney Wold and her husband and to die as close as she can get to her dead lover's grave is taken silently. Her choice is not narrated as a subjective event, though we are given the text of the suicide note she leaves behind. It is directed to Esther and declares her intention, with a concluding performative request for forgiveness. It is a speech act because it puts Esther in the position of saying either yes or no to the request: "The place where I shall lie down, if I can yet get so far, has been often in my mind. Farewell. Forgive" (59).

At two crucial points in her life Esther herself makes a silent or private decision in the solitude of her room. The first occurs when she is as a child told by her aunt that it would have been better if she had never been born. She then silently resolves to be good and to do good, speaking her resolution to her doll, whether out loud or silently is hard to tell: "I . . . confided to her that I would try, as hard as ever I could, to repair the fault I had been born with (of which I confusedly felt guilty and yet innocent), and would strive as I grew up to be industrious, contented and kind-hearted, and to do some good to some one, and win some love to myself if I could" (3). Though this resolution is no doubt constantly renewed throughout her life, Esther's second moment of explicit decision is overtly defined as a repetition or renewal of the first. It occurs when she learns from Lady Dedlock that the latter is her mother. After a solitary vigil attempting to come to terms with this, Esther decides once more to be good and to do good. Her narrative account of this decisive event is given after the fact, from a point seven years after her happy marriage to Allan Woodcourt. Her account begins with constative statements of fact: "I saw very well that I could not have been intended to die, or I should never have lived: not to say should never have been reserved for such a happy life" (36). It leads to the performative assertions of renewed resolution and prayer I have cited in my second epigraph. To renew a resolution: it is an odd kind of performative utterance. In this case the resolution is apparently spoken silently by Esther to herself. First, at one time in your life, you make a resolution in response to a disastrous discovery about yourself. That resolution determines the whole course of your life. Years later, in response to a new discovery that changes your entire sense of yourself once more, you "renew" that first resolution in the changed circumstances, still speaking silently to yourself. In a somewhat similar way, employing a different performative, a man in debt and his creditor, for example Trooper George and Grandfather Smallweed in this novel, agree, with proper signatures, to "renew" the bill that signifies the former's indebtedness and its terms. A third moment, repetition of the first two, is also involved in Esther's account. This is the moment of Esther's narration of these events, her (somewhat inexplicable, given what she tells us about her modest reticence) decision to write down as a first-person autobiography the story of her life.

It might seem easy enough to decide that Esther's report of her two moments of decision is "mention" rather than "use" of the speech acts involved. Surely my narrative account of speech acts I uttered long ago is not itself a speech act, any more than reading aloud the Declaration of Independence is a declaration of independence. A moment's reflection will show, however, that matters are not so simple. Even the "mention" of a speech act, however much one attempts to neutralize it, still contains some residue of "use." In this case Esther's narration of her prior speech acts changes them by making them public and by making an implicit appeal to the reader to endorse, ratify, or approve of what she long ago said to herself, or to her doll, her alter ego.

This aspect of Esther's narration is made explicit in one place near the end of the novel: "Full seven happy years I have been the mistress of Bleak House. [She means the new Bleak House, repetition of the first. John Jarndyce builds the new one as a wedding present for Esther and Allan Woodcourt.] The few words that I have to add to what I have written, are soon penned; then I, and the unknown friend to whom I write, will part for ever. Not without much dear remembrance on my side. Not without some, I hope, on his or hers" (67). This demand on the reader for a response of "remembrance" and bearing witness is another speech act. It puts the reader in a new position, the position of responding or not responding to the demand made on him or her. Do you, or do I, say "Yes, she did right," or do we not? Can we ratify her decision and in effect do as Kant says we should do, make it a general law valid for all mankind that all should decide and act as Esther does?

The novel, you can see, demands that the reader distinguish legal public performatives from the silent ones that accompany quiet doing good to those nearest. The only wholly felicitous written performatives in the novel are Sir Leicester's writing on his slate as he lies speechless after his stroke, "Full forgiveness. Find – " (56), and its echo in the last words of Lady Dedlock's final note: "Farewell. Forgive" (59).

Should an ethical decision always be expressed in language and made public thereby? Walter Benjamin thought so. Speaking in condemnation of Ottilie's silent decision in Goethe's *Die Wahlverwandtschaften* (*The Elective Affinites*) to starve herself to death, Benjamin says: "No moral decision (sittlicher Entschluß) can enter into life without verbal form (sprachliche Gestalt) and, strictly speaking, without thus becoming an object of communication

(Gegenstand der Mitteilung)."[5] For Kierkegaard in *Fear and Trembling*, on the contrary, and for Jacques Derrida in his commentary on Kierkegaard in the third chapter of *Donner la mort*, the reverse is the case. The validity of Abraham's decision to obey Jehovah and to go forth to sacrifice his beloved son Isaac depends on its remaining silent. To express it in language would be to fall into generality and to betray the unspeakable singularity of his decision.[6]

Dickens appears to side with Kierkegaard and Derrida on this point. He believes that silent resolution accompanied by efficacious local action, like Esther's mute housework accompanied by the cheerful jingling of her house-keeping keys, or Jarndyce's quiet charities to those immediately around him, are infinitely superior to any sort of public decision that is ratified by legally institutionalized convention or by speech acts that are written, signed, and duly registered. Esther affirms this commitment in a firm put-down of Mrs. Pardiggle's appeal to her to go in for the Pardiggle sort of noisy "philanthrophy": "I thought it best to be as useful as I could, and to render what kind services I could, to those immediately about me; and to try to let that circle of duty gradually and naturally expand itself" (8). Sir Leicester would speak if he could to proffer forgiveness to Lady Dedlock. His writing is a prosthesis for his version of the spoken or silent performative decision followed by practical doing that has Dickens's highest approval in *Bleak House*.

What then about *Bleak House* itself? It is certainly not silent, nor is it an oral performative. It is a noisy written document almost a thousand pages long. Is *Bleak House* predominantly constative, a representation of things as they were in Victorian society at that time, or does it have a performative component? If the latter is the case, the novel, by Dickens's own accounting, would seem to fall under the anathema he directs at almost all written documents, especially those legally executed. Even if they sometimes make something happen, that something is almost always bad, an infelicitous felicity at best. It is clear, however, that Dickens intended and hoped that *Bleak House* would not just describe or represent, but that it would be performatively efficacious, that it would be a way of doing something good with written words. Dickens wanted *Bleak House* to persuade its readers to detest the Court of Chancery and to work to reform or abolish it. It is also clear that he wanted *Bleak House* to persuade people to accept and act on the Victorian ideology that said a woman's place is in the home and that her highest vocation is being a wife and mother, as well as being a good house-keeper. How can *Bleak House* do that? How it can plausibly be said to have a possibly efficacious performative dimension, how can it work as a political and ethical intervention?

The answer is complex. One way is through transformation of the realities of English society into language by means of the invention of a swarm of characters each with his or her idiosyncratic way of speech and behavior: Bucket, Tulkinghorn, Snagsby, Boythorn, Chadband, Grandfather and Grandmother Smallweed, and the rest. *Bleak House*, moreover, is organized around a system or rather non-system of recurrent competing and conflicting figures of speech, each through its repetition implicitly aiming, unsuccessfully, at totalizing mastery. This double transformation is a complex speech act changing Victorian reality into a Victorian imaginary in the form of the weird and even hallucinatory characters that people *Bleak House*. This in turn makes it possible, at least hypothetically, for *Bleak House* itself to work on its readers not just as the description of a historical state of things but as an efficacious performative. The novel then would do something with words. It would bring its readers to judge differently and to act differently. Dickens hopes they will act to shovel Law and Equity away once and for all and that all women will take Esther as a model.

Moreover, the overall action of the novel is concocted in another way to exert a magic transformative power over the reader. It is, after all, not just a static series of portraits but a dramatic action or what Kenneth Burke called "a strategy to encompass a situation." This dramatic action identifies a whole series of characters with the evils of the legal system, either as its perpetrators or as its victims, and then kills off that pollution as it is embodied in those characters, in a wholesale purgation or catharsis. It does this in order that Esther and Allan may live happily ever after. This parallels the classic tragic action: the separating of the good from the evil, the identifying of the bad with its symbolic representatives and then the elimination of the bad by killing off its embodiments. Oedipus must blind himself and go into exile in order to cure Thebes of the plague. Hamlet must die to carry off that "something rotten" in Denmark so that Horatio may absent himself from felicity a while and survive to tell Hamlet's story in a cleansed Denmark. What is extravagant or hyperbolic about *Bleak House* is the number of characters who must die to carry off the pollution that is identified with mud, disease, law, and illicit sex: Hawdon, Krook, Jo, Gridley, Richard Carstone, Tulkinghorn (because he knows too many dirty secrets; in his death he carries them to his grave), Hortense, Lady Dedlock, the brickmaker's baby, who dies in Esther's place, so Esther may live. The novel is strewn with rotting corpses, perhaps the ultimate form of the pollution the novel so fears and is so obsessed with. The two main plots, the case of Jarndyce and Jarndyce and the uncovering of Lady Dedlock's secret, are only tangentially related in the dramatic actions. They are most strongly joined in both being cases of pollution that must be removed if the body politic is to be brought back to health. The novel works powerfully to persuade the reader that illicit sex is as bad as an unjust legal system and that both can only be purged by death.

Where did Dickens get his inspiration for these complex transformations of material reality into performative language? In response to what demand made on him did he write down, one by one, over a period of two years, the chapters and number parts that make up this novel? What is the mode of existence of these imaginary characters and their lives and deaths? That they have a curious sort of existence is testified to in the preparatory notes to the number parts. In Dickens's mind they preexisted in some strange realm of virtuality and needed only to be actualized in his words in a given chapter, one by one or in small groups, with gaps between signaled in the breaks between chapters. The number notes are "memos" from Dickens to himself. They consist for the most part of lists of characters or phrases attributed to them, followed by the "yes" or "no" of performative assent or dissent to the imperative demand each of these characters makes to be represented in words. It is as though they were all crowding forward like the ghosts Ulysses invokes in the *Odyssey* and saying in a cacophonous chorus: "Please do me!" One example out of many is in the notes for chapter 19:

> Mr. Guppy – His mother? Not yet
> Mr. Krook? Yes.
> The Turveydrops No. Next time
> Tom-all-Alone's Do. Yes.
> Miss Flite – Her friend? Not yet [7]

Just as the novel itself when we are not reading it sits closed in on itself on our bookshelf waiting to be actualized through reading, so all the swarm of *Bleak House* characters exists in some strange somewhere with each going on being himself or herself waiting for Dickens to allow them to manifest themselves in his words. The great dark illustrations for *Bleak House* by Phiz (Hablot K. Browne) are a striking graphic representation of this mode of existence. With their somber clarity and their fuzzy, irregular, edges, they look as if they had been just brought into focus by a great effort out of a dark background that still to some degree inhabits them. Those irregular edges remind the viewer of what has been left out, the surrounding margin that remains blank or invisible.

The greatest performative events of *Bleak House* are those by which Dickens, the inimitable Boz, calls all these characters down from the nowhere/somewhere where they await embodiment in language. This language, Dickens hopes, will intervene in the body politic and in the daily lives of his readers to change them, to make them behave and choose differently. Dickens used the popular media of his day – the novel, periodicals, popular theatre, his public readings – as forms of ethical and political intervention, just as television, cinema, and talk shows are used today to impose and support ideological assumptions, sometimes to expose and criticize them. *Bleak House* itself is a striking hyperbolic example of a felicitous way to do things with written words.

NOTES

1 J. Hillis Miller, "Introduction" to *Bleak House*, ed. Norman Page (Penguin, 1971). Reprinted as "Interpretation in Dickens' *Bleak House*," *Victorian Subjects* (Duke University Press, 1991), pp. 179–99.

2 Two recent collections, one of essays on *Bleak House*, the other of essays on Dickens's work generally (though it includes two essays on *Bleak House*) will give some idea of the great number and range of this recent work. Both collections include extensive bibliographies: *Charles Dickens*, ed. Steven Connor, Longman Critical Reader (Longman, 1996); *Bleak House: Charles Dickens*, ed. Jeremy Tambling, New Casebook Series (St. Martin's Press, 1998).

3 An example of this rigor in thinking about the body is Jacques Derrida's recent book on touching: *Le toucher, Jean Luc Nancy* (Galilée, 2000).

4 J. L. Austin, *How to Do Things with Words*, 2nd edn., ed. J. O. Urmson and Marina Sbisà (Oxford University Press, 1980), p. 12.

5 See Walter Benjamin "Goethe's *Wahlverwandstschaften*," *Illuminationen* (Suhrkamp, 1969), pp. 121–22 ("Goethe's *Elective Affinities*," trans. Stanley Corngold, *Selected Writings*, vol. 1, ed. Marcus Bullock and Michael Jennings [The Belknap Press of Harvard University Press, 1999], p. 336).

6 See Søren Kierkegaard, *Fear and Trembling*, in *"Fear and Trembling" and "The Sickness Unto Death"*, trans. Walter Lowrie (Doubleday, 1954), and Jacques Derrida, "À qui donner (savoir ne pas savoir)," *Donner la mort* (Galilée, 1999), pp. 79–114 ("Whom to Give to (Knowing Not to Know)," *The Gift of Death*, trans. David Wills [University of Chicago Press, 1995], pp. 53–81).

7 *Dickens's Working Notes for His Novels*, ed. Harry Stone (University of Chicago Press, 1987), p. 219.

FURTHER READING

Bigelow, Gordon. "Market Indicators: Banking and Domesticity in Dickens's *Bleak House*." *ELH* 67 (2000), 589–615.

Dever, Carolyn. "Broken Mirror, Broken Words: *Bleak House*," *Death and the Mother from Dickens to Freud*. Cambridge University Press, 1998, pp. 81–103.

Miller, D. A. "Discipline in Different Voices: Bureaucracy, Police, Family, and *Bleak House*," *The Novel and the Police*. University of California Press, 1988, pp. 58–106.

Miller, J. Hillis. "Introduction" to *Bleak House*, edited by Norman Page. Penguin, 1971. Reprinted as "Interpretation in Dickens' *Bleak House*," *Victorian Subjects*. Duke University Press, 1991, pp. 179–99.

Newsom, Robert. *Dickens on the Romantic Side of Familiar Things: Bleak House and the Novel Tradition*. Columbia University Press, 1977.

Robbins, Bruce. "Telescopic Philanthropy: Professionalism and Responsibility in *Bleak House*." In *Nation and Narration*, edited by Homi Bhabha. Routledge, 1990, pp. 213–30.

Schor, Hilary. *Dickens and the Daughter of the House*. Cambridge University Press, 1999.

Stewart, Garrett. "The New Mortality of *Bleak House*." *ELH* 45 (1978), 443–87.

5

HILARY SCHOR

Novels of the 1850s: *Hard Times, Little Dorrit*, and *A Tale of Two Cities*

The novels Charles Dickens wrote in the 1850s, with their capacious social canvases and their voice of social reform, seem to invite readings of their political message. No less so does the career of Dickens himself in that energetic decade, when one nonconformist preacher claimed, "There have been at work among us three great social agencies: the London City Mission; the novels of Mr. Dickens; the cholera."[1] Dickens's wide-ranging undertakings in both speeches and the pages of the journal *Household Words*, which he founded in 1850 (undertakings which included his earnest discussions of sanitation reform, prostitution, and the need for protection of authors and their copyright) made him a powerful public figure. However, recent accounts have stressed that his private life was lived almost as obsessively in the public eye: the growing discontent with his ever-increasing family; his painful encounter with his former sweetheart, Maria Beadnell, now a nervous and foolish middle-aged woman; the meeting with the young actress, Ellen Ternan; and the decision to separate from his wife Catherine, which he announced in the pages of *Household Words*. In all this flurry of social and erotic activity, it has been hard to focus on the real and complicated achievements of the novels of this decade, when Dickens was to command his greatest sales and to reach a wider sphere of commitment in all of his literary endeavors.

The novels themselves, it is true, tempt us to read them purely as social doctrine, much as they did many Victorian readers – and this is inevitable when the novels are so clearly "about" something in the social realm, be it the industrial revolution in *Hard Times*, the increasing bureaucratization of government and the imprisonment of the individual citizen in *Little Dorrit*, or the revolution of a down-trodden populace in *A Tale of Two Cities*. But I am less interested in the novels' mimetic possibilities (their ability to reflect accurately a world outside of themselves) than in the imaginative properties such an attempt at mimesis unleashed, and the possibilities of fiction-writing Dickens learned from his political activities. The "Dickens imagination" became something different in the process of writing the major social-problem novels of the 1850s: the effort at encompassing a broader social sphere led to a change in the forms of realism – to systems of reference that rely less on reported fact than on metaphor; ideas of character that break with models of a solid and impermeable individualism. These transformations are more than mere formal experimentation. As Dickens came to realize, to understand literary fiction differently is finally to transform the structures, fantasies, and even the politics of a culture – to reconceive the fictions that govern our public and private lives.

From his earliest novels, Dickens was concerned with issues of the public sphere. Even before *Oliver Twist*'s concerted attack on the New Poor Law of 1834, "Boz" had wandered the darkest streets of lower-class London, gazing into pawn shops, gin shops, and prison yards. Critics have traced convincingly the progress of Dickens from these earlier, satiric social experiments through the more engaged and carefully plotted novels of the 1840s. *Martin Chuzzlewit*, with young Martin's journey to America, and *Dombey and Son*, with its extended attack on Mr. Dombey's selfishness and his reliance on the laws of business rather than domestic relations, seem to expand Dickens's social gaze, while muting somewhat the radicalism that tinged the earlier, wilder attacks – the freeing of the boys of Dotheboys Hall; the starving seamstresses of *Nicholas Nickleby*; the grimy boatmen and hungry maidservants of *The Old Curiosity Shop*. As Dickens's "art" matured, so his social vision at once deepened and (or so most argue) became more conservative; bringing more of England into view, so he also became less able to name convincingly the solutions to England's woes.

These more critical accounts of Dickens's increasing conservatism must argue against those essayists who, since at least George Bernard Shaw, have seen in the later Dickens a true radical, one whose vision reveals the profound rifts in English society. It was *Little Dorrit*, Shaw maintained, which made him a socialist; T. A. Jackson claims that Dickens himself was a Marxist; examples like these could be multiplied – even if they could be equalled almost instantly by those who see Dickens as increasingly reactionary, bourgeois, and downright cranky.[2] In part, these critical contradictions grow out of a confusion of social vision with an interest in political or social reform: as Humphry House noted long ago, "Good as the old days were, the new are in some ways better, and Dickens helped to make them so."[3] But as House also noted, "while it is generally accepted that Dickens did a great deal of good, there is a genial vagueness about what exactly he did and how he did it." "Nearly all" the scholars who have written on Dickens's history and reformism, House concludes, have "interpreted Dickens more through their own belief than through the beliefs of his time."

To take up the question of what Dickens believed about the social sphere, what he thought needed reformation, and what good these novels did, is to take up as well the question of what Victorian readers believed fiction could do for them and for their world – for no writer has ever addressed more self-consciously and with more skill the desires of a wide reading public. Thomas Carlyle, prophet and scourge to his society, ranted compellingly against the proliferation of fiction in his essay on "Biography," but went on to announce that even the most foolish of novels could offer some powerful vision of the world. While Carlyle condemned that arriviste-Cockney novelist Dickens, he was so moved by the power of Dickens's "A Christmas Carol" that he sent Jane Welsh Carlyle off to purchase and stuff a turkey for his Christmas feast. It was this very power to move that frightened Dickens's critics. Quick to acknowledge what critic George Henry Lewes called the "fun" of Dickens's fiction, they were less ready to see in it a serious social statement, and where they did, less willing to see that social engagement as a good. "It is a thousand pities," said a reviewer in *The Rambler*, "that Mr. Dickens does not confine himself to amusing his readers, instead of wandering out of his depth in trying to instruct them"; Edmund Whipple claimed that "Dickens's mind was so deficient in the power of generalization, so inapt to recognize the operation of inexorable law, that whatever offended his instinctive benevolent sentiments he was inclined to assail as untrue"; "Who, it may be asked," or so James Fitzjames Stephen wondered, "takes Mr Dickens seriously?"[4]

Stephen, however, answers his own question most seriously, and in a series of essays in the 1850s (including a sustained attack on *Little Dorrit*) lays out precisely the dangers for readers in (mis)taking fiction for fact. To those who take Dickens as "nothing more than any public performer," he offers the reminder that to the "vast majority of mankind [who] think little, and cultivate themselves less . . . such writers as Mr. Dickens are something more than amusement." At one moment, he claims that Dickens's critiques are "just exaggerated enough to make the subject entertaining"; at another, that "he only wants to sell his books," and "spices them with a certain amount of advocacy of social reform . . . by way of persuading himself that he is of some use in the world." All this would be dangerous enough ("scattered fire," as Stephen calls it) without the added danger of what to Stephen seems Dickens's absolute ignorance. This man "with a very active fancy, great powers of language, much perception of what is grotesque, and a most lachrymose and melodramatic turn of mind" is "utterly destitute of any kind of solid acquirements," a "gad-fly" who "does not know his own meaning" or "see the consequences of his own teaching." The danger of Dickens's ignorance would be far less great, Stephen seems to say, were the power of his fiction less. The "most influential of all indirect moral teachers," the contemporary novelists, matter precisely because they appeal to the imagination;[5] though they "caricature instead of representing the world,"[6] the world they represent is appallingly seductive, one not of "truth" but of "romance"; one not of "sense and cultivation" but of "speculation" (Stephen, "Mr. Dickens," p. 345).

To rehearse these concerns about Dickens and the social realm is not to be so far from today's ordinary anxieties about art. Stephen's concerns are least risible when he fears that Dickens will encourage readers to take politics less rather than more seriously; the dangers of mere caricature are now, in an age of parody and cynicism, clearer than ever. But what is most instructive in these debates is the anxiety we share about the nature of fiction itself: is it, as Stephen has it, mere "speculation," a "romance" that distorts the "real truth"; or is it, as a more favorable reader in the period asserted, "more real and determinate, in so far as it can convey matter of fact, more earnest, in so far as it can be made a vehicle for matter of speculation, and more conscious, at the same time, of its ability in all matter of phantasy?"[7] If that critic, David Masson, is one of the few of Dickens's contemporaries *not* to fear the power of "phantasy," he might perhaps be offering us some ways of reading the social novels of the 1850s as at once "real," "earnest," and fantastic; as operating in a powerful fictional and social realm of their own.

Hard Times is the Dickens novel that asks most clearly to be read not as a mere fictional world but as a commentary on a contemporary crisis. It is, after all, *Hard Times for These Times*, and it is dedicated to Thomas Carlyle, the social thinker whose vision of a society of human connections (one that transcended the mere "cash-nexus" he articulated in works like *Past and Present* and *Sartor Resartus*) influenced Dickens so profoundly in the 1840s and 1850s. The climate of the time would have led contemporary readers to expect a novel of industrialism and class violence. Following the remarkable literary successes of novels like Elizabeth Gaskell's *Mary Barton*, and the recent strife at the Preston factory (which Dickens had visited before he began writing *Hard Times*), there was every reason to expect Dickens to engage the issues that surrounded the "Condition of England novel," so called after the great question of workers and masters identified by Carlyle himself in his pamphlet on Chartism. True, the more violent strikes of the 1840s had given way to a general sense of urban well-being, but Dickens had never been one to let sleeping social issues lie.

Nonetheless, the first pages of *Hard Times* put us not within a factory but within a schoolroom, and the most industrious workers we see in the novel are the jugglers, riders, and clowns of Sleary's travelling circus, from which the strolling-girl, Sissy Jupe, is exiled when she joins the family of the

Utilitarian theorist and politician Thomas Gradgrind, whose children, Louisa, Tom, Malthus, and Adam Smith have begun early their education in things metallurgical, mathematical, and "somethingological" (1.4). Readers in quest of the grittier realism of Gaskell, Benjamin Disraeli, or Charles Kingsley, all authors of important industrial novels, would be disappointed in Dickens's chief representative of the working class, a factory worker ("one of the fluffy classes" [2.10]) named Stephen Blackpool, who resists joining the union, offers as political analysis only the tag-phrase "'tis a muddle" (1.10), and ends the novel in an abandoned mine shaft, brought up only to see the evening star and die.

Despite a flurry of scholarly articles connecting *Hard Times* to the Preston lock-out and other contemporary "factory controversies," the novel in fact seems far less topical in its references than *Bleak House*, a novel completed the year before and one which, despite being set in the 1830s, resonates with a range of contemporary "key-notes." Whereas falling buildings, urban poverty, the revitalized Metropolitan Police Force, and current debates over contagious diseases make their way into *Bleak House*, *Hard Times* seems far more fantastical, taking its opening notes not from discussions of pauper education but fairy-tales and Ali Baba – the little children in the Gradgrind school are compared to the forty thieves, hiding in jars until boiling oil is poured in. The narrator asks, "dost thou think that thou wilt always kill out-right the robber Fancy lurking within – or sometimes only maim him and distort him" (1.2), and the distortion of the children's imagination (particularly Tom and Louisa's) remains central to the novel's plan. Similarly, the first description of the industrial city, Coketown, is of "a town of unnatural red and black like the painted face of a savage"; the chimneys give off not what Gaskell would describe as "unparliamentary smoke" (*North and South*, chapter 7) named for its defiance of new laws governing pollution, but "interminable serpents of smoke [which] trailed themselves for ever and ever, and never got uncoiled"; and the repetitive piston of the factory's steam-engine is "like the head of an elephant in a state of melancholy madness" (1.5). The novel's own repetitive machinery generates metaphors at the same remarkable rate. Mr. Bounderby, "rich man: banker, merchant, and what not," has a "metallic laugh" (1.4); Mr. Gradgrind works "as if an astronomical observatory should be made without any windows" (1.15); the lights in the great factories look "like Fairy palaces" – or so "travellers by express-train said" (1.10). No logic seems to underwrite these metaphors (how else could Mr. Bounderby have "a pervading appearance on him of being inflated like a balloon, and ready to start"? [1.4]), and yet they consistently pull the novel away from its tract-like message, and toward some realm of pure fantasy, in which Bounderby's dependent-housekeeper, Mrs. Sparsit, gets to be a "bank fairy" and Louisa Bounderby to compare herself to "the Coketown works," in which "there seems to be nothing . . . but languid and monotonous smoke" (1.15). "Yet when the night comes, Fire bursts out, father!" Louisa says, and the reader foretells Louisa's own plot – its bursting out, and its final conversion, like the "realities" she fails to grasp, into dust and ash.

Hard Times works less by argument than by such metaphorical or analogical groupings: the education which "distorts" the young Gradgrind children is a part of the same repressive force which keeps the workers from experiencing any pleasure, or the industrialists from imagining the lives around them. The failure of "fancy" is part of the systematic failure of imagination that results in the bad marriages, ruined homes, and selfish strivings of virtually all of the characters. In that way, the work *Hard Times* performs is less to present in some mimetic way the miseries of industrialism (though it offers the bleakness of such a life far more evocatively than its critics sometimes notice) than to represent the systems of thought that both produced and sustain it. When Louisa Gradgrind, now married to Bounderby, the "bully of humility," is led by the plot into the dark home of Stephen Blackpool, it is "the first time in her life Louisa had come into one of the dwellings of the Coketown Hands" (the synecdoche refers to their reduction from full humanity to their labouring parts). More than that, "for the first time in her life she was face to face with anything like individuality in connexion with them" (2.6). For her, they have been

> Something to be worked so much and paid so much, and there ended; something to be infallibly settled by laws of supply and demand; something that blundered against those laws, and floundered into difficulty; something that was a little pinched when wheat was dear, and over-ate itself when wheat was cheap . . ., something that occasionally rose like a sea, and did some harm and waste (chiefly to itself), and fell again.

But, the narrator concludes, "she had scarcely thought more of separating them into units, than of separating the sea itself into its component drops" (2.6). And Louisa, confronted for the first time with the individuality which is suddenly connected to *her*, "stood for some moments looking round the room," at "the few chairs, the few books, the common prints, and the bed." Far from littering the novel with details of a realistically drawn worker's room (Gaskell would have added domestic implements; Disraeli described the prints), Dickens stresses instead Louisa's itemization of "common" elements. However few they possess, workers, too, must sit on chairs and sleep on beds; Louisa must learn to see the similarities as well as the differences between her life and that of these "common" people.

It is not that *Hard Times* contains no coherent political ideas, nor even that its political representatives fail absolutely. Stephen does not join the strike, but he explains quite clearly to Bounderby what it is his fellow-workers want. In a passage that appears in the book's manuscript but not in the printed volume, Stephen makes clear to Rachael the violence that is directed against the workers' bodies;[8] and Louisa's growing sympathies direct our attention to the poverty of imagination under which they (like she) are asked to live. But unlike the essays Dickens was publishing at the same time in *Household Words*, *Hard Times* holds up little hope for public solutions to public ills. Rather, its imaginative heart is with Louisa Bounderby's struggle to escape her father's educative and her husband's sexual bondage, to move from the utter negativity of the caricatured Utilitarian training she has received ("Never wonder!" says her father repeatedly) to Sissy Jupe's simpler and more imaginative universe. At the novel's end, Louisa stares into the fire and sees the exoneration of Stephen Blackpool, the quiet earnestness of Rachael's continued labour, the death of her lonely brother Tom, the happy children of Sissy Jupe. What she does not see is "herself again a wife – a mother – lovingly watchful of her children" and giving them the life she did not have – for "Such a thing was never to be" (3.9). Dickens is as interested in the ruin of the individual as in the tangles of the system, and *Hard Times* offers little hope for the resurrection of the passionate fires that Louisa Gradgrind once kept banked inside her.

For the Dickens of the 1850s, society in general seems to hold little hope for individual renewal, and it is an almost equally vexed question if individuals can do anything to renew the social sphere. If *Hard Times* offers up somewhat ironically its three volume titles ("Sowing," "Reaping," "Garnering"), *Little Dorrit* weights its two-book structure ("Poverty" and "Riches") almost as harshly; indeed, by the book's end it seems easier for a camel to pass through the eye of a needle than to get any rich people into the book's happy ending. And where fantasy held out the promise of some more imaginative life elsewhere (even Sissy Jupe's father loved the stories of the Sultana Scheherezade, and hearing of her "kept him, many times from what did him real harm"), in *Little Dorrit*, fantasy seems dangerous, story-telling either pathetic compensation or lethal self-delusion, and the social sphere not infinitely expansive but terminally reducible to carceral metaphor. The vast analogies of *Little Dorrit* – the Marshalsea Prison which spreads its image across all of society, the Circumlocution Office, whose bureaucracy strangles all individual invention – offer not the hope of changing the key-note, but a death-knell for the imagined connections *Hard Times* held on to so persistently.

Except, that is, for the novel's heroine, Amy Dorrit. Interestingly, Amy is herself a friend to fiction – indeed, quite a fabulist. The night she visits Arthur

Clennam in his rooms in Covent Garden, she says she has told her father she has gone to a party. "Oh, no, certainly!" she says, "I never was at a party in my life"; but she adds, "I hope there is no harm in it. I could never have been of any use, if I had not pretended a little" (1.14). In addition to signaling the heroine's excessive modesty, her speech suggests an interesting permutation in Dickens's thinking about fiction: not only is some fiction harmless, at best it may also be "of use." For Amy, story-telling is part of maintaining the fiction of a family (her debtor father does not know his children work; Amy lies to Arthur about her love for him to continue seeing him; she allows the child–woman Maggy to believe she is helpful in running errands and carrying messages), but it is also part of envisioning a place for herself in society. Were Amy ever to see herself as merely "a common prison-child," as her sister regards her, she would be incapable not only of helping others but of sustaining her own life. Without fiction, Dickens seems to say, we would lead lives more truly impoverished than that of the poorest debtor in the Marshalsea.

But such a view of fictions of usefulness (attractive though it might be to novel-readers!) does not go far in examining the political implications of that expansive, imprisoned vista which is *Little Dorrit*. Sylvia Manning has noted that *Little Dorrit* has been spared some of the more reductive readings *Hard Times* has endured for the simple reason that imprisonment for debt had already been ended in England;[9] no one could think of *Little Dorrit* as the same kind of "novel with a purpose" that *Hard Times* in some ways resembles. And yet, as we have seen, *Little Dorrit* did elicit some of the most violent reactions Dickens received from social-minded critics. If imprisonment for debt is a thing of the past, the labyrinthine bureaucracy Dickens identified in the Circumlocution Office (whose motto is "How not to do it") suggests if anything a heightened anxiety about the metaphorical nature of political structures at that time.

Dickens's exposé of government inefficiency (and James Fitzjames Stephen's immediate and rather vicious response) suggests that the problems of describing or delimiting the social are turning rapidly into the problem of describing government itself. One of the fascinating things about *Little Dorrit* is how exactly the terms of "How not to do it" are mirrored by that government's opposing figure, Amy Dorrit. For Amy, who has "always been strong enough to do what [she] want[s] to do" (2.24), despite her size, femininity, and poverty, the only question that matters is "What is to be done?" At times, in his invocation of her fanatic loyalty and her obedience to "duty," Dickens seems to pose Amy herself as a social principle, what Lionel Trilling referred to as "the female paraclete," a figure of cultural salvation.[10] But the genius of *Little Dorrit* lies not so much in its marking of systems of oppression (the Marshalsea; the quarantine) or its observation of smaller, more personal deprivations (the Plornishes and their shop; old Nandy in the uniform of the poor house; Mr. Dorrit, pretending to a dignity he never had) as in the bleakness that follows the good characters: Amy, Arthur, even Flora Finching, unable to recover from some early, fatal blow that froze her in her own self-imprisonment.

The novel seems to invoke a kind of self-governance we have come, after Foucault and such trenchant readers of Dickens as D. A. Miller, to call disciplinary.[11] Only the characters who embrace their limitations (Amy, her poverty and her prison-status; Arthur, his will-lessness; Tattycoram, the counting of one-and-twenty) are allowed anything like a happy ending, but the novel is unusually sharp even for Dickens in registering the quality of their suffering: the exact extent of what they are lacking.

Nowhere is this truer than in the novel's other great metaphor, that of the "shadow" of the prison. Amy who (in telling her own story) "condenses the narrative of her life into a few scanty words about herself" (1.24), goes in and out of the prison "like a little ghost, and vanish[es] away without a sound." Even the novel's conclusion, in which "the noisy and the eager, and the arrogant and the froward and the vain, fretted and chafed, and made their usual uproar," cannot make Amy noisy or arrogant or even conspicuous. Far from undoing the power relations that *Little Dorrit* tracks so compellingly, Amy's entrances and exits from "the prison of this lower world" merely seem to cast their own small shadow over the "long bright rays, [the] bars of the prison" (2.30). In a world of such a glaring (and such a betraying) sun, the shadow-narrative suggests a darker world of masochism, secrets, and promises – a world that may not ultimately transform systems of power, but has the ability to unsettle and disrupt them.

We might take our cue for this reading (a reading of Amy's gothic power as a more subtle form of undoing the world of "How not to do it") from another shadow, Sydney Carton, whose nocturnal ramblings through the Paris of the French Revolution suggest a city more dead than alive; more unreal than palpable. Dickens began *A Tale of Two Cities* with the roads of both Paris and London already haunted by the forces of unrest: the woodman is preparing the axe which will chop down the trees that will make up the guillotines and the tumbrils which will bring them their prisoners; the wine which spills on the streets of Paris foreshadows blood; the grief-maddened, imprisoned Doctor Manette has already written the memoir that will indict his own son-in-law, Charles Darnay, whom he has yet to meet at the novel's opening. The "fact" that will save Darnay, his uncanny resemblance to his otherwise unlike double, Carton, is a trick of mere appearances. Again, as with Amy Dorrit's fictions, resemblances and shadows are hardly enough to keep at bay the terrifying social forces of dissolution and mob violence which, for most of the novel, give us our sense of revolutionary France.

A Tale of Two Cities seems to raise few of the political questions the earlier two novels have done. Deliberately set back in time, it poses none of the questions of topicality and sensationalism Stephen complained of in Dickens, nor can it be imagined to have the immediate reformist impulses of the other. Its claims to a mimetic or social realism seem undercut immediately by its satiric opening, and any social realism it allowed to persist would surely be undone by the novel's clearly prophetic ending, in which the self-sacrificing Sydney Carton not only imagines that "it is a far, far better thing that I do, than I have ever done," but claims to see "this place," the bloody square where he is going to his execution, at some day in the future "then fair to look upon, with not a trace of this day's disfigurement" (3.15). Much as Amy Dorrit's fantasies seemed to take her out of this "lower world," so Carton's seem to take him (and the novel) not only out of society but out of history itself.

Nonetheless, A Tale of Two Cities returns to the same social and political concerns we have seen so far – not only the problems of industrial workers (echoed oddly in Doctor Manette's obsessive work as a shoemaker both inside and after he leaves the Bastille) but the grinding poverty, sexual violence, and familial disruption which have been the sign of class warfare in all three novels. In this novel, as in Hard Times and Little Dorrit, it falls to women to make sense of the social order – in this novel, to both the gentle Lucie Manette, who travels to France and witnesses the revolution in order to rescue her husband (and who herself runs the risk of being arrested as a spy for making "signs and signals" [3.12]) and the tiger-like Madame Defarge, who pursues Darnay and his family not for their economic oppression of the people, but for the rape and murder his uncle and father carried out on her sister, her father, and her brother. "Those dead are my dead," she says, threatening to lay waste all of France in her vengeance. Indeed, her loyal hench-woman is called The Vengeance, and Dickens's mob is most powerful (and most terrifying) when it resembles not the malcontented factory workers of Coketown, but the passionate Louisa Bounderby, waiting for the fires to burst out, or even Amy Dorrit, obsessive observer of the Marshalsea-like miseries of a poverty-stricken Italy. Both social consciousness and the violence that seeks to give it a voice, in these novels, are the property of women.

But A Tale of Two Cities insists even more fiercely on the gothic or nightmare quality of social rage – and even of social justice. Not only Sydney Carton but his companion in the tumbril, the unnamed seamstress who goes to her death accused of "plots," imagines a world made better by revolution.

Speaking of her cousin, living far away and unable even to read the news of the seamstress's death ("she knows nothing of my fate – for I cannot write – and even if I could, how should I tell her!" [3.15]), the seamstress imagines a world transformed:

> "If the republic really does good to the poor, and they come to be less hungry, and in all ways to suffer less, she may live a long time: she may even live to be old . . . Do you think . . . that it will seem long to me, while I wait for her in the better land where I trust both you and I will be mercifully sheltered?"

Carton, further undoing history in the interest of messianic time, reassures her that "there is no Time there, and no trouble there," but her question echoes Dickens's own interests, fictional and political. What is the nature of social change? What would it mean for a revolution to allow the poor, as they never have, "even" to "live to be old"? Can the novel imagine an end to narrative, a place of shelter outside of time?

A Tale of Two Cities balances its promise of redemptive history (the fair place, no longer disfigured; the better land of merciful shelter; the Republic that "does good to the poor") with an interest we can only call, after Stephen, Masson, et al., "speculative." However sympathetic Dickens is to the cause of revolution (and he is deeply unsympathetic to the "lords of the State preserves of loaves and fishes," as he calls those in authority), he is not proposing that the Madame Defarges of the world be allowed to sacrifice women and children on the guillotine at will, however "pretty" a spectacle they make. He is, however, making a spectacle of his own here: one in which historical action provides an arena for private virtue, as Sydney Carton goes to his death "to keep a life you love beside you!" (2.14; 3.11). Dickens's image of the already dead Carton, walking the mysterious street paved with secrets, is of an individual heart that stands opposed to social invasiveness, that defends a realm of individualism not imaginable to the state. Precisely why Madame Defarge cannot anticipate the plots of Carton is that unlike Louisa, Amy, and Lucie, she cannot imagine going to her death, turning herself into a spectre, for the love of another.

The end of Little Dorrit ("Went down into a modest life of usefulness and happiness . . . inseparable and blessed") suggests initially a world of individual connections, what J. Hillis Miller has called "the relation of love" – the relation, he argues, which Dickens proposes in lieu of a "fictive" society, one which is merely the "projection of the selfish desire of individuals."[12] But for Dickens the answer is never wholly private, even when the novels end with the solitary reflections of characters like Louisa Bounderby and Sydney Carton. These conclusions push us, rather, toward two very different definitions of the social world in the Dickens novel, definitions that focus our attention on what the Dickens novel includes, and what it deliberately leaves out. What it leaves out, most powerfully, is any social engine for transformations. Neither unions nor charity; neither parliamentary machinations nor reformist politics; none of these external forms of political transformation works, or is even seriously considered in these novels, despite our knowledge that in his journalism Dickens considered them all in turn. But Dickens does not close the novels with a vision of solitary individuals unwilling to look beyond themselves; instead, these characters seem if anything haunted by too many versions of themselves and those they love. Louisa sees the image of her dying brother and her unborn children; Sydney Carton addresses the as yet unborn son of Lucie Manette Darnay, who he imagines can redeem his name in that brighter, "fairer," future. Much as *A Tale of Two Cities* tried to imagine the workings of the crowd, the collective political desires of the women and men dancing the Carmagnole (and try it did, though it hardly succeeds), so it tries to imagine the individual consciousness as caught up in some larger force – call it prophecy; speculation; or some shadowy sense of a self beyond mere individualism, as much as it is beyond mere politics.

The real genius of these later novels of Dickens is, as I have tried to suggest, the power of imagination each unleashes, and the amazingly wide ends (social, cultural, legal, moral) each pursues. The power of analogical thinking in *Hard Times*, like that of metaphors of society in *Little Dorrit* and of ghostly narratives in *A Tale of Two Cities*, suggests a world in which social injustices could in turn be reimagined. Dickens nowhere suggests that "beginning the world again," as he calls this impulse in *Bleak House*, the other great social novel of the 1850s, is an easy or even an achievable goal; it is, however, the failure to make imaginative leaps, whether of sympathy or charity, which has landed England in the rigor mortis of industrial, carceral, and political despair. When Louisa Bounderby looks around Stephen Blackpool's room, as when Amy Dorrit offers her sympathy to Mrs. Clennam or the Plornishes, or Sydney Carton embraces the seamstress on the tumbrils of the revolution, the possibility of some connection at once individual and social is made less speculative, less "romance" and more "truth"; something more (because differently) real is left to believe in at the end of these novels.

We might close these reflections on politics and history in the Dickens novel with his final completed work, *Our Mutual Friend*, a novel set more clearly "in these times of ours" (1.1), and caught up in the absolute materiality of Victorian culture: the horse dung on the streets; the petty vengeances of ballad-sellers and money-lenders; the mounds of dust that offer a fortune to the men who collect, sift, and resell them. The novel offers itself as truly the "dust heap of history," for so many of the ideas of Dickens's fiction come to rest here, most powerfully his earlier faith in fictions of social transformation, rendered more fairy-tale-like and less "realistic" than ever. In this world everything turns to muck, and a thin layer of grime covers it all.

But the novel's "golden dustman," Mr. Boffin, asserts otherwise: when the lawyer Mortimer Lightwood, "with a light laugh," asserts that "everything wears to rags," Mr. Boffin demurs. "'I won't go so far as to say everything,' returned Mr. Boffin, on whom his manner seemed to grate, 'because there's some things that I never found among the dust'." (1.8) The "rags" Lightwood won't find in the dust-heaps are the affection and remembrances Boffin and his wife bear for the orphaned John Harmon; the transformation of the selfish Bella Wilfer into the "truest golden gold"; and the Boffins' cheerful renunciation of their fortune in favor of Bella and John and their baby. Speculative and certainly romantic; and yet not entirely individual, limited, apolitical. The power of Dickens's metaphoric constructions to conjure up a social vision beyond the personal, something that individuals participate in beyond their own imaginations, was the most powerful social force of his age; it is only by renaming the fictions of social *mis*representation that the novel can represent a universe beyond the dust-heap. The effort to transform the novel so that it incorporates a social vision beyond the limitations of mimesis, beyond the world of rag-and-bottle shops and hard-edged misery, led to a world of speaking shadows: a world of gothic and prophetic vision. That powerful vision, which was Dickens's best gift to novel-readers, is what endures, and it is what turns the dusty world to gold.

NOTES

1 The nonconformist preacher was James Baldwin Brown; quoted in G. M. Young, *Portrait of an Age: Victorian England* (Oxford University Press, 1977, orig. published 1936), p. 69; the citation is provided by G. Kitson Clark in his annotated edition, p. 276.

2 Monroe Engel nicely defined the "best modern critics of Dickens," by whom he means George Orwell and Edmund Wilson, as describing an "enigmatic mixture of radicalism and conservatism in his novels" and trying to "find a commonsense rationale for the mixture" (Engel, "The Politics of Dickens' Novels," *PMLA* 71 [1956], 945–74; quotation at 945). Nicholas Coles's subtle reading of the difference between "Dickens the novelist" and "Dickens the reformer" argues that working in "different discourses enables him to articulate [sic] represent the necessarily ambivalent response of an alert and concerned middle-class Victorian to his society" (Nicholas Coles, "The Politics of *Hard Times*," *Dickens Studies Annual* 15 [1986], 145–79, quotation at 146).

3 Humphry House, *The Dickens World* (Oxford University Press, 1941), pp. 10–11.

4 The review in *The Rambler* is by Richard Simpson (October 1854); Whipple's in *Atlantic Monthly* (March 1877); both are quoted in *Charles Dickens: The Critical*

Heritage, ed. Philip Collins (Routledge and Barnes and Noble, 1971), pp. 303 and 315 respectively. Stephen's remarks are from "Mr Dickens as a Politician," *Saturday Review* (3 January 1857). Quoted in Collins, *The Critical Heritage*, pp. 344–49.

5 This passage, uncited in Collins, *The Critical Heritage*, is on p. 125 in the original.

6 This phrase is from Stephen's review of *Little Dorrit*, "The Licence of Modern Novelists," *The Edinburgh Review* (July 1857). Quoted in Collins, *The Critical Heritage*, p. 367.

7 *British Novelists Since Scott* (Macmillan, 1859), quoted in *Victorian Criticism of the Novel*, ed. Edwin M. Eigner and George J. Worth (Cambridge University Press, 1985), p. 152.

8 See *Hard Times*, ed. George Ford and Sylvère Monod (Norton, 1990, 1966), p. 247.

9 Sylvia Manning, *Dickens as Satirist* (Yale University Press, 1971), pp. 156–57.

10 Lionel Trilling, "Little Dorrit," *The Opposing Self* (Viking, 1955), p. 57.

11 See in particular, D. A. Miller, "Discipline in Different Voices: Bureaucracy, Police, Family, and *Bleak House*," *The Novel and the Police* (University of California Press, 1988), pp. 58–106.

12 J. Hillis Miller, *Charles Dickens: The World of His Novels* (Harvard University Press, 1958), p. 226.

FURTHER READING

Carlisle, Janice. "*Little Dorrit*: Necessary Fictions." *Studies in the Novel* 7 (1975), 195–214.

Carr, Jean Ferguson. "Writing as a Woman: Dickens, *Hard Times*, and Feminine Discourses." *Dickens Studies Annual* 18 (1989), 161–78.

Gallagher, Catherine. *The Industrial Reformation of English Fiction: Social Discourse and Narrative Form, 1832–1867*. University of Chicago Press, 1985.

House, Humphry. *The Dickens World*. Oxford University Press, 1941.

Humpherys, Anne. "Louisa Gradgrind's Secret: Marriage and Divorce in *Hard Times*." *Dickens Studies Annual* 25 (1996), 177–96.

Hutter, Albert J. "Nation and Generation in *A Tale of Two Cities*." *PMLA* 93 (1978), 448–62.

Manning, Sylvia. *Dickens as Satirist*. Yale University Press, 1971.

Newsom, Robert. "'To Scatter Dust': Fancy and Authenticity in *Our Mutual Friend*." *Dickens Studies Annual* 8 (1980), 39–60.

Nunokawa, Jeff. *The Afterlife of Property: Domestic Security and the Victorian Novel*. Princeton University Press, 1994.

Schor, Hilary. *Dickens and the Daughter of the House*. Cambridge University Press, 1999.

Stewart, Garrett. *Death Sentences: Styles of Dying in British Fiction*. Harvard University Press, 1984.

Trilling, Lionel. "*Little Dorrit*." *Kenyon Review* 15 (1953), 577–90. Reprinted as "Introduction," the New Oxford Illustrated edition of *Little Dorrit*. Oxford University Press, 1953. And as "*Little Dorrit*," *The Opposing Self*. Viking Press, 1955.

6

BRIAN CHEADLE

The late novels: *Great Expectations* and *Our Mutual Friend*

Dickens's last two completed novels are "dark" with a sense of social estrangement. Their keynote is the orphaned Pip's intuition of life as a "universal struggle" (*GE* 1), their arena increasingly London, the site of modernity. By the 1860s Dickens's domestic life was in tatters, with his wife discarded, his home sold, his family a disappointment (even Kate, his favorite daughter, having married precipitately to get away from it all), the letters enshrining the past put to the bonfire, and his relationship with Ellen Ternan illicit. He had long despaired of the institutions of social power. Increasingly, and despite his reactionary tendencies as he grew older, a profound questioning of such basic conditions of Victorian life as class privilege and the effects of capital became the ground bass of his work.

Near the end of the first movement of *Great Expectations*, Pip watches in the gloom as the recaptured Magwitch is rowed out to the black Hulk moored off the marshes. As the convict disappears over the side of the ship, "the ends of the torches were flung hissing into the water, and went out, as if it were all over with him" (5). This evocation of the archetypal ferrying-off of the damned by torchlight to the underworld, coming as it does after the whole community has enjoyed the ritual of a hunting down, has something of the purgative force with which, at the climax of melodrama, the villain is hissed and flung out in a circle of dying stage fire. The import is all the more intense in that the climax of the hunt, Magwitch grappling with Compeyson in a grotesque version of a ruffianly assault on a gentleman, taps into the primal bourgeois fears of lower-class violence and of losing class. The plot pivots on the expunging of Magwitch, and it is a mark of Dickens's capacity to pinpoint fundamental social issues that this transportation should reflect not only the colonial extension of the nineteenth-century system, but also the extent to which that system entailed a brutal suppression of the "low." As John Stuart Mill put it, more circumspectly but no less trenchantly, "One of the effects of civilization (not to say one of the ingredients of it) is, that the spectacle, and even the idea, of pain, is kept more and more out of the sight of those classes who enjoy in their fulness the benefits of civilization."[1]

But the "moving on" (*BH* 18) of the convicts is seen through Pip's eyes, and made poignant partly by his relief, and partly by his sense of a terrible complicity with Magwitch. In the long perspective of the narrative, in which Pip's theft replicates Magwitch's theft of turnips, with both made resonant by Jaggers's account of an evil system generating children "in great numbers ... for the hangman" (*GE* 51), there is no immunity from pain or criminality. The novel makes it clear too that the shipping of the convicts is no more than the extreme form of the control by "othering" seen in Mrs. Joe's bringing Pip up by hand. Pip's sense of guilt is so vivid in the encounter with the victimized "Abel" because he has already been conditioned to think of himself as "naterally wicious" (4), much as the young Dickens working at the Blacking Factory felt himself to be a "small Cain," though he "had never done harm to any one" (Forster, 1.2). The casual indifference with which the spent torches are flung onto the water, and the pathos of their going out, thus crystallize the sense of a disciplinary, uncaring regime. From Mrs. Joe slapping butter grudgingly on the slice, to Magwitch "chopping a wedge off his bread, and soaking up with it the last fragments of gravy round and round his plate, as if to make the most of an allowance" (*GE* 40), from Jaggers bullying his sandwich to Wopsle bullying the "Amens" (4), Dickens presents a society in which life's basic exchanges are permeated with the resentful violence of power relations and a competitive economy. Moreover, he understands that the resentment endemic to class society provides the impulse for the policing of the hierarchy; for it is Mrs. Joe's frustration with her class position that leads her to find a compensation in bullying those beneath her. Such commonplaces are worth rehearsing, if only to reinvigorate Raymond Williams's judgment that what gives distinction to Dickens's social criticism is his ability to suffuse innumerable details with a single "structure of feeling" which defines the "general condition" of society.[2]

Pip proves his right to be the hero of his tale by turning repugnance into a love for the outcast; and it is a mark of the book's audacity that this is presented as no more than the heart's proper instinct, an exchange of right feeling as natural and desirable as the love of a son for a father. The softening of Pip's heart is confirmed by, and helps to release, impulses of forgiveness all round, the book holding firm to Dickens's ethic of moral sentiment. Straightforward readings of *Great Expectations* of this kind are legion,[3] though differing widely in emphasis and on such key issues as Pip's guilt or the two endings.[4] Recently, however, an influential tendency in criticism has been a neo-Marxist or new historicist tradition of critique, aimed not so much at interpreting a novel's intentions as at suggesting how its ideas and assumptions are politically conditioned.[5] The discussion of *Great Expectations* that follows begins by suggesting some of the ways in which this is so.

There is something pyrrhic about Pip's moral victory. The poet and critic W. H. Auden has said: "There are . . . two competing sources of guilt: one arising from the breaking of the human law in the rightness of which one believes . . . and the other from the consciousness that the human law no longer corresponds to the divine, a conviction that unless the human law is broken society will perish."[6] In his penitence toward Magwitch and Joe, Pip absolves himself from the first kind of guilt. But though he holds Magwitch's hand in solidarity when he is sentenced, Pip's own pietistic verdict, "Lord, be merciful to him, a sinner" (58), conveniently forgets the imperative to align the human law with the divine. Estella's initial disdain fills Pip with an intense "smart" of injustice (8), and Magwitch's anger focuses on the injustice of Compeyson's getting off lightly; but Pip, as a young gentleman, himself attempts to "move on" both Orlick and Trabb's boy from their jobs, and he would have Orlick outlawed from the country. Moreover, Pip comes to feel it was the chance encounter with Magwitch and not his whole upbringing that has "chained" him, and his final clerkship suggests that resentment of oppression has given way to a willing self-repression. It is not disconcerting that Pip should find virtue in gentlemanly capitalism, for few manage to live outside the system; but when he insists that Clarriker's has "a good name," and "worked for its profits" (58), he seems haunted by the need to justify and excuse, as though affirming a diminished notion of personal integrity were the only chance of wholeness within a shifty world. Pip's eleven-year exile in Cairo (an expiatory replication of Magwitch's banishment), preceded as it is by violent encounter, symbolic drowning, and sickness unto death, has the force of an emasculation. Pumblechook observes with gratification that Pip is no longer "as plump as a Peach" (58), and the thinness is felt in the flat prose of the final chapters. The chastened mood is anticipated by nothing so much as the description of Barnard's Inn (where Pip finds temporary lodging with Herbert when he comes to London), whose desolation might seem a decisive intimation that urban society can afford the self only a subdued provisionality. Small wonder that for D. A. Miller, Dickens simultaneously "censures policing power," and "reinvent[s] it."[7]

The elevation of "right feeling" helps to construct a specifically bourgeois form of virtue. The "good feeling" (34) on which the Finches of the Grove pride themselves is, by contrast, a genteel clubbishness. In Bentley Drummle, the coarseness of snobbish disdain is exposed; and the upper-class tendency to treat love as a heartless power-play is revealed as a degradation, fittingly enough, through his "breaking" of Estella. At the other social extreme, bourgeois inner worth is set against Orlick's rancor, the feared discontent of the uncouth masses who do (or shamelessly shirk) physical work. Bourgeois self-betterment is saved from any comparable implication of upward aggression in that Pip's education is presented as an attempt to make himself *worthy* of an exalting love. And the ultimate bourgeois consolidation of right feeling as its "cultural capital"[8] comes through the accommodation of manners to morals in the disciplining of Pip to that "gentleness of heart" which a century earlier the novelist Samuel Richardson had presented as central to the idea of a gentleman (*Clarissa* 2, Letter 21). The term tended to suggest someone who did not need to work, but Dickens wrests it from this implication not just by exposing the dream of great expectations as an aspiration to false gentility and idleness, but by making Joe the yardstick of right feeling. It is a shaming lesson that the lowly Joe's trustworthiness and tolerance, and his payment of Pip's debts, should best exemplify the essential bourgeois virtues. But Forster's praise of Dickens's humor as the quality through which he most effectively "discovered the affinities between the high and the low . . . which bring us all upon the level of a common humanity" (Forster, 9.1) suggests how the comic treatment of Joe's goodness also helps to naturalize the bourgeois myth of society as a commodious family of the deserving. By divesting the notion of the gentleman of any suggestions of rank, and by presenting it as an absolute moral counter, Dickens makes it central to the fable of bourgeois virtue.[9]

Embourgeoisement of feeling depends on binding such socially turbulent energies as desire and aggression, a binding centered on Estella and Magwitch. Estella is most alive when she invites Pip, with "a bright flush" (11), to kiss her cheek after he has knocked down Herbert; but the plot of desire is sacrificed to the moral plot, and Estella's perverse upbringing is the logical extension of the barring of respectable Victorian women from desire. The aggressive "maleness" which feeds off libidinal energy is equally fettered: Pip and Drummle are allowed to lock themselves in *their* later combat for Estella only by squaring up in straining immobility for the direct warmth of the fire, like a pair of sumo hearth-dogs.

In his handling of Magwitch, Dickens achieves a more complex binding, both of the aggression associated with work and money, and of social anger. Pip's attempt to buy off Magwitch with clean notes, only to be reminded of the sweated money wrapped around the file, reveals that work and money link the high and low more decisively than any potential for right feeling. But by displacing Magwitch's labor to the colonial periphery, the novel largely suppresses its insight into the exploitative basis of the class system and the economic grounding of social relations. One does not have to take seriously work done in Australia – even Micawber can become a magistrate there. When Magwitch's first emissary returns, he finds Pip's marsh world a "most beastly place. Mudbank, mist, swamp, and work; work, swamp, mist and mudbank" (28), but even the work done at the forge is not imaginatively realized, the book proving itself sympathetic to Pip's fear that Estella might see him toiling as a blacksmith. The effective displacement of work to the colonies thus allows for the almost total suppression of the competitive and aggressive energies of what Walter Bagehot called the "multifarious, industrial, fig-selling world."[10] Moreover the returned Magwitch himself renounces his desire to "exhibit" his gentleman, regretting it as "lowness" (40), a failure in morals and manners; and as this entails renouncing too his desire to be revenged on genteel society, the renunciation has the effect of neatly suppressing his residual social anger.

Ideological readings of a text, however, tend to be selectively focused and simplified. It is all too easy to rewrite the moral fable of *Great Expectations* as serving to bind the very energies through which society might be changed or even redeemed, and there is something overbearing in the current insistence on political demystification. When John Bayley sees the terror the returned Magwitch unleashes in Pip as deriving from the fear of being possessed by another, and calls this "the direst threat Dickens's unconscious knows,"[11] the insight is hardly upstaged by an insistence that the Victorian unconscious is politically constructed to enshrine the idea of creative selfhood. Moreover, to think of Dickens's volatile texts, with their wild comic eruptions, their violence, and their sudden symbolic illuminations, as singlemindedly inscribing bourgeois ideology, is to erase all sense of their tone and texture. It is also to ignore their capacity for challenging and destabilizing cultural formations.

Because the prevailing symbolic economy exists to iron over contradictions in the social formation, it is extremely unstable and prone to slippages. One such is Joe's attempt to whitewash his brutal father with the lie that he was "good in his heart" (7). Joe's "lie" pinpoints the deceit in the notion of innate goodness which sustains the family myth; and it reinscribes the sense of lower-class violence which the myth attempts to sublimate. Slippages are not, however, inevitably subversive. Transgression, after all, provides the resistance necessary for any work to generate its closures. Trabb's boy mocks Pip's pretensions by exaggerating the bodily forms of deference, turning them into derisive, transgressive gestures. He similarly reduces Pip's unpracticed *hauteur* by strutting with limbs akimbo, hair twined, and an extravagantly wriggling gait – and by wearing his bag as though it epitomized the straight-jacketing effect of new clothes and good manners. The performance inevitably attracts a knot of spectators, suggesting the power of carnival to unite the low. The mockery precipitates in Pip an acute sense of the dislocation and dispersal of self inherent in crossing classes, for he feels himself "ejected" or vomited into the open country (30) as though by a reflex of the protesting public body. Yet only the element of falsity in Pip's pretensions, and not the norm itself, is being shown up: Pip ruefully reassures himself that "to have exacted any lower recompense from [Trabb's boy] than his heart's best blood would have been futile and degrading" (30), but this restraint confirms that he has risen above the anarchic impulses the boy represents. Even when raised to an inspired pitch, the grotesque reversals of carnival thus reinscribe respectable norms.

Similarly, Dickens's fascination with violence almost invariably works toward its containment. Orlick looms large in the latter phases of the book, seething like "Cain, or . . . the Wandering Jew" (15), and he is often seen as figuring Pip's repressed hostilities and desires.[12] But it is as compelling to see him as the demonical obverse of the victimized and far-wandering Abel Magwitch. On this reading, the binding of Magwitch's social anger finally depends on its being repellently displaced into the brutal rancor of Orlick.

What, however, seems most to characterize both the humor and the violence in Dickens, is that they refuse to stay bound. Trabb's boy won't be moved on; and in the large economy of the novel this is a very good thing, for it is his mobile curiosity that ensures Pip's rescue from the lime-kiln. Then too, the lime-kiln imbroglio renews Pip's irrational sense of guilt, as though Dickens were subliminally reraising the issue of social injustice in the very act of putting it to bed. There are shifts and slippages wherever one looks. The scandalous dependence of Pip's gentility on the sweated work of an ex-convict is no sooner on the way to being offset by the refiguring of Magwitch as Pip's loving "father," than the plot plunges into the discovery that Estella is the daughter of Magwitch and Molly. No sooner is Magwitch seemingly softened than he leaps at Compeyson in the galley as though to drag him under. The futile attempt to disguise Magwitch by putting powder on his hair might seem an epitome: "I can compare the effect of it, when on, to nothing but the probable effect of rouge upon the dead; so awful was the manner in which everything in him, that it was desirable to repress, started through that thin layer of pretence, and seemed to come blazing out at the crown of his head" (40). At every point of seeming or attempted closure there is fresh seepage. Dickens's urge to abrogate boundaries would seem irrepressible: even the Miss Havisham subplot originates in the birth of a rotten half-brother within a secret second marriage to a cook.

As with plot, so with character. Stallybrass and White indicate in their discussion of the politics of transgression that the approved self is constituted only through a continuing repudiation of the delinquent other, but, this makes a hankering for the low an essential constituent of the fantasy life of the center.[13] The stronger the repression, the more powerful the fantasies. This is well illustrated in the figure of Molly, the murderess whom Jaggers forces into domestic dutifulness in a weird parody of the angel in the house. Jaggers's obsessive disciplining of her has an intense erotic charge. With equal measures of sadism and an epicure's delight in a prize specimen, he displays the power of the arm with which she had strangled a rival, but over which, at her trial, he had "so skilfully contrived" her sleeves that it "had quite a delicate look" (48). In defending her, he explains away the scratches on her wrists as marks of her having pushed through a bramble thicket, tearing her dress and lacerating her skin – images whose suggestion of rape subliminally reinforce a gipsy wildness of passion. Wemmick describes how Molly had been married (to Magwitch) when very young, and "over the broomstick" (48); and if the reference is to an informal wedding marked by the pair jumping over a broomstick, the metaphorical implication is that the woman is already pregnant, or about to be. In every detail, from "lithe nimble figure," to hair "streaming," and face "as if it were all disturbed by fiery air" (26), Molly is thus invested with all the energy and authority of that sexuality which Foucault sees Victorian texts as actively constructing. Jaggers overtly binds Molly, but Pip equally overtly unbinds her by reading Estella in her hands. Filiation is here achieved not by dredging up hidden documents or a dying nurse who tells all, which are the processes whereby the bourgeois reclaims its own in the conventional family romance, but by recognizing that the culturally proscribed sexuality remains scandalously embodied in the elegant daughter.

To return to the passage where Magwitch is taken off to the hulks is thus to read in it a more intense haunting. Dickens picks up its elemental imagery in the scene where Magwitch returns, and he revisits it directly later, making Wopsle share with Pip his sense of how, when the torches were extinguished, he felt lost in "an outer ring of dark night all about us" (47). The sense of a definitive loss seems an intuition of a society so intent on maintaining its purity by purging all pollutants that it is in danger of divesting itself of vital energy. Nonetheless, the narrative keeps turning back on itself with restless disquiet, as Dickens's imagination compulsively spawns incidents and occasions which threaten the novel's stability.

To move from one novel to the next is to realize that this habit amounts to a deep but intuitive *thinking* at what Browning called "the dangerous edge of things" ("Bishop Blougram's Apology," 400). This claim might seem dubious when the main plot of *Our Mutual Friend* is so conventional and implausible. The following discussion of the novel, rather than engaging with current critical tendencies, will suggest why the main plot is as it is, and then locate the book's greatness in Dickens's greater preparedness to confront painful issues he had previously evaded.

The Harmon plot reworks that of *Great Expectations*. It again attempts to subdue the aggressive, self-seeking aspects of material success, divesting the scheming "donors" of all Magwitch's threatening anger and making them dutiful servants, the Boffins, who voluntarily accept the rights of their betters to financial advantage. It presents John Harmon, returned from the Cape like Pip from Cairo, as guiltless and fit to be rewarded, as though wealth sanctioned true selfhood rather than distorting identity. And in having the heroine, the lively Bella Wilfer, repudiate her initial veneration of money, it re-establishes the role of woman as the repository of domestic virtue and ground of inner value.[14]

Harmon, however, is not, as Pip was, a temporary sojourner in London; for the city is now unquestionedly the place where the debased inheritance of modern life has to be taken up, and the book is quintessentially urban. Pip's lime-kiln sense of a frighteningly attenuated hold on identity is momentarily intensified in John Harmon's apprehension, in his account of near-death by drowning, that "there was no such thing as I" (2.13); but within the extended canvas of *Our Mutual Friend* an individual's fears about being seem insignificant. The city is not amenable to the anguished autobiography of the ordinary man; in its vast anonymity it hardly matters whether one is Radfoot, Handford, Rokesmith, or Harmon. Opportunistic self-aggrandizement is one response to this belittling condition. But the appalling example (and fate) of the Lammles and Veneerings makes it clear that sanity and the hopes of a stable identity lie rather in embracing the ordinary decencies – such as marrying, setting up home, establishing a small circle of friends, and having children. John and Bella find (as most people still do) that such mundanities can be given the generous glamour of Romance. What seems at stake is not so much a bourgeois myth as a necessary fiction.

The main plot nonetheless has an enforced jauntiness, an upbeat and sentimental striving. Modern readers are tempted to dismiss it as simply coy, but the plotting itself foregrounds the benign deceit involved; and Dickens goes to the length of having Boffin achieve his elaborate deception at the expense of temporarily destroying, in a most disconcerting way, the gratifying complicity between author and reader which had hitherto been crucial to Dickensian narrative.

If the Harmon plot accepts the city as the ground of modern existence, the rest of the novel foregrounds its dominant conditions, notably the imperative of work which *Great Expectations* had tended to repress. Everywhere, those not speculating or trading in purchasable identities – the vast majority who are not falsely presuming to realize great expectations – are subject to its routines, or caught up in an improvisational economy of survival. The details are precise: Rumty Wilfer trudges homeward through a suburban Sahara energized as a place where "tiles and bricks were burnt, bones were boiled, carpets were beat, rubbish was shot, dogs were fought, and dust was heaped by contractors" (1.4), and the opening description of Gaffer busy on his boat carefully discriminates his accoutrements from those of a fisherman, waterman, or lighterman. Yet, like almost everything else in Dickens, work is theatrically transmuted, its specific actualities not the point. Thus Rumty embodies the pathos of clerkship (Clarriker's writ small). With Podsnap work is the grid of self-esteem, with Mr. Venus the source of pride, with Jenny a chance to be imaginatively revenged on the waste of life. If it scars Pleasant Riderhood, it gives Lizzie (idealized in the same circumstances) the skills and strength to save Eugene. Work enables the narrative: it provides "Secretary Rokesmith" with the pretext to stay at the Boffins', thus initiating the ordering impulse of the main plot, and it calls Mortimer Lightwood out, with Eugene in tow, toward Lizzie and the radical decentering in the subplot. Eugene and Mortimer pass "down by Ratcliffe, and by Rotherhithe; down where accumulated scum of humanity seemed to be washed from higher grounds, like so much moral sewage" (1.3), and there might seem nothing to distinguish Dickens's distaste from Eugene's. At the height of the search for Gaffer, however, Dickens makes it clear that the distaste is Eugene's, and that it affords him no defense against the contingency of the working river:

> Not a ship's hull, with its rusty iron links of cable run out of hawse-holes long discoloured with the iron's rusty tears, but seemed to be there with a fell intention. Not a figure-head but had the menacing look of bursting forward to run them down . . . Not a lumbering black barge, with its cracked and blistered side impending over them, but seemed to suck at the river with a thirst for sucking them under. (1.14)

The indecent impingement of a life squalid and scarred from hard use, and the apprehension of being at once insignificant and physically threatened, are a traumatic shock to Eugene's cushioned middle-class consciousness. Far deeper than distaste is the intuition of vulnerability and of absolute responsibility for one's own life. It is this awareness, attuned to what Mill calls "pain" and Pip "the terror of childhood" (28), which produces the drive to survive discoloring tears. And Eugene's awareness of his exclusion from this massively alien purposefulness is the ground of his need for Lizzie.

The threats to selfhood which the Harmon plot, no less than *Great Expectations*, prudently sidesteps are directly faced in the presentation of Bradley Headstone and Eugene. In Bradley, Dickens openly explores the anxieties of crossing class boundaries (kept at bay in the comic treatment of the Boffins and in Pip's encounter with Trabb's boy). Like Orlick, Bradley is corroded by the class anger he vents in his jealous hatred of Eugene. But in Bradley, Dickens lays bare too the masochism inherent in the middle-class self-discipline to which Pip deferred. For years Bradley has bottled up an essentially violent nature, and the excess of his repressed passion precipitates the intuition, recognizable only in the extreme case, and virtually un-narratable within the Victorian context, of something dangerously destructive in the ascetic denial of libidinal energies which is central to bourgeois selfhood. In Eugene's attempts to find a ground for being, Dickens goes further, threatening to subvert the base on which the approved self is constructed. For in Eugene he mercilessly scrutinizes the beliefs that we are free moral agents and that innate decency of feeling will prevail – the very beliefs which ground both liberal humanism and classical realism.

The assumption that good and bad characters can be readily differentiated is the key normalizing function of the Dickensian narrative, but it goes awry with Eugene. His gesture of trifling "quite ferociously with his dessert-knife" (1.2) at the Veneerings' dinner party epitomizes his attempt to dissociate himself from genteel society; and both Dickens's own recoil from its mores and his residual dandyism make him sympathetic to Eugene. When Eugene falls in love with Lizzie it thus seems inevitable that he, no less than Bella, will prove his good-heartedness. But Eugene's dilemma goes deeper than Dickens first anticipated. At the moment of "crisis," the logic of the exclusions in Eugene's "Out of the question to marry her . . . out of the question to leave her" makes seduction the only possibility; and this is confirmed by Dickens's judgment that Eugene is now moving on an irresistible "current" of "wickedness" (4.6). The focus on a decent character moving toward real evil is something new in Dickens's work, for the seduction is not consigned murkily to the wings, as with Steerforth's ruining of Little Emily, and it is preempted only by Bradley Headstone's murderous attack.

In *Bleak House* Dickens confronted for the first time the infections of the will and the heart's incapacity to rise above its circumstances. Richard Carstone shows himself a very willing party to being in Chancery; and in Nemo's perverse self-abandonment Dickens goes further, tapping the primal middle-class fear that ultimately what lies within is simply the exhaustible will. He develops this possibility in *Little Dorrit*, where Arthur Clennam says flatly at the outset, "I have no will" (2). In character after character in the later works, from Esther, Miss Wade, and Miss Havisham to Sidney Carton, George Silverman, and Bradley, Dickens explores cases of social maiming. Eugene, in contrast, is by no means presented as the *victim* of particular circumstances.

In helping Lizzie to become educated, Eugene tries to rise above the selfish irresponsibility ingrained by social privilege. He believes himself in saying, "You have struck [my carelessness] dead" (4.6), and he tries to center his best impulses in her. But when she flees from his advances, particularly because he lacks the ballast of purposeful work, he is thrown back upon his habituated self. Carelessness remains the pose with which he meets the world: he flaunts it in putting down Bradley and in fumigating Mr. Dolls with the fire-scuttle before deigning to bribe him, and he assumes that a witty detachment cleanses such deeds of harm. The habit of carelessness has eroded his capacity to make decisions, weigh consequences, and act with principled purpose. Consequently, and because society casts him only in the part of philanderer, he becomes locked into this role without fully realizing what is happening. In trying to persuade Jenny Wren to reveal Lizzie's whereabouts, he says, with seeming casualness, "I think of setting up a doll, Miss Jenny" (2.2). Jenny's subsequent rebuff, "If you want one, go and buy one at the shop" (3.10), shows that she understands the implications, for hers is as close a reference to paying for a prostitute at a brothel as the Victorian novel will allow. Through such exchanges, Dickens shows how Eugene, step by step, and despite all his good intentions, finds himself inserted into the amoral stereotype cynically prescribed by the Voice of Society in which the girl is "set . . . up" with beefsteak and porter (4.17).

The novel consistently foregrounds the regulatory power of the Voice of Society, whose final vigorous persistence, along with Podsnappery, is a mark of the deepening pessimism which "darkens" Dickens's late work. His inability even to acknowledge his liaison with Ellen Ternan made him acutely aware of the realities of a serious involvement with a person as low in the social scale as Lizzie, and of how easy it was to become socially trapped. But with Eugene, Dickens does not stop at showing how hard it is to sustain the illusion of being a free moral agent in a restrictive society. Nor is Eugene's ennui simply the "fatal paralysis" of the will that Carlyle recognized.[15] Because Eugene's "utterly careless" pose (2.6) carries the implication that "everything is ridiculous" (1.13), it makes him dangerously susceptible to the casual cynicism for which anything is permissible. His male and class prerogatives give him enormous power over Lizzie; and Dickens shows that once he is inserted into the role of seducer, he finds a relish in his mastery. Eugene says exultingly, "I have gained a wonderful power over her" (4.6). It is easy to lament the suppression of libidinal energy, as one is tempted to do with Pip, without facing up to its anarchic quality. When Eugene forces Lizzie to admit that she loves him, the narrator comments: "There was something in the attitude of her whole figure as he supported it, and she hung her head, which besought him to be merciful and not force her to disclose her heart. He was not merciful with her, and he made her do it" (4.6). This is perversely cruel and virtually a prefigured rape. After Lizzie has gone, Eugene weeps, but Dickens registers his "little rising resentment against the cause of the tears" (4.6); and in another even more appallingly masterful touch he makes Eugene conclude with callous fatalism, "She must go through with her nature, as I must go through with mine" (4.6). In recklessly resolving "to try her again" (4.6) and in brutally shutting himself off from any prompting of a "better nature," Eugene shows that it *is* true of both him and Bradley that "their struggles are *toward* [the crime]" (3.11).

There is, however, a moral countermovement within the presentation of Eugene which is equally complex. When he first looks in unobserved at Lizzie weeping by the fire, he asks Mortimer, "Do you feel like a dark combination of traitor and pickpocket when you think of that girl?" (1.13). If this shows that he feels his power over Lizzie from the first, it also suggests that his self-consternation is not just a pose, and it opens upon a fundamental apprehension of social guilt. As his relationship with Lizzie develops, Eugene subliminally channels repressed guilt into a self-destructive impulse, which takes the form of goading Bradley Headstone to murder him. It is as though Eugene "knows" that he can change his "nature" and forfeit privilege only by the most extreme self-violation; and that he is recklessly prepared to precipitate a wasteful maiming at the hands of Bradley, as the only way of saving Lizzie and himself from a recklessly wasteful self-expenditure in sexual passion. If Eugene discovers an eroticized need to feed off Bradley's unrestrained energies, the impulse is yet resolutely deathward, and working against his overt will-to-power over Lizzie. Indeed, in making Eugene and Bradley the book's ultimate birds of prey (ultimate in that they prey finally upon themselves), Dickens holds hard, in both cases, to the belief that the self is, however obscurely, centered upon moral impulses, with the will to self-destruction to be seen as the will to self-punishment. Henry James complained that Dickens did not know what he was doing with Eugene and Bradley,[16] but far more compelling is John Bayley's view of him as an inspired "sleep-walker" whose genius lay in not needing to be on top of the extraordinary products of his mind.[17]

In *Great Expectations* there is still a sense that the low impinge scandalously on the genteel; but by *Our Mutual Friend*, only Podsnap absurdly assumes that the low can be "moved on" out of view. When Mr. Dolls is described as experiencing "two fits of trembles and horrors in a doorway on which a woman had had out her sodden nap a few hours before" (4.9), the casualness of "nap" surmounts distaste, and the detail reflects a very modern kind of dispassionate, unguarded attentiveness within the zone of pain and chaos. The final presentation of Eugene is equally dispassionate and hard.

Pip ends up by justifying his compromise; but in Eugene's fears for himself *after* his reclamation by Lizzie, there is a renewed intuition of radical self-division which ensures that such simple categories as free will, innate goodness, unitary selfhood, or the exculpatory autobiography remain as shell-shocked as Eugene himself. This intuition of radical self-division was to be further explored in Jasper, the central character of Dickens's last, uncompleted, novel, *The Mystery of Edwin Drood*. Where Eugene moves *across* the city toward possible redemption, Jasper actively seeks out the East End opium den, not as one discovering the life and energies of the socially other, but as one explicitly using this displacement to encounter the otherness within. In Eugene, and more fully in Jasper, Dickens takes up Jaggers's uncompromising sense of an essential evil in life, qualifying the belief in innate goodness on which his aesthetic of moral sentiment had depended, and exploring the ways in which evil impulse is intrinsic to the possibilities of the self.

NOTES

1 John Stuart Mill, "Civilization," in *Essays on Politics and Society*, ed. J. M. Robson (Routledge, 1977), p. 130.
2 Raymond Williams, "Social Criticism in Dickens: Some Problems of Method and Approach," *Critical Quarterly* 6 (Autumn 1964), 214–27, at 226.
3 Still among the best are Queenie Leavis's in F. R. and Q. D. Leavis, *Dickens the Novelist* (Chatto and Windus, 1970) and Robert Garis's in *The Dickens Theatre* (Clarendon, 1965), which also includes an excellent essay on *Our Mutual Friend*.
4 The classic essay on guilt and doubling is Julian Moynahan, "The Hero's Guilt: the Case of *Great Expectations*," *Essays in Criticism* 10 (1960), 60–79. On the two endings, and on a range of more formal matters, students will find Edgar Rosenberg's New Norton Critical edition of the novel very helpful. The new edition by Janice Carlisle (Bedford Books, 1996) usefully outlines a range of critical approaches and surveys the novel's reception.
5 The pace was set by D. A. Miller, *The Novel and the Police* (University of California Press, 1988). For an outline of a new historicist approach see the essay by Mary Poovey listed in Further Reading.
6 W. H. Auden, *The Prolific and the Devourer* (The Ecco Press, 1993), p. 39.
7 Miller, *The Novel and the Police*, p. 20.
8 Pierre Bourdieu, *Distinction* (Routledge, 1971), pp. 41–65.
9 See Robin Gilmour, *The Idea of the Gentleman in the Victorian Novel* (Allen and Unwin, 1981).
10 Walter Bagehot, "Charles Dickens," in *Dickens: The Critical Heritage*, ed. Philip Collins (Routledge, 1971), p. 390.
11 John Bayley, *The Uses of Division* (Viking, 1976), p. 93.
12 See Moynahan, "The Hero's Guilt."
13 Peter Stallybrass and Allon White, *The Politics and Poetics of Transgression* (Methuen, 1986), "Introduction."

14 Students considering this novel might well start with J. Hillis Miller's "*Our Mutual Friend*," *Victorian Subjects* (Duke University Press, 1991) and with Nancy Metz's "The Artistic Reclamation of Waste," *Nineteenth-Century Fiction* 34 (1979), 59–72.

15 Thomas Carlyle, *Past and Present*, ed. Richard Altick (New York University Press, 1965), p. 11.

16 See Henry James, "*Our Mutual Friend*," in *The Future of the Novel*, ed. Leon Edel (Vintage Books, 1956).

17 John Bayley, "*Oliver Twist*," in *Dickens and the Twentieth Century*, ed. John Gross and Gabriel Pearson (Routledge and University of Toronto Press, 1962), p. 49.

FURTHER READING

Baumgarten, Murray. "Calligraphy and Code: Writing in *Great Expectations*." *Dickens Studies Annual* 11 (1983), 61–72.

Brooks, Peter. "Repetition, Repression, and Return: the Plotting of *Great Expectations*," *Reading for the Plot: Design and Intention in Narrative*. Knopf, 1984.

Gallagher, Catherine. "The Bio-Economics of *Our Mutual Friend*." In *Fragments for a History of the Human Body*, vol. III, edited by Michel Feher. Zone, 1989.

Jordan, John O. "The Medium of *Great Expectations*." *Dickens Studies Annual* 11 (1983), 73–88.

Kucich, John. "Dickens' Fantastic Rhetoric: Semantics of Reality and Unreality in *Our Mutual Friend*." *Dickens Studies Annual* 14 (1985), 167–90.

Miller, Andrew H. "Rearranging the Furniture of *Our Mutual Friend*," *Novels Behind Glass: Commodity, Culture, and Victorian Narrative*. Cambridge University Press, 1995.

Moynahan, Julian. "The Hero's Guilt: the Case of *Great Expectations*." *Essays in Criticism* 10 (1960), 60–79.

Poovey, Mary. "Reading History in Literature: Speculation and Virtue in *Our Mutual Friend*." In *Historical Criticism and the Challenge of Theory*, edited by Janet Levarie Smarr. University of Illinois Press, 1993.

Sedgwick, Eve Kosofsky. "Homophobia, Misogyny, and Capital: the Example of *Our Mutual Friend*," *Between Men*. Columbia University Press, 1985, pp. 161–79.

Tambling, Jeremy. "Prison-Bound: Dickens and Foucault," *Essays in Criticism* 37 (1986), 11–31. (On *Great Expectations*).

7

ROBERT NEWSOM

Fictions of childhood

Dickens is conventionally credited with having imported into a central role in the novel the figure of the innocent child – often suffering and orphaned, abandoned, or simply neglected – from Romantic poetry, where it (and its healthier and happier siblings) had been celebrated, notably if esoterically, by William Blake and, far more popularly, by William Wordsworth. Since a growing concern with children was itself a central feature of the evolving ethos of the middle class throughout the nineteenth century, especially in Britain and the United States, it is an interesting albeit impossible speculation to imagine what might have happened to our ideas of the family had Dickens opted for a career as an actor, say, instead of that as a novelist – much less what the fictions of Emily and Charlotte Brontë, George Eliot, Robert Louis Stevenson, Henry James, Mark Twain, Lewis Carroll, Rudyard Kipling, James Joyce, among many others, would have been like without the example of Dickens before them. Impossible though the speculation may be to complete, it seems clear that Dickens has, via such characters as Oliver Twist, Little Nell, Tiny Tim, Paul Dombey, and a host of others, made an enormous difference in the way our culture thinks about children.

An oversimplified account of Dickens's role in this story[1] would run thus: in the early modern period and undoubtedly associated with the emergence of "individualism" and the rise of the middle class and the "domestic," there emerged an idea of the child quite unlike earlier conceptions, which had assumed children to be essentially animalistic and uninteresting, or merely deficient, undeveloped, and incomplete adults.[2] By the late eighteenth century, however (classically in Jean Jacques Rousseau's *Émile*), the child came to be recognized as a *qualitatively* different being, perhaps closer to humankind's original, natural, even prelapsarian state, and deserving of special care – both for the sake of its healthy cultivation and to preserve its innocence for as long as possible. In its most important Romantic treatment in England (in Wordsworth and especially in his famous "Ode: Intimations of Immortality"), the child was in addition imagined as literally closer to the divine ("trailing clouds of glory do we come / From God, who is our home") and, both in this closeness to the divine and as determining and forming the character of the adult, peculiarly and even incongruously a figure of some authority ("The Child is Father of the Man"). (In Wordsworth's account there are already the seeds of the twentieth century's most important elaboration of the theme – Sigmund Freud's theory of psychoanalysis.)[3] Dickens's "hard experiences in boyhood," as his biographer John Forster styles them – his father's imprisonment for debt while young Charles, just turned twelve, was sent to work for several months with lower-class men and boys at Warren's Blacking, a dismal factory where shoe polish was made – were clearly felt by him to have rung down the curtain on the innocence of his own childhood and also to have been critically determining of his adult character: "all these things have worked together to make me what I am," he writes in the autobiographical fragment first published by Forster (1.2). Pity for his own lost childhood undoubtedly made him especially receptive to the Wordsworthian conception of childhood, and this sensitivity (as was recognized by Dickens himself and has long since become conventional critical wisdom) was intensified by the loss of his beloved sister-in-law Mary Hogarth, who was suddenly taken ill one night and died in his arms when she was only seventeen (and he just twenty-five). Hence not just a reverence for the child, but an often intense fear for the child's welfare and a sometimes morbid sentimentality hover about Dickensian children, many of whom die young.

But several factors require us to complicate this tale. For one thing, a competing version of the child, no less widespread among Victorians than that of the Romantic child, held that children are especially vulnerable to wicked temptations and especially given to disobedience, the hallmark of original sin (Grylls, *Guardians*, p. 24). Such was the image of childhood popular among Puritans, Calvinists, and Evangelicals, an image descended from earlier conceptions of childhood and that bypassed, so to speak, the conception of the child idealized by the Romantics. While Dickens invariably set himself against religious severity (which he always associated with the spirit of the Old Testament), he was nevertheless as adept at imagining wicked children as spotless ones – for example, the Artful Dodger and the boys in Fagin's gang, or Tom Scott, the imp who is attached to Quilp in *The Old Curiosity Shop*, or, much later on, Tom Gradgrind in *Hard Times*, a veritable "monster" of selfishness who grows into a young man given to "grovelling sensualities" (2.3).[4] For another thing, while Dickens may himself be counted among those who more often than not adopted the Romantic line, Wordsworthian child-worshipers are rare indeed in the world he portrays, and such devotees of the Romantic child as we do find are generally impaired and ineffective, like Master Humphrey and Little Nell's grandfather and the several other old men, also mostly nameless bachelors, who trail after Nelly without being able in the end to protect her. (We might expect the most avid worshipers of children to be their mothers, but there is a notable failure of mothering in Dickens's world – a fact that has reverberations as well for the topic of Dickens and women. What tender and affectionate mothers we do find in Dickens tend to die young.) Or the devotees of children may be positively dangerous. At the very beginning of *Oliver Twist*, the narrator speculates that if the new-born Oliver "had been surrounded by careful grandmothers, anxious aunts, experienced nurses, and doctors of profound wisdom, he would most inevitably and indubitably have been killed in no time" (1). While this idea is certainly expressed jokingly – the point of the novel's opening is to underscore the miserable neglect that accompanies the birth of a child in a workhouse – still it gives rise to the troubling image of smothering, over-protective love as the alternative to the starvation that comes with a lack of love. (In this connection we may note Henry James's recollection that when he read *Oliver* as a small boy, the illustrations of the "nice people and the happy moments" frightened him "almost as much as the low and the awkward.")[5] Little Nell's grandfather, when he is not being neglectful (routinely leaving her home alone at night, for example, while he is off gambling), can be more positively dangerous, as when he sneaks into her bedroom while she sleeps in order to steal the money she has sewn into her garments (*OCS* 30). At such moments, the person who pretends to be devoted to her is hardly distinguishable from her nemesis Quilp, the demonic and abusive dwarf, who asks if Nell would like to be his "number two" if his present wife should die and who frolics in her little bed once he has evicted Nell and her grandfather (11).

In fact, it is a striking characteristic of the children in the early novels especially that, far from being revered, they are often objects not just of neglect, but of an abuse that is active and sadistic. Sadism is of course by definition sexual, but the sexuality of Quilp's sadism is a good deal more explicit than we might expect in Victorian fiction. Here is a fuller version of Quilp's proposal to Nell:

> "How should you like to be my number two, Nelly?"
>
> "To be what, sir?"
>
> "My number two, Nelly; my second; my Mrs. Quilp," said the dwarf.
>
> The child looked frightened, but seemed not to understand him, which Mr. Quilp observing, hastened to explain his meaning more distinctly.
>
> "To be Mrs. Quilp the second, when Mrs. Quilp the first is dead, sweet Nell," said Quilp, wrinkling up his eyes and luring her toward him with his bent forefinger, "to be my wife, my little cherry-cheeked, red-lipped wife. Say

that Mrs. Quilp lives five years, or only four, you'll be just the proper age for me. Ha, ha! Be a good girl, Nelly, a very good girl, and see if one of these days you don't come to be Mrs. Quilp of Tower Hill."

So far from being sustained and stimulated by this delightful prospect, the child shrunk from him, and trembled. Mr. Quilp, either because frightening anybody afforded him a constitutional delight, or because it was pleasant to contemplate the death of Mrs. Quilp number one, . . . only laughed and feigned to take no heed of her alarm.   (6)

Elsewhere Quilp delights in kissing her, "smacking his lips," and exclaiming, "what a nice kiss that was – just upon the rosy part," and he extols her as "such a chubby, rosy, cosy, little Nell . . . so small . . . so compact, so beautifully modelled, so fair, with such blue veins and such transparent skin, and such little feet, and such winning ways . . ." (9). It is hard to distinguish here if Quilp wants to have sex with Nell or to eat her – or perhaps both.

Before we too quickly distance ourselves from what must seem the self-evident perversity and evil of Quilp's (or her grandfather's) relations with Nell, however, we should notice that it is the very beauty, innocence, and vulnerability of the child as imagined here – her intense lovableness – that create the conditions for that perversity. As James Kincaid points out in *Child-Loving*,

If the child is desirable, then to desire it can hardly be freakish . . . The pedophile is thus our most important citizen, so long as he stays behind the tree or over in the next yard: without him we would have no agreeable explanation for the attractions of the empty child. We must have the deformed monster in order to assure us that our own profiles are proportionate.[6]

From this perspective, Dickens simply plays out the logic implicit in Wordsworthian child-worship and that continues to be played out today in a culture that, if anything, places even greater value on childhood than did the Victorians.

Like other sadists in Dickens who delight in torturing children (e.g., Wackford Squeers in *Nicholas Nickleby* – "I never threshed a boy in a hackney-coach before . . . There's inconveniency in it, but the novelty gives it a sort of relish too!" [38] – or Mr. Creakle in *David Copperfield* – "he had a delight in cutting at the boys, which was like the satisfaction of a craving appetite" [7]), Quilp is a brilliant *comic* creation, and we participate in his sadism by laughing at it even as we feel for his victims. Likewise we laugh with Fagin and his gang as they play upon Oliver's innocence and pretend that a coaching session for the young pick-pockets is just "a very curious and uncommon game." And we are amused too that Oliver can't recognize whores when he sees them ("They were not exactly pretty, perhaps; but they had a great deal of colour in their faces . . . Being remarkably free and agree-able in their manners, Oliver thought them very nice girls indeed. As there is no doubt they were" [9]). So an additional complication in the story of Dickens as the chief importer of the figure of the Romantic child into the novel, beyond the facts that there are some very wicked children in the Dickens world and relatively few successfully nurturing adults, is that we are actually invited to take some pleasure ourselves (and most readers do) in the spectacle of the abused child, even, or perhaps especially, when it is pecu-liarly grotesque and over the top.

The abused child, moreover, may feel – in fiction as in life – some real attraction for the abuser. Not that Smike or David Copperfield can muster any affection for Messrs. Squeers or Creakle, but Fagin's fondness for his "dears" (Gary Wills has written effectively about the novel's hints at the old man's pederasty)[7] is to some extent reciprocated; Oliver certainly appreciates the fact that it is Fagin who gives him his first really tasty meal – indeed we first see Fagin standing at the fire grilling sausages (8), and while *we* may see in his toasting fork an emblem of the devil, Oliver sees in him a generous provider. Little Nell is as ga-ga in everything to do with her grandfather as is he about her (and the world more generally); her greatest terror is that she will be separated from him if people see just how out of his mind he really is. Much later in Dickens's career, Little Dorrit's tenderness for her father, in spite of his self-absorbed exploitation of her, will be even more painfully and plausibly rendered. And in his last completed novel, *Our Mutual Friend*, the dolls' dressmaker Jenny Wren will pretend to feel nothing but vexation with her drunken father – indeed, her habitual mode is to pretend that he is *her* child – but when he collapses just before dying she is distraught and help-less: "My poor bad, bad boy! and he don't know me, he don't know me! O what shall I do . . . when my own child don't know me!" (4.9).

It is hard to imagine Oliver Twist ever grown up, but the examples of Nell, Amy Dorrit, and Jenny Wren all point to what Malcolm Andrews calls the theme of "the grown-up child" and what Arthur Adrian had earlier referred to as the theme of "inverted parenthood" in Dickens.[8] Not only are effective mothers and fathers in short supply in the Dickens world, not only does this seem to be the normal if not the ideal state of affairs, that is ("The universe," says Mr. Jarndyce in *Bleak House*, "makes rather an indifferent parent, I am afraid" [8]), but Dickens stands the Romantic child on its head, as it were, by making so many of his children precociously responsible and acute. Or perhaps he simply literalizes in a weird way Wordsworth's formula (already quoted), "The Child is Father of the Man." Nell's grandfather knows this perfectly well when he remarks to Master Humphrey, "It is true that in many respects I am the child, and she the grown person" (1).

While Dickens generally decries the conditions that produce such precocity ("It always grieves me," he has Master Humphrey say in the same chapter, "to contemplate the initiation of children into the ways of life, when they are scarcely more than infants"), it is also true that we are invited to find such precocity charming, though Dickens shows signs of being progressively troubled by it as time goes on. The uncanniness of Little Nell is subdued (especially in contrast to that of her grandfather); by the time we arrive at Jenny Wren, however, it has become flamboyant. In his review of the novel, Henry James writes of her, "Like all Mr. Dickens's pathetic characters, she is a little monster; she is deformed, unhealthy, unnatural; she belongs to the troop of hunchbacks, imbeciles, and precocious children who have carried on the sentimental business in all Mr. Dickens's novels; the little Nells, the Smikes, the Paul Dombeys."[9] Not all readers, of course, would have agreed with James that Nell was "a little monster," but we may say that as the child evolves in Dickens, it becomes proportionately less childlike and attractive as its weirdness becomes more manifest. Thus Nell has in the course of Dickens's career in effect developed, by the time of Jenny Wren, into a being much more like Master Humphrey or Quilp or Nell's grandfather.

Paul Dombey provides an interesting example of a child halfway along this trajectory and one who, perhaps because of his intermediate position, exhibits a peculiarly rich number of traits ranging from the pathetic to the monstrous. These are epitomized in the equivocal phrase "old-fashioned," applied to him on several occasions. Initially, this seems to mean "precocious" or more literally "made like an old person" (the *Oxford English Dictionary*, indeed, cites a quotation from *Dombey* chapter 14 with this meaning). But in addition to precocity, the term also suggests something uncanny:

> He was childish and sportive enough at times, and not of a sullen disposition; but he had a strange, old-fashioned, thoughtful way, at other times, of sitting brooding in his miniature armchair, when he looked (and talked) like one of those terrible little Beings in the Fairy tales, who, at a hundred and fifty or two hundred years of age, fantastically represent the children for whom they have been substituted. (8)

The novel plays quite insistently too on a more familiar sense of "old-fashioned," which comes up when the instrument-maker Sol Gills remarks that "seven-eighths of my stock is old-fashioned. I am an old-fashioned man in an old-fashioned shop, in a street that is not the same as I remember it" (4). This sense of "old-fashioned" as antiquated and therefore on the verge of dying out eventually also attaches itself to little Paul.

He overhears himself thus described and cannot fathom what it means: "What old fashion could that be, Paul wondered with a palpitating heart, that was so visibly expressed in him; so plainly seen by so many people!" (14). As his health gradually but steadily fails, the term takes on new meanings: "And now it was that Paul began to think it must surely be old-fashioned to be very thin, and light, and easily tired, and soon disposed to lie down anywhere and rest . . . " (14). He never does fully comprehend the phrase, which the narrator famously glosses thus at the little boy's death:

> The old, old fashion! The fashion that came in with our first garments, and will last unchanged until our race has run its course, and the wide firmament is rolled up like a scroll. The old, old fashion – Death!
>
> Oh thank GOD, all who see it, for that older fashion yet, of Immortality! And look upon us, angels of young children, with regards not quite estranged, when the swift river bears us to the ocean! (16)

The pathos of Paul's death is intensified by his failure to appreciate what is so apparent to everyone around him, that he is dying. This representation of a *limited* consciousness is indeed an important technique that Dickens deploys in many places to heighten pathos and especially the pathos of children (the crossing-sweeper Jo in *Bleak House* provides a good example). We feel for those who do not know what we know; they are, compared with us, innocents. Yet it comes as a surprise to the reader too that the phrase "old-fashioned" will in the end not just refer to death itself, but evoke the story of the Fall through a turn to the sense of "fashion" that refers to a manner of dress (when Adam and Eve put the fig leaves on, they also "put on" the "garment" of mortality). So the reader, in spite of foreseeing Paul's death, is nonetheless like Paul in being only half-aware of what the term "old-fashioned" means, or will come to mean. Our consciousness turns out to be, like Paul's, limited and imperfect, even at the moment when we are most sure that we know what is coming. And thus Dickens plays an artful trick upon us and gives us one unexpected further chance to experience something like the child's limited perspective – as well as to realize that we have experienced it.

An imperfect consciousness and the contrast between that limited consciousness and some broader one are critical elements in what is surely an aspect of Dickens's interest in childhood equally important as his thematizing of it – his recreations of the feelings of childhood and what it is like to be a child. Far more than Wordsworth, for example, Dickens helps us recover the thoughts and sensations peculiar to childhood.

At the beginning of Dickens's career, that recovery notably takes place not through the direct representation of a child's consciousness, as will later be the case in the first-person narratives of *David Copperfield* or *Bleak House* or *Great Expectations*. It takes place, rather, as we have seen above in the case of little Oliver's mistaking Nancy and her fellow prostitutes for "very nice girls indeed," through precisely the *gap* between a child's limited understanding and a grownup's – the same gap that simultaneously creates pathos. And for these purposes, the more limited the understanding the better. The very absence of personality that critics have often complained of in Oliver or Nell thus helps achieve the effect of verisimilitude (just as, James Kincaid would no doubt remind us, the child's purity, selflessness – essential emptiness, in short – provides a blank field which we are free to fill up with our own desires and idealizations). When the third-person narrator of *Bleak House* invites us into the consciousness of an illiterate boy who "don't know nothink" by exclaiming, "It must be a strange state to be like Jo! To shuffle through the streets, unfamiliar with the shapes, and in utter darkness as to the meaning, of those mysterious symbols, so abundant over the shops, and at the corners of streets, and on the doors, and in the windows!" (14), the effectiveness of the narrator's move is somehow and curiously not undermined by the fact that he pretends, omniscient though he clearly is, that he can only imagine the state of Jo's mind. The effectiveness may instead actually be enhanced by that pretense.

It is not until the middle of his career that Dickens presents sustained first-person narratives that recall their writers' childhoods. It was during this time too that he composed the fragment of an autobiography that he showed to Forster and his wife and only a little later incorporated much of, with little alteration, into early chapters of *David Copperfield*. The best estimates (see Nina Burgis's "Introduction" to the Clarendon edition of *Copperfield*) are that most of the fragment was written in 1848, and several personal events (the death of his sister Fanny; the chance recollection told to Forster by a friend of Dickens's father that he recalled having seen him at work as a boy at Warren's) may have triggered it.

But it seems likely too that a more public literary event played an important part in Dickens's turn to first-person narratives: the publication in the fall of 1847 of Charlotte Brontë's *Jane Eyre*. (While Dickens apparently said in conversation that he had never read *Jane Eyre*, his claim is scarcely credible; *David Copperfield* and, even more so, *Bleak House*, are full of its traces; the latter, indeed, can be read as virtually an anti-*Jane Eyre*, the story of how governesses who conquer their anger and social resentments can also in the end marry the men they love.)[10] Charlotte Brontë's first novel caused a great stir and, with William Makepeace Thackeray's *Vanity Fair* (published the same year), was heralded by many critics as signaling the arrival of a new generation of novelists capable of challenging the preeminence Dickens had enjoyed for a decade. It is hard to imagine Dickens letting such challenges go unanswered, and it is impossible to imagine so good a reader as he not learning from his rivals. If Jane Eyre owes much to Oliver Twist, so too surely do David Copperfield, Esther Summerson, and Pip owe much to her.

It is with the hero most closely modeled on himself (and whose initials mirror his own) that Dickens gives us his first extended account in the first person of what it feels like to be a child. In the early chapters of Copperfield Dickens finds what we might call a "mode" for such writing. I mean something less personalized – or even gendered – than a "voice," for Dickens will adapt this mode to narrators as different as David Copperfield, Esther Summerson, and Pip, and will adopt it as well in several frankly autobiographical essays written for his periodicals Household Words and All the Year Round.[11] Here is the opening of the chapter "I Observe":

> The first objects that assume a distinct presence before me, as I look far back, into the blank of my infancy, are my mother with her pretty hair and youthful shape, and Peggotty, with no shape at all, and eyes so dark that they seemed to darken their whole neighbourhood in her face, and cheeks and arms so hard and red that I wondered the birds didn't peck her in preference to apples. (2)

This conveys a genuine feeling for how children actually perceive and think. How strange and coarse adult skin felt to us when we were very young is something most of us can surely recall, and the easy inference that such skin might be attractive food for birds wonderfully captures how open the child's mind is to possibilities that adults would find shocking (just the sorts of possibilities exploited by the logic of fairy-tales).

Clearly as important as the phenomena of childhood here, however, are the phenomena of the adult's *memory* of childhood and therefore as well the mediation of the phenomena of childhood by adult consciousness. Charlotte Brontë had written Jane Eyre's account of her childhood in what is straightforwardly the voice of an adult. What is so strikingly authentic in her early chapters is not the child's voice, therefore, but rather the vivid memory of the child's angry sense of powerlessness in the face of the injustices of unsympathetic and even cruel adults. Dickens will achieve similar effects in the autobiographical fragment and in the Murdstone chapters of Copperfield, the Miss Barbary chapters of Bleak House, and the Mrs. Joe and Miss Havisham chapters of Great Expectations. But he wants in these places also to get at the feeling of being a child under happier and more ordinary circumstances and seems to want to recover that feeling merely for its own sake, as something interesting in itself. Thus David Copperfield rather leisurely and digressively asks himself, "What else do I remember? Let me see."

The most extended and complicated example of Dickens's writing in this mode – because it so intertwines the perspective of the child with the adult's retrospection of the original experience – comes with the justly famous beginning of *Great Expectations*, where Pip describes how he came to name himself: "My father's family name being Pirrip, and my christian name Philip, my infant tongue could make of both names nothing longer or more explicit than Pip. So I called myself Pip, and came to be called Pip"; how he imagined his dead parents' appearances based upon their tombstones: "my first fancies regarding what they [my father and mother] were like, were unreasonably derived from their tombstones. The shape of the letters on my father's, gave me an odd idea that he was a square, stout, dark man, with curly black hair"; and how one "memorable raw afternoon toward evening" he came to form his "first most vivid and broad impression of the identity of things":

> At such a time I found out for certain, that this bleak place overgrown with nettles was the churchyard; and that Philip Pirrip, late of this parish, and also Georgiana wife of the above, were dead and buried; and that Alexander, Bartholomew, Abraham, Tobias, and Roger, infant children of the aforesaid, were also dead and buried; and that the dark flat wilderness beyond the churchyard, intersected with dykes and mounds and gates, with scattered cattle feeding on it, was the marshes; and that the low leaden line beyond was the river; and that the distant savage lair from which the wind was rushing, was the sea; and that the small bundle of shivers growing afraid of it all and beginning to cry, was Pip. (1)

There is of course a lot going on here beyond the desire to recreate the feeling of what it is like to be a child and think as a child. Or we might say rather that that desire leads Dickens, as it had Wordsworth, to far larger questions – about language, identity, authority, self-consciousness, and, perhaps most insistently, death.

What the opening of *Great Expectations* presents is in effect what we might name Dickens's Mortality Ode, a decidedly *post*-Romantic account of a child who has evidently never trailed clouds of glory, but rather (like Esther Summerson and Little Dorrit before him), has been born into a fallen world essentially and already marked by what Pip will later call "this taint of prison and crime" (32). A stronger way to put this would be to say that the opening of Pip's narrative is not really about childhood at all, but about growing up – the loss of innocence that is already evident in the self-conscious act of self-naming, his "infant tongue" notwithstanding. Not, of course, that Pip's growing up is anything like complete on this first memorable afternoon; it will not be complete until the novel's very end, if then. But neither childhood nor innocence have ever really been his, and a nostalgia for the childhood he never had – if such a nostalgia is possible – haunts him throughout his story. ("Nostalgia" is literally the pain of wanting to return home; the mysterious note from Wemmick that Pip will be handed as a warning that he is being watched – "DON'T GO HOME" (44) – at once serves as an ironic motto for the boy whose greatest wish has been to leave the world of the forge and begs the question whether Pip really has ever had a proper home he could later come back to.)

The development of a new conception of the child is necessarily accompanied by a new conception of the grownup, and as much as the Victorians are notable for their delight in children, they are no less famous for all those contrasting qualities that comprise the stereotype of the grownup: responsibility, respectability, earnestness, stability, seriousness. While Dickens is withering in his scorn for such archetypal enemies of childhood as Mr. Dombey, Miss Barbary, the Murdstones, and Mrs. Clennam, he can be almost equally severe on those who refuse to grow up, such as Harold Skimpole, or Flora Finching, or even David Copperfield's beloved "child-wife" Dora (44), whom David cannot bring himself seriously to scold, but whom Dickens purposively kills off in order to clear the decks for the more mature Agnes and thus rescue David from "the first mistaken impulse of an undisciplined heart" (45). The benevolent grownups who, early in Dickens's career, were notable for their childish innocence (Mr. Pickwick is of course the great original here; he is quickly followed by the Cheeryble brothers in *Nickleby*) have later incarnations whose childishness is either more seriously limiting (Mr. Dick in *Copperfield*) or that turn out to be not quite so childish as they had at first appeared (Mr. Boffin in *Our Mutual Friend*). And while Dickens always applauds the persistence of childhood memories in the adult, believing that it is accompanied by "a certain freshness, and gentleness, and capacity of being pleased" (*DC* 2) and will even celebrate his own inability to grow out of a long list of childhood impressions (e.g., in "Where We Stopped Growing," *HW* [1 January 1853], discussed at length and reprinted entire by Andrews, *Dickens and The Grown-up Child*, pp. 57–70 and pp. 193–98); and while he is happy to assert that "it is good to be children sometimes, and never better than at Christmas, when its mighty Founder was a child himself" (*ACC* 3); and while by all accounts he was delightful company for little children and a fabulous party-giver, clown, and magician, nevertheless all that attraction to the childish was defined and qualified by his keen and thoroughly adult sense of the seriousness of life and the eminently Victorian need always to be up and doing something useful and productive.

By most accounts, including some from his own children, Dickens was an extraordinarily affectionate parent when his children were very little, but his powerful need for control – for neatness, punctuality, and order – were manifest even then, and he grew progressively demanding and distant as his children grew up. He himself refers to "a habit of suppression . . . which I know is no part of my original nature, but which makes me chary of shewing my affections, even to my children, except when they are very young" (to Mrs. Winter, 22 February 1855, Pilgrim 7.543). Dickens ascribed this restraint to his having been rejected by his first love (to whom this letter was written twenty years later), but it seems no less likely that it would have had earlier roots as well in what he felt to be his first rejection by his own parents (and especially his mother) at the time of his father's imprisonment and his own exile to the Blacking Factory.

Dickens's depiction of himself in the autobiographical fragment at that critical juncture is interestingly divided: on the one hand he presents himself as an abandoned waif, exposed to all sorts of evil ("I know that, but for the mercy of God, I might easily have been, for any care that was taken of me, a little robber or vagabond" [Forster, 1.2]); on the other he takes pride in the quality of his work, his street smarts, and general pluckiness (though he had scarcely enough money on which to live, one day he walked up to the landlord of a pub and demanded a glass of "your very best – the VERY *best* – ale . . ., if you please, with a good head to it"; the episode is recorded both in the fragment and in *DC* 11, where it is illustrated as well in one of Phiz's best-known plates). It would require much more space than we have available to explore the very complicated ways in which Dickens has split up his own representations and indeed understanding of himself in the autobiographical fragment.[12] But we should note here that the project of such splitting is carried forward in the fiction and that such apparently diametrically opposite characters as, for example, Oliver Twist and the Artful Dodger each reflect aspects of Dickens that lived side by side, so to speak, within him – whether they coexisted happily or even whether they were conscious of one another, it would be very hard to say. Thus the complication that we noted at the outset of this chapter in the story of Dickens as the first great importer of the idea of the Romantic child into a central place in the novel reflects not just that he drew upon a very different but equally available tradition of thinking about childhood from the Wordsworthian – a tradition that we may identify most simply as Puritan – but reflects as well his own complicated and conflicted experience of himself as a child, an experience that he was forever returning to in his fictions and that he was through his fictions forever reinventing.

NOTES

1 English literature generally and Dickens in particular have been extremely well served by criticism interested in childhood. Peter Coveney, *Poor Monkey* (1957; reprinted and revised as *The Image of Childhood* [Penguin Books, 1967]), is the classic starting point. Coveney argues that there is a general decline in the quality of representations of the child after the Romantics. The indispensable subsequent study of the child in nineteenth-century literature generally is David Grylls, *Guardians and Angels* (Faber and Faber, 1978), which draws on a rich array of interdisciplinary secondary sources. The major studies of the child in Dickens are Angus Wilson, "Dickens on Children and Childhood," in *Dickens 1970*, ed. Michael Slater (Chapman and Hall, 1970) and, most recently, Malcolm Andrews, *Dickens and the Grown-up Child* (University of Iowa Press, 1994).

2 The classic statement of the "discovery" of the child is Philippe Ariès, *Centuries of Childhood*, trans. Robert Baldick (Alfred A. Knopf, 1962). His account, which tends to assume that the discovery of childhood was accompanied by parental and institutional anxiety to impose new forms of discipline upon children, is significantly qualified by Lawrence Stone, "The Massacre of the Innocents," *New York Review of Books*, 14 November 1974, who later, in *The Family, Sex and Marriage in England 1500–1800* (Harper and Row, 1977), stresses the mutual affection of parents and children that accompanies these developments and that is so important in Romantic and Victorian conceptions of childhood. See Roger Cox, *Shaping Childhood* (Routledge, 1996) for an interesting study that carries the history and debate through the twentieth century.

3 Ned Lukacher, in "Freud's *'Dickens'scher Styl,'*" *Primal Scenes: Literature, Philosophy, Psychoanalysis* (Cornell University Press, 1986), provocatively argues for Dickens as himself the deepest, most powerful influence on "the most fundamental aspects of Freud's thinking . . . the problem of memory and . . . the necessity, indeed the compulsion, to construct alternate scenes in those instances where memory has become unreliable or somehow suspicious." "In the culture of psychoanalysis," he writes, "Dickens has always been the figure of both its pre-history and its future" (p. 330).

4 Barry Qualls, "Transmutations of Dickens' Emblematic Art," *The Secular Pilgrims of Victorian Fiction* (Cambridge University Press, 1982), amply demonstrates how Dickens's works are steeped in the extremely popular Puritan works of John Bunyan and Francis Quarles especially. See pp. 98–100 for a discussion of Dickens's treatment in this context of the Romantic child.

5 *Autobiography*, ed. F. W. Dupee (Criterion Books, 1956), p. 70.

6 (Routledge, 1992), pp. 4–5.

7 "Love in the Lower Depths," *The New York Review of Books* 36:16 (26 October 1989), 60–67.

8 Arthur Adrian, "Dickens and Inverted Parenthood," *Dickensian* 67 (1971), 3–11; and see also his *Dickens and Parent–Child Relationships* (Ohio University Press, 1984), especially pp. 119–31.

9 Quoted in *Dickens: The Critical Heritage*, ed. Philip Collins (Routledge and Barnes and Noble, 1971), pp. 470–71.

10 Peter Ackroyd, *Dickens* (HarperCollins, 1990), p. 837, quotes a transcription of Dickens's conversation first published by Jerome Meckier. See also Lisa Jadwin,

"'Caricatured, Not Faithfully Rendered': *Bleak House* as a Revision of *Jane Eyre*," *Modern Language Studies* 26 (1996), 111–33.

11 Peter Rowland has compiled and edited just about all Dickens's identifiably autobiographical writings (whether found in the autobiographical fragment, the letters, or the fiction) in *My Early Times* (Aurum Press, 1997). Although necessarily synthetic and to some extent fanciful (since it is not always clear in the sources where fact ends and fiction begins), his entertaining compilation is also of considerable scholarly value, being scrupulous in identifying its components.

12 A good place to start would be Steven Marcus's brilliant essay, "Who Is Fagin?" in his *Dickens: From Pickwick to Dombey* (Chatto and Windus, 1965), pp. 358–78. See also Albert D. Hutter, "Reconstructive Autobiography: the Experience at Warren's Blacking," *Dickens Studies Annual* 6 (1977), 1–14; Robert L. Patten, "Autobiography into Autobiography: the Evolution of *David Copperfield*," in *Approaches to Victorian Autobiography*, ed. George P. Landow (Ohio University Press, 1979), pp. 269–91; and Alexander Welsh, "Young Man Copperfield," *From Copyright to Copperfield: The Identity of Dickens* (Harvard University Press, 1987), pp. 156–72.

FURTHER READING

Andrews, Malcolm. *Dickens and the Grown-up Child*. University of Iowa Press, 1994.

Ariès, Philippe. *Centuries of Childhood*. Translated by Robert Baldick. Alfred A. Knopf, 1962.

Coveney, Peter. *Poor Monkey* (1957). Reprinted and revised as *The Image of Childhood*. Penguin Books, 1967.

Cox, Roger. *Shaping Childhood*. Routledge, 1996.

Grylls, David. *Guardians and Angels*. Faber and Faber, 1978.

Stone, Lawrence. "The Massacre of the Innocents." *New York Review of Books*. 14 November 1974.

The Family, Sex and Marriage in England 1500–1800. Harper and Row, 1977.

Wilson, Angus. "Dickens on Children and Childhood." In *Dickens 1970*, edited by Michael Slater. Chapman and Hall, 1970.

8

MURRAY BAUMGARTEN

Fictions of the city

Realism in Dickens's time was magical, for the city was a fairy-tale come to life, grim, exhilarating, and transformative. To describe this urban world was to create a new Bible, encompassing heaven and earth, and all that lies between, the keynote struck at the beginning of *Bleak House*:

> London. Michaelmas term lately over, and the Lord Chancellor sitting in Lincoln's Inn Hall. Implacable November weather. As much mud in the streets, as if the waters had but newly retired from the face of the earth, and it would not be wonderful to meet a Megalosaurus, forty feet long or so, waddling like an elephantine lizard up Holborn Hill.   (*BH* 1)

Personal experience fed the literary work: when Dickens was born on 7 February 1812, London was a city of horse-drawn carts and carriages, entered through city gates like Charing Gate, Newgate, with its formidable prison, and Kennington Toll Gate. When Dickens died fifty-eight years later in 1870, the gates and city wall had been pulled down and built on, and London turned into a sprawling monumental city, transformed by the industrial revolution, especially the railroad and entrepreneurial capitalism as well as the British imperial venture, into the first world-city.

During Dickens's lifetime, London was more excavated, more cut about, more rebuilt, and more extended than at any time in its previous history.[1] A huge sewer system had been built by 1853, when *Bleak House* was published, and a viaduct had been completed that brought clean drinking water to all parts of the city, thus ridding it of the fear of cholera and typhus that had plagued it for centuries. Victoria Station and Euston Station had become the termini of the railroad, effectively bringing the commerce of the world and its people into the city; the underground was under construction by 1864, when Dickens was writing *Our Mutual Friend*, and the Thames, relieved now of carrying the city's waste to the sea, had been organized into a pleasing promenade via the great Embankment projects. Spacious new boulevards graced the city, among them Victoria Street, Garrick Street, and the newly extended Oxford Street. Now there were four times as many streets and roads in London as when Dickens had arrived in the city with his parents at the age of eleven. The remaining fragments of the city gates were now surrounded by universes of urban activity rather than the rural countryside.

By 1870, Greater London, as the metropolitan area came to be known, had swallowed up nearby villages to become 4 million strong, and as if to echo its power the census revealed that the majority of the people of England now lived in cities. Single family houses were the rule with new ones by the end of the century equipped with indoor plumbing. Londoners for the most part did not live in apartment blocks, like the French; there were small plots of green around the houses, larger gardens for the wealthier, with servants for all classes living by the back stairs. And there were the great institutions, like the Law, with its Inns of Court, that combined legal offices, housing, and the court rooms. London was a governmental center. The Bank of England and the Houses of Parliament, rebuilt on their present location along the Thames after the great fire of 1819, were in London. Together with the Stock Exchange they dominated what was still referred to in Dickens's time as "the city," and that had become the economic center of the world.

As Dickens's fictions record these transformations and respond to this era of unprecedented rapid and radical social change, they articulate contradictory and complicated attitudes to city life, and stamp London with their characteristic perspectives. His contemporaries (like our own) saw the city through the eyes he provided. For Dickens, this magical place evoked the "attraction of repulsion," for it was "such a gritty city; such a hopeless city . . .; such a beleaguered city (*BH* 12), a waste and wasteland, and yet also a celebration "of the city as the most impressive embodiment of change" (Schwarzbach, *Dickens*, p. 195), increasingly the dominant fact of modern life.

Before Dickens wrote about London, beginning with *Sketches by Boz* and *The Pickwick Papers*, the city had not for decades figured in fiction except as an occasional setting for domestic action. It had, however, been a major presence in the work of some of the important graphic artists of the late eighteenth and early nineteenth century, including Hogarth and Cruikshank. They had been joined by lesser artists in providing images of the city for a public avid for news of the metropolis. Dickens's focus on urban life thus coincided with the project of *Pickwick*, which brought together text and image and fed a popular market; the London he describes was a city of explosive force, growing two and a half times its size in two generations. No wonder then that London, the modern city writ large, is the central protagonist of his fiction and one of the defining elements of his popular success.

As a mature writer, Dickens continued to draw on the experience of the young newspaper reporter who had written *Sketches by Boz* in his spare time, capitalizing on his walks through the city to outline the different neighborhoods and their distinctive inhabitants. "What inexhaustible food for speculation, do the streets of London afford!" he comments in beginning one of his *Sketches*. We "have not the slightest commiseration for the man who can take up his hat and stick, and walk from Covent Garden to St. Paul's Churchyard, and back into the bargain, without deriving some amusement – we had almost said instruction – from his perambulation." (*SB* "Shops and Their Tenants"). A sense of joy and exuberance informs the many sketches that describe London's amusements and recreations: "The River," "Astley's," "Greenwich Fair," "Vauxhall Gardens by Day." He was particularly drawn to Covent Garden, the food and vegetable market, with its striking contrasts of plenty and poverty. In the 1860s, he had rooms nearby and often stayed there. Throughout his life he thought of himself as a walker in the city, a vagabond of the streets. His close friend, biographer, and literary executor, John Forster, notes that for the young Dickens "to be taken out for a walk into the real town, especially if it were anywhere about Covent Garden or the Strand, perfectly entranced him with pleasure. But, most of all, he had a profound attraction of repulsion to St. Giles's. If only he could induce whomsoever took him out to take him through Seven Dials, he was supremely happy. 'Good Heaven!' he would exclaim, 'what wild visions of prodigies of wickedness, and beggary, rose in my mind out of that place'" (Forster, 1.1). This part of the city evoked his childhood, and all those places in the neighborhood of Warren's Blacking Factory and Hungerford Stairs are central to his writing: Covent Garden, the Temple, St. Giles, Waterloo Bridge, the Strand, and Temple Bar.

Even when Dickens was abroad, London loomed large in his thoughts: in many of his letters from different parts of Europe he writes of his desperate need to be there, to experience the crowds, the teeming street-life of the metropolis, the diversity of its people. Walking the streets inspired him. In 1844, he commented from Genoa: "Put me down on Waterloo Bridge at eight o'clock in the evening [the time he finished working as a child at Warren's], with leave to roam about as long as I like and I would come home, as you know, panting to go on [writing]" (Forster, 4.5). Among his friends, Dickens was famous for working all day and then, after supper, getting them to join him in sallying forth for a night-time walk of twenty miles or more through the London streets. His daughter Kate notes that "he would walk through the busy, noisy streets, which would act on him like a tonic and enable him to take up with new vigour the flagging interest of his story and breathe new life into its pages" (Schwarzbach, *Dickens*, p. 27).

Parts of the London that his novels envision so vividly had been the subject of other writers and great painters. Carlyle satirized the pretensions of its aristocratic dandies and newly arrived middle classes; Wordsworth wrote a magnificent sonnet about it; and Turner and Whistler painted its bridges. But they were not part of the city as Dickens was. Wordsworth made Grasmere in the Lake District his home; and Carlyle, Whistler, and Turner set up households in Chelsea, then a village quite separate from the city, their home base. From its embankment they could look back at bustling London and render it as part of the pastoral vision of Wordsworth's splendid poem:

COMPOSED UPON WESTMINSTER BRIDGE,
SEPTEMBER 3, 1802

Earth has not any thing to show more fair:
Dull would he be of soul who could pass by
A sight so touching in its majesty:
This City now doth, like a garment, wear
The beauty of the morning; silent, bare,
Ships, towers, domes, theatres, and temples lie
Open unto the fields, and to the sky;
All bright and glittering in the smokeless air.
Never did sun more beautifully steep
In his first splendour, valley, rock, or hill;
Ne'er saw I, never felt, a calm so deep!
The river glideth at his own sweet will:
Dear God! the very houses seem asleep;
And all that mighty heart is lying still!

The stately rhythms of this poem are the poetic equivalent of the emblematic paintings of the city by Turner and Whistler. Unlike Wordsworth or Carlyle, Turner and Whistler, Dickens was a cockney – then the term meant a Londoner – who lived in the city, earned his daily bread there, and took his recreation in its theatres and shows. It marked him in everything, and he reveled in its ambience, living in it continuously for forty years, with time out for foreign travel, seaside summer vacations, and even, after he bought the estate of Gad's Hill in Rochester in 1856, maintaining rooms near Covent Garden above the offices of *All the Year Round*, which he edited. The evening before his death at Gad's Hill he had prepared to go into the city the next day. And he is buried in London in Westminster Abbey. Unlike most of his artistic contemporaries, his life was lived at the London pace: ambitious, all-encompassing, swift, full of contradictions, energetic, and dynamic. And these are of course the signatures of his prose style.

When Dickens signed the contract for his first novel, *The Pickwick Papers*, and married Catherine Hogarth, he moved to the house at 48 Doughty

Street, not far from the British Museum and the University of London, and lived there while finishing that novel, writing *Oliver Twist* and his third, *Nicholas Nickleby*. It was the house in which his beloved sister-in-law Mary died on the evening of 7 May 1837 in Dickens's arms. That June was the only time in his professional career that he ever missed a deadline. There were other dark experiences in Dickens's London. Unlike Turner's and Wordsworth's, Dickens's London was brilliantly lit by gaslight at night, but filled with coal smoke from its heating systems and factories and railroad, effectively darkening it by day. Dark it was in another sense since it was the center of immigration and flooded with refugees from the margins of the British empire; and dark with the difficulties of industry and the beginnings of industrial capitalism, captured by the many photographs of nineteenth-century London that have come down to us.

These pictures reflect part of Dickens's personal experience in London. Not only the city of his success as a novelist, it was also the place of his humiliation as a child: even as an adult he could not walk past the Hungerford Market without shuddering, for there as a young boy he had been put to work in a blacking factory, pasting labels on the pots of shoe-polish, to rescue his family from their sudden fall into poverty and debtors' prison. In his fiction this theme recurs in the tumbledown houses encountered by his protagonists that list crazily in what he called the wilderness of streets. As early photographs reveal, this first modern city was a place of enormous hope and simultaneously desperate need, the city at once of the optimism of modernity in all its technological force and of its grim exploitation, and both are essential to Dickens's vision. It is worth noting that 1837–38, the year of the first book publication of *Pickwick* and of *Oliver*, is also the moment when Daguerre and Talbot invented modern photography. Dickens is the modern artist of London whose vision includes the realism of the photographers of urban grime and misery and the graceful, ideal pleasures of the painters of pastoral London. He is the writer who takes Wordsworth's subject, the child growing up, and makes that rural boy into a city figure, a trajectory central, among others, to the main characters of *Oliver Twist*, *David Copperfield*, and *Great Expectations*. The contradictions of his personal life, from work as a court reporter, theatre-goer, newspaper man, novelist, editor of magazines, philanthropist, and amateur theatrical producer and actor, to marriage, child-raising, separation, and divorce, Dickens lived through in London, the first modern city – the city of the contradictions of modern life.

The narrative of his novels takes us on a tour through this city of contradictions, their intricate plots the engines driving us on this journey. His prose moves us rapidly between London scenes at once pastoral and intensely urban. Thus in *Nicholas Nickleby* the grim search for a job leads Nicholas to the counting house of the brothers Cheeryble, which looks out upon a bit of grass where birds are always singing. In bringing these contradictions together, Dickens's prose is magical in its realism. In his fictions, the city is always present as a looming shape – the dome of St. Paul's, the many church steeples defining its skyline – and yet at the same time the novels present a personal, limited, individual view. The city is chaotic; the city is ordered; personal vision is juxtaposed against the panoramic. The two perspectives play against each other powerfully, for example, in the Todgers episode in *Martin Chuzzlewit*. And Dickens's prose, like his city, like his own life, is always dynamic, always moving us through change.

One clue to how, in Dickens's writing, London can be both "that mighty heart" of Wordsworth and the roaring steam-engine of change is offered by the Crystal Palace, which Dickens visited in 1851. This astonishing house of glass was designed and built by Joseph Paxton, architect and greenhouse gardener, and displayed the new technology that was transforming the world. Built to house the first world's fair, it gave us the Machine in the Garden, with trees and shrubs growing inside the glass house. Framing machinery with greenery, drawing the viewer into an exploration of the world's riches all assembled under the largest glass house ever built at that time, the Crystal Palace made breathtaking drama out of modern technological achievements. It was a place Dickens often found congenial, reinforcing his sense of modern English possibility.[2]

Dickens understood that his was a world in transition, and that it was defined not just by the modern habits it was moving toward but the traditional habits it was leaving behind. This was a world in which the stagecoach would coexist with the railroad, whose advent Dickens compares to the great natural disaster of an earthquake, which destroys and levels Staggs's Gardens in a notable passage in *Dombey and Son* and calls forth the rebuilding of a city. The iron horse not only transforms the countryside and the city but brings with it new ways of seeing, notably panoramic vision,[3] as well as a new range of sounds and sights.

The train stations created new entrances to London, functioning as the new gates to and from the city, themselves the cathedrals of the new technological order. Industrial capitalism changed England; where it destroyed, it also rebuilt.[4] Dickens's novels are filled with the sounds of the city, which articulate the interplay of traditional and modern senses of time, in the symphonic chorus of London life. The grating shriek of the railroad and its booming whistle resonate against the cries of street vendors hawking their oysters and greens and old clothes. These sounds in counterpoint express a modern sense of time, rendered onomatopoetically, for example, in *Dombey and Son*.[5] To the ear as well as the eye, the city is on display in Dickens.

Like the great river Thames that runs through it, Dickens's London is in constant motion. And that changing experience is one of the reasons city life in Dickens makes its impact not as a completed image but as a fragmented experience that depends upon the partial point of view of the (inevitably involved) participant–observer. Thus, *Our Mutual Friend*, the last novel Dickens lived to complete, begins, "In these times of ours," locating reader and narrator as engaged observers who see "a boat of dirty and disreputable appearance, with two figures in it," floating "on the Thames between Southwark Bridge, which is of iron, and London Bridge, which is of stone, as an autumn evening was closing in." Instead of the clarity of omniscient narration, this narrator resembles a camera-eye just slightly out of focus, peering into the scene in tandem with the reader to ascertain why the man in the boat "had no net, hook, or line . . . his boat . . . no cushion for a sitter, no paint, no inscription, no appliance beyond a rusty boathook and a coil of rope." This man, we are told, "could not be a fisherman . . . he could not be a waterman . . . he could not be a lighterman or river-carrier." Who he is and what his functions are is displaced from description to action, as the activity he engages in – of scavenging – at one and the same time becomes a personal act and an urban task. And the conflict engendered by his work, which surfaces a page later when his ex-partner accuses him of murder, turns into a quarrel about the use and abuse of urban space.

Like the river on which this scene takes place, the city is in constant motion. Though the livelihood of its inhabitants depends on their abilities to read its changes, it resists deciphering as it simultaneously invites decoding like a modern version of the Book of Revelation; repeatedly character, narrator, and reader discover that this city cannot easily be charted.[6] Furthermore, this city is not single or whole, but differs at different times and places for narrator and reader, just as it does for different characters who experience it variously as labyrinth, marketplace, prison, and redeemer. This city becomes the prism of personality, be it Coketown in *Hard Times* or London in *Great Expectations*, and everywhere it is the principle of change and motion animating Dickens's fictions, the subtext of their plots, and the informing idea of scene, character, and tale.

His modern vision articulates the city scene as a site of dialectical contradictions. For Dickens London is not only a conflicted city, in transition, but one whose explosive urban vitality depends upon the yoking together of its contradictions. Note that while the scene with which *Our Mutual Friend* opens has a panoramic scope, there is nevertheless no one place from which to view it as a whole. Rather, it is distinguished by the ceaseless flow of change and transformation. Crowd scenes and individual figures repeatedly evoke the liminal moment of change.

Dickens is the first novelist to theatricalize the city, articulating scenes and situations that would in later fiction become an urban convention. Dickens brought the stock-in-trade of early nineteenth-century picture books into his novels. His crowd scenes, like his streets, have a Hogarthian vitality, swarming with character types and dramatic situations that are snapshots of experience in motion. His power as a creator of urban fiction is remarked on by the pioneers of film, who acknowledge the ways in which they learned their craft by reading him.[7] Perhaps they filled their motion pictures with urban arrival scenes because they noted how such scenes punctuate Dickens's novels, as do the chase sequences. Let one stand for many:

> Having made sure of his watching me, I tempt him on, all over London. One night I go east, another night north, in a few nights I go all round the compass. Sometimes, I walk; sometimes, I proceed in cabs . . . I study and get up abstruse No Thoroughfares in the course of the day. With Venetian mystery I seek those No Thoroughfares at night, glide in them by means of dark courts, tempt the schoolmaster to follow, turn suddenly, and catch him before he can retreat. Then we face one another, and I pass him as unaware of his existence, and he undergoes grinding torments. Similarly, I walk at a great pace down a short street, rapidly turn the corner, and, getting out of his view, as rapidly turn back . . . Night after night his disappointment is acute, but hope springs eternal . . . and he follows me again to-morrow. Thus I enjoy the pleasures of the chase . . .
>
> (*OMF* 3.10)

Not that Dickens invented the motion picture *avant la lettre*; rather, he grasped the potential of the daguerreotype and participated in the technological efforts of many, including his friend, the actor and theatrical producer, William Macready, to create the illusion of motion in their art. Not only was he alert to the illusionism of the Diorama – a three-dimensional scene which, by means of images painted on transparencies and viewed through a small aperture, produced the effect of movement and change – he was steeped in the machinery of the Romantic Theatre, whose stock-in-trade was the simulation of movement, change, and transformation.

Thus to read Dickens is to encounter an urban writer whose work does not only rely on the city for the setting of plot and character, but rather situates London at the center of his fictions: it is the generator of plot and the determining element of scene and setting. Even the coaching episodes in his novels, which articulate a pastoral and rural nostalgia, depend upon the city as their definitional counterpart. In this way, his novels complicate the binary structure of country and city that Raymond Williams has seen as among the central, defining characteristics of his writing.

Dickens articulated in his writing the connection between the making of urban fiction and the invention of modern urban life. He charts the impact of the city that was the central railroad station of the nineteenth century: everything in that world passed through it. In the process of coping with its extraordinary fullness, Dickens explores his world-city's modern world-making power. In describing this London, he makes it our living presence.

In this Dickens universe, urban life takes the forms of a theatrical code. London, a synecdoche for the "attraction of repulsion"[8] in Dickens's realm, yet carries the sign of the hurly-burly transformative optimism of theatrical experience. At once magic-lantern show, ballad opera, and the gestural encounter of nineteenth-century melodrama, the great city informs Dickens's fiction – which constructs London as a panoramic vision of the music hall out of the materials of labyrinth and marketplace. This is not to deny the sociological aspect of the fiction but, rather, to apprehend its metaphoric subtext. For Dickens this city is real, *and* it is a set of nested tropes.

Historians note his accuracy in this regard. Nineteenth-century industrial capitalism helped to define the modern city in theatrical terms. Not only was this a function of the reconstruction of the cities, and of massive new investment in plazas, parks, and squares; it was also the result of the accumulation of capital and the growing democratization of everyday life. In the city, crowds now gathered, not only on ritualized occasions and events – executions, coronations, royal weddings, progresses, and parades – they also congregated in the course of daily business, including commuting to work.

The new spaces created by the urban reconstruction of London (which was in full swing by the 1850s, having taken shape shortly after the Napoleonic wars) served as impromptu theatres for street performers who could now take their activities from local side-streets and neighborhood building courts to the potentially larger audiences congregating in these public arenas. Such urban theatrical phenomena punctuate Dickens's novels: Pip and Wemmick in *Great Expectations*, to take only one example, meet on the street amid the crowds going to and from work. Their encounters bear witness to these new experiential conditions, which shape their lives. As Wemmick changes into Jaggers's law-clerk on the way into the city, and back into the benevolent son of the Aged P. on his return journey to Walworth, Pip, standing-in for the Dickensian reader, discovers the transformative theatrical experience that defines this urban world.

Creating the infrastructure that made the modern city possible, the monumental building projects paradoxically also provided a glimpse of the easier pace of the past in the informal street performances they made possible by the new dramatic staging of the city. At the same time, they made everyone a performer. Lewis Mumford underlines the function of the modern city as encouraging and inciting "the greatest potential number of meetings, encounters, challenges between all persons, classes and groups, providing, as it were, a stage upon which the drama of social life may be enacted, and with the actors taking their turns as spectators and the spectators as actors."[9]

In spite of the new power-relations that maximized competition and that Noddy Boffin defines in *Our Mutual Friend* as "scrunch or be scrunched" (3.5), nineteenth-century London was also the place of "playful self-making" for all – especially for the working and lower classes. They asserted through their "convivial laughter, their sympathy, their nonhegemonic speech, and their imaginative exuberance [that] life is not warfare against sin, nor is it only competitive struggle." Without "wealth or status" they yet become "imaginatively adept at exploiting language, gesture, and common reality to transform, with a sense of ceremony, existences which would otherwise be overwhelmed by necessity and utility."[10] From the Artful Dodger in *Oliver Twist* to Rogue Riderhood in *Our Mutual Friend*, Dickens's novels are a portrait gallery of such figures of transformation.

While Dickens's representations of lower-class life echo those of journalists of his time, including Leigh Hunt and Henry Mayhew, they also provide a dynamic sense of character and possibility. Where other writers reinforce conventional stereotypes of the poor that, sustained by an emergent anthropology, would develop spurious racial distinctions and make class division a seeming fact of nature, Dickens's characters dramatize their situations as part of a strategy of overcoming such barriers. While Silas Wegg is poor and a rogue, the way in which he accepts Boffin's offer to read to him – "No, sir. I never did 'aggle and I never will 'aggle. Consequently, I meet you at once, free and fair, with – Done, for double the money!" (*OMF* 1.5) – is but one of many instances in *Our Mutual Friend* in which theatrical self-presentation functions to bridge class and social divisions as well as further economic gain.[11]

Dickens, even in his darker novels, does not speak for the class divisions so evident in the city or accept them as natural or a social given; rather, his plots enforce the possibility that the urban world is the site of moral self-making precisely because it brings people together across class and social lines. The serial format of Dickens's novels enforces this transformational context, as does the city with its ephemeral, transitory, changing experiences of repetition with variation.

Rather than being tied to place, competence, and craftsmanship as measures of value, clothing was now in this city one way of indicating the realm of desired identity. Perhaps that is why the sketch of Monmouth Street Dickens provides in *Sketches by Boz* is so vivid, the clothes turning into the lives of the people who wore them in a dreamer's dance of the imagination.

> We love to walk among these . . . and to indulge in the speculations to which they give rise; now fitting a deceased coat, then a dead pair of trousers, and endeavouring, from the shape and fashion of the garment itself, to bring its

former owner before our mind's eye. We have gone on speculating in this way, until whole rows of coats have started from their pegs, and buttoned up of their own accord, round the waists of imaginary wearers; lines of trousers have jumped down to meet them; waistcoats have almost burst with anxiety to put themselves on; and half an acre of shoes have suddenly found feet to fit them, and gone stumping down the street with a noise which has fairly awakened us from our pleasant reverie, and driven us slowly away, with a bewildered stare, an object of astonishment to the good people of Monmouth Street, and of no slight suspicion to the policemen at the opposite street corner.

(*SB* "Old Clothes")

In Dickens's world the opportunities for self-presentation are manifold. They take place in the Victorian parlor, in which Mr. Podsnap dismisses everything "not English" and Mr. Bounderby reiterates his rise from birth-in-a-ditch to industrial and financial eminence in *Hard Times*, as well as in Edith Dombey's and Bella Wilfer's self-definition before the bedroom mirror. It is not accident then, or merely a taste for sociological completeness, that brings the poor and the homeless to the center of Dickens's stage; rather, it is in their relations to the hegemonic middle class that Dickens explores the range of possibilities offered by the urban theatre of modern life.

His exploration focuses on the public world as well as the private realm; he takes us into Chancery and the Inns of Court, and the places in between. In his world, the homeless, whether Silas Wegg or Nicholas Nickleby, perform their self-making in the new public arena articulated by and in nineteenth-century European culture, in and along the modern street. Given its public status and accessibility, the throngs passing through it, and its availability for many purposes, this modern street superseded all other venues. *Little Dorrit* concludes on its last page with Arthur Clennam and Amy Dorrit, freed of the imprisonments of the past, leaving the Marshalsea prison, and going out of the church where they have been married into "the roaring streets" —

They paused for a moment on the steps of the portico, looking at the fresh perspective of the street in the autumn morning sun's bright rays, and then went down.

Went down into a modest life of usefulness and happiness. Went down to give a mother's care, in the fulness of time, to Fanny's neglected children no less than to their own, and to leave that lady going into Society for ever and a day. Went down to give a tender nurse and friend to Tip for some few years, who was never vexed by the great exactions he made of her, in return for the riches he might have given her if he had ever had them, and who lovingly closed his eyes upon the Marshalsea and all its blighted fruits. They went quietly down into the roaring streets, inseparable and blessed; and as they passed along in sunshine and shade, the noisy and the eager, and the arrogant and the froward, and the vain, fretted, and chafed, and made their usual uproar.

(*LD* 2.34)

Now the homeless and dispossessed individual is part not of the picturesque pastoral or rural Wordsworthian landscape but of the stage of urban life. Dickens's characters are part of the panorama of the street – of crowds and action and constant movement – a characteristic feature of Dickens's art. The picturesque individual has been turned into the unusual, eccentric performer on the stage of urban life.

The first great practitioner of the detective novel, Dickens creates a linguistic universe that in the energy, deftness, and surprise of its syntax thereby simulates the theatrical experience of life in the modern city. As we read his writing we participate in the modern theatrical project of urban life: modern identity has become staged identity. Like the detectives of the London Metropolitan Police, founded in 1829, whom he admired and wrote about in *Household Words*, Dickens teaches us how to decode that city world and navigate through its darker streets. His fiction trains us in keen and swift observation, careful judgment, and thoughtful commitment. As his co-editor W. H. Wills noted, "If thieving be an Art [then] thief-taking is a Science." Like Inspector Bucket of *Bleak House*, these detectives "every man of them, in a glance, immediately takes an inventory of the furniture and an accurate sketch of the editorial presence. The Editor feels that any gentleman in company would take him up if need should be, without the smallest hesitation, twenty years hence" ("A Detective Police Party," *HW* [27 July 1850], pp. 409–10). They are the great readers of this city world.

In 1866, Dickens proudly noted, "I know London better than any one other man of all its millions."[12] By that time his knowledge had reached around the world, fusing his understanding and the metropolis itself: for his readers Dickens and London were virtually the same. The myriads of tourists since then who have made the Dickensian sites of London, whether real, imagined, or commercially constructed, into places of pilgrimage, attest to the power of "the Inimitable."

The careful reader of Dickens encounters a metropolis that is at once the "wilderness of London," which Nicholas Nickleby faces at the beginning of the novel, as well as the cozy, pastoral world of the Cheerybles where many of Nicholas's problems, be they economic, familial, sexual, or urban, are resolved. The criminal realm of *Oliver Twist*, counterbalanced by the haven of the Maylies, is echoed and complicated by the dark world of Tom-All-Alone's in *Bleak House*, to cite another example. Nemo's and Miss Flite's lodgings at Krook's stand in vivid, sharp contrast to Chesney Wold and Bleak

House itself. The "attraction of repulsion" that Dickens felt on his nocturnal wanderings with his detective friends as well as visits to prison and morgue surfaces in the contrasting realms of *Our Mutual Friend*, which pits old Harmon's house, Boffin's Bower, Bella Wilfer's familial domicile, and her Doll's House against Venus's – as well as the streets of Bradley Headstone's wandering and Wegg's homelessness. The immensity of this imperial city overwhelms the reader, while the resting place of achieved home comforts us.

The mystery of this city is the mystery of modern personality, as Dickens noted in *A Tale of Two Cities*:

> A wonderful fact to reflect upon, that every human creature is constituted to be that profound secret and mystery to every other. A solemn consideration, when I enter a great city by night, that every one of those darkly clustered houses encloses its own secret; that every beating heart in the hundreds of thousands of breasts there, is, in some of its imaginings, a secret to the heart nearest it! Something of the awfulness, even of Death itself, is referable to this.
>
> (*TTC* 1.3)

Dickens's city is the stage on which we engage in the modern theatre of self-making. For Dickens's London was the theatre in which the visions of the imagination, and all the contradictions of modern life, were realized, acted-out, and displayed. For him and thus for us, his readers, London is a magic-lantern picture show. Reveling in the contradictions of this first world-city, Dickens leaves us not with one of its many aspects but its multifariousness; thus he engages us in the mystery of the city through his fiction, and thereby charts its biblical possibilities.

NOTES

1 F. S. Schwarzbach, *Dickens and the City* (Athlone Press, 1979), p. 195.
2 Tatiana Holway compares Dickens's writing to the panoramic vision of modern culture offered by the Crystal Palace. See her "Speculation and Representation: Charles Dickens and the Victorian Economic Imagination," Ph.D. dissertation, Columbia University, 1999, and "The Most Singular and Peculiar Feature of the Exhibition: the Crystal Palace, Charles Dickens, and the 'Coup d'Oeil' of 1851," paper delivered at the Dickens Project annual summer weekend conference, "Victorian Spectacle," 1–4 August 1996, University of California, Santa Cruz.
3 Wolfgang Schivelbusch, *The Railway Journey* (University of California Press, 1987), chapter 4, passim.
4 Humphry House, *The Dickens World* (Oxford University Press, 1941), p. 138.
5 Murray Baumgarten, "Railway/Reading/Time: *Dombey and Son* and the Industrial World," *Dickens Studies Annual* 19 (AMS Press, 1990), 65–67.
6 Philip Collins, " Dickens and the City," in *Visions of the Modern City*, ed. William Sharpe (Proceedings from the Heyman Center for the Humanities, 1983), pp. 101–2.

7 Sergei Eisenstein, "Dickens, Griffith and Ourselves," *Film Theory and Criticism*, ed. Leo Braudy and Marshall Cohen (Oxford University Press, 1999), pp. 426–34.
8 Rick Allen, "John Fisher Murray, Dickens, and 'the Attraction of Repulsion,'" *Dickens Quarterly* 16:3 (September, 1999), 139–59.
9 Lewis Mumford, *The Urban Prospect* (Harcourt Brace, 1968), p. 184.
10 Pam Morris, *Dickens's Class Consciousness: A Marginal View* (London, 1991), pp. 34–35.
11 Michal Ginsburg has articulated the formal aspects of this radical turn of Dickens's fiction, especially of *Our Mutual Friend*. The plot of this novel makes it possible, she notes, for Dickens "to think of history as a process of transformation." "The Case Against Plot in *Bleak House* and *Our Mutual Friend*," chapter 7 of *Economies of Change: Form and Transformation in the Nineteenth-Century Novel* (Stanford University Press, 1996), p. 147.
12 Quoted in *Dickens: Interviews and Recollections*, vol. II, ed. Philip Collins (Macmillan Press, 1981), p. 326.

FURTHER READING

Altick, Richard. *The Shows of London*. Harvard University Press, 1978.
Baumgarten, Murray and H. M. Daleski (eds.). *Homes and Homelessness in the Victorian Imagination*. AMS Press, 1998.
Briggs, Asa. *Victorian Cities*. Odhams Books, 1964.
Collins, Philip. *Dickens and Crime*. St. Martin's Press, 1962.
Dyos, H. J. and Michael Wolf. *The Victorian City*. Routledge & Kegan Paul, 1973.
Garis, Robert. *The Dickens Theatre*. Clarendon Press, 1965.
Marcus, Steven. *Engels, Manchester, and the Working Classes*. Random House, 1974.
Maxwell, Robert. *The Mysteries of Paris and London*. University Press of Virginia, 1992.
Nord, Deborah. *Walking the Victorian Streets: Women, Representation, and the City*. Cornell University Press, 1995.
Sanders, Andrew. *Dickens and the Spirit of the Age*. Clarendon Press, 1999.
Schwarzbach, F. S. *Dickens and the City*. Athlone Press, 1979.
Sharpe, William and Leonard Wallock. *Visions of the Modern City*. Columbia University Press, 1983.
Welsh, Alexander. *The City of Dickens*. Clarendon Press, 1971.

9

CATHERINE WATERS

Gender, family, and domestic ideology

" – Be it ever," added Mr. Wegg in prose as he glanced about [Mr. Venus's] shop, "ever so ghastly, all things considered there's no place like it."

Our Mutual Friend 3.7

As the editorial manifesto he wrote in 1850 to accompany the first number of *Household Words* indicates, Dickens had always aspired "to live in the Household affections, and to be numbered among the Household thoughts" of his readers. He saw himself as a prophet of the hearth, and his contemporaries hailed his reputation as the purveyor of cozy domestic bliss. As a reviewer of *David Copperfield* in *Fraser's Magazine* wrote, "There is not a fireside in the kingdom where the cunning fellow has not contrived to secure a corner for himself as one of the dearest, and, by this time, one of the oldest friends of the family."[1] This reviewer attributes Dickens's widespread popularity to "his deep reverence for the household sanctities, his enthusiastic worship of the household gods." Yet despite this reputation as the prophet of domestic bliss, any close examination of Dickens's novels reveals very few portraits of happy and harmonious families. According to George Newlin, a statistical analysis of the novels yields 149 full orphans, 82 with no father, and 87 with no mother, making a total of 318 full or partial orphans: "only fifteen named characters we deem significant in the major works (novels and Christmas Books) had or have two parents, and in nearly half of these cases their families today would be considered dysfunctional."[2] Silas Wegg's amusing application of the well-known early nineteenth-century lyric about "home, sweet home" to the unprepossessing abode of the taxidermist in the epigraph to this chapter wittily captures the ambivalence of Dickens's representation of domesticity in his fiction. Renowned as the celebrant of the hearth, Dickens nevertheless invested his imaginative energy in the depiction of grotesque or fractured families. He used familial relations – often represented in transposed or distorted forms – to explore the social, political, and economic tensions of his age. In the process, his fiction participated in a larger cultural discourse about the family and helped to form those gender and class differences which were fundamental to the workings of Victorian domestic ideology.

Household Words marked the fulfillment of Dickens's long-held desire to establish a periodical that would be characterized by what he described, in an 1845 letter to Forster, as "*Carol* philosophy, cheerful views, sharp anatomisation of humbug, jolly good temper . . . and a vein of glowing, hearty, generous, mirthful, beaming reference in everything to Home and Fireside" (Forster, 5.1). *Carol* philosophy had been defined in 1843 with the publication of Dickens's first and most famous Christmas Book, and it found a new vehicle of expression in the Christmas numbers of *Household Words* and, later, *All the Year Round*. Dickens's identification with Christmas was noted by his reviewers, Margaret Oliphant wryly describing him as "the first [writer] to find out the immense spiritual power of the Christmas turkey,"[3] and J. W. T. Ley nominating him in the 1906 Christmas issue of *The Dickensian* as "The Apostle of Christmas."[4] This association with the great domestic festival of the nineteenth century is a major source for Dickens's reputation as the prophet of the hearth: a worship of the home that is encapsulated in the Christmas Book descriptions of bustling little women – like Mrs. Cratchit in *A Christmas Carol* or Dot Peerybingle in *The Cricket on the Hearth*, whose superintendence of a small, snug home, crisp fire, and tempting supper manifests their domestic virtue – as well as in the potent winter contrasts drawn between indoor and outdoor settings. Dickens had in fact exhorted the audiences attending his public readings of *A Christmas Carol* to "make themselves as much as possible like a group of friends, listening to a tale told by a winter fire"[5] and, as one commentator remarked of the *Carol* on the first Christmas following Dickens's death, "Of a Christmas Eve night, the red curtains drawn close, the coals stirred up, the boys and girls home from school and gathered round, father might well read them this enchanting little legend."[6]

The characterization of the home as an enclave of family warmth and harmony and its superintendence by a woman who embodies the domestic ideal are key elements in the ideology of the Victorian middle-class family. From earlier usage to describe a household or a lineage, the term "family" underwent a specialization between the seventeenth and nineteenth centuries to describe a small kin-group sharing the same house.[7] In the fields of sociology and history, much study has been devoted to analyzing the development of family forms in relation to wider social and economic structures, a number of Marxist accounts, for example, explaining the emergence of its nuclear form as a result of the relations of production that obtain under capitalism. Dickens's fictional representations of the family have traditionally been examined as an index to social realities, the political force of his writing being held to depend upon the adequacy and accuracy of his social critique. But research within Victorian studies over the last two decades has sought to resituate literature within a larger cultural discourse in an effort to reveal its continuities with other contemporary modes of representation. Feminist critics, in particular, have sought to explore the role of literary culture in the wider formation of sexual identities by uncovering the ways in which the construction of the middle-class family depended upon a division of gender roles which confined women to the private sphere. Such studies focus on the effects of power generated by the differentiation of normal and deviant behavior, emphasizing the political force of language. Instead of asking whether Dickens's fictional representations of the family are passive reflections of the age (whether true or false), his novels can be assigned a more active role in the discursive construction of the family and of gendered identity. Dickens's fiction is one of the discourses which helped to formulate normative definitions of the family and female identity – the two are inseparable – in the nineteenth century, and rather than assessing the faithfulness of their correspondence to reality, his novels must be understood in more dynamic terms. His fiction exploits the shifts in meaning given to the notion of the family in the nineteenth century – away from an earlier emphasis upon lineage and blood toward a new ideal of domesticity seen as "right" for everyone – and reveals the ways in which class and gender differences were implicated in the affirmation of the values of the middle-class family.

The idealization of the home in the Christmas Books entails a definition of women as domestic creatures and a sanctification of the hearth that were part of the ideology of "separate spheres" in the nineteenth century. According to this supposed division between "private" and "public" domains, women were responsible for creating and maintaining the home, while men were associated with the working world of industry and commerce. One of Dickens's *Sketches of Young Couples* (1840), "The Nice Little Couple," includes a description of Mrs. Chirrup that reveals the way in which the idealization of the home depended upon a particular definition of female subjectivity – one that was determined by the embodiment of domestic virtue, rather than social position or economic value: "She is a condensation of all the domestic virtues, – a pocket edition of the young man's best companion, – a little woman at a very high pressure, with an amazing quantity of goodness and usefulness in an exceedingly small space."[8] The virtues of the home-making woman are embodied in a number of Dickensian heroines, including Little Nell, Agnes Wickfield, Esther Summerson, Little Dorrit, and (after some initial blunders) Bella Wilfer, and they are often highlighted by contrast with the qualities of those women whose value is "extrinsic" and manifested in a preoccupation with wealth and display of social position.

The representation of these domestic angels helps to define the middle-class ideal of the family in opposition to the values and practices held to characterize other social groups.

The narrator's description of Mrs. Chirrup lays great emphasis upon her diminutive stature, and it is notable that two of the domestic heroines listed above are given the sobriquet, "Little" (although the designation of Nell as "Little" was added later). Size is a recurrent motif in Dickens's representations of the domestic ideal. "Whether it is that pleasant qualities, being packed more closely in small bodies than in large, come more readily to hand than when they are diffused over a wider space, and have to be gathered together for use, we don't know," says the narrator in "The Nice Little Couple," but Dickens's domestic angels are always diminutive and his scenes of familial harmony tend to be set in small spaces. The littleness of Dot Peerybingle is captured in her shortened first name and relished by the narrator in Chirp the First of *The Cricket on the Hearth*, as he describes "her little figure" and "very doll of a baby." "As briskly busy as a child at play in keeping house," her stature is in keeping with her cozy home. The jocularity and intimacy of the narrator's tone work to reinforce the suggestions of warmth and togetherness associated with the Peerybingle hearth, projecting a domestic context for the reader who ideally enjoys Dickens's Christmas Book by his or her own family fireside. The young David Copperfield attributes his captivation with Mr. Peggotty's boathouse to the fact that it had never been intended to be lived in on dry land. But his description dwells upon its compact size and snugness (gliding over the class-differentiation implied in the special provisions made for Master David) as it provides "just enough" security for the orphaned child (*DC* 3). Similarly, much of the charm of Wemmick's castle depends upon its miniature scale (although the very idea of "fortification" itself acknowledges the vulnerability of the private sphere in this prison-dominated novel). Throughout his fiction, Dickens draws a contrast between such cozy homes, which harbor the domestic ideal, and great houses, like Chesney Wold, Satis House, or the cold mansion of Mr. Dombey, which are inhabited by alienated or embittered occupants. Such mansions fail to maintain the division between private and public spheres, allowing the worlds of business, politics, or "Fashion" to intrude upon the sanctity of the home.

The social significance of housing and interior design is shown with particular self-consciousness in *Our Mutual Friend*, where the narrator deplores the "hideous solidity" of the Podsnap plate (1.11) or where the curious interior of Boffin's Bower is described. The room that Silas Wegg enters in Book the First, chapter 5, has its furnishings strangely mixed to accommodate the contrasting aspirations of Mr. and Mrs. Boffin. As a "highflyer at Fashion,"

Mrs. Boffin has her sofa, footstool, and table forming a centerpiece on a patch of flowery carpet; Mr. Boffin, in contrast, "'don't go higher than comfort,'" and prefers two homely settles by the fire on the uncarpeted floor, together with some "compensatory shelves on which the best part of a large pie and likewise of a cold joint were plainly discernible among other solids" (1.5). The ideological coding of domestic furnishings is made explicit in Book the Second, chapter 6, when Eugene Wrayburn explains to Mortimer Lightwood that he has fitted out a kitchen in their "Private" chambers, complete with miniature flour-barrel, rolling-pin, "charming kettle," and so on, in order to secure "'the moral influence of these objects, in forming the domestic virtues.'"

Eugene ironically articulates the workings of domestic ideology whereby possession of the ideal middle-class home (suitably superintended by an Angel in the House) becomes the sign of moral virtue and guarantor of male identity. But as he learns, miniature flour-barrels and rolling pins are no substitute for the home influence of a domestic angel. "[H]ome is yet wherever she is,"[9] and even in the midst of uncongenial surroundings, the virtues of the true homemaker shine through. In *The Old Curiosity Shop*, the narrator, Master Humphrey, is particularly struck by the incongruity he observes in Nell's residence within her grandfather's shop. He remarks the appearance of the place as being "so unsuited to her," and muses on her image "surrounded and beset by everything that was foreign to its nature, and furthest removed from the sympathies of her sex and age" (1). No doubt Nell would appear to him to be more "at home" in the midst of a loving family circle gathered around a brightly burning hearth. Her domestic skills – she busies "herself immediately in preparing supper" (1) for her grandfather and their visitor upon her safe return to the shop – identify Nell's embodiment of those virtues associated with the hearthside angel, thus adding to the bachelor-narrator's sense of her uncongenial placement in this context and affirming a normative conception of the middle-class family.

Nell and her grandfather are forced onto the road by Quilp, who invades their domestic space first by encamping in the back parlor and then by "coil[ing] himself" upon her bed (11). While Nell's exposure to the open spaces of the countryside elicits the narrator's concern for her insecurity and dispossession, she retains the virtues of the domestic angel earlier remarked by Master Humphrey. She mends Judy's clothes for the showmen in chapter 16, and while staying with the schoolmaster in chapter 25, she busies herself "in the performance of such household duties as his little cottage stood in need of." But although able to make a home wherever she is, Nell remains just as much "out of place" on the road as she was in the shop. Instead of finding herself among "suits of mail," "fantastic carvings," and the other paraphernalia of the shop (1), once she flees London, Nell encounters a series of human curiosities in the itinerant showmen: Codlin and Short, the "exhibitors of the freaks of Punch" (16); "Grinder's lot" (17); Jerry and his dancing dogs; Mr. Vuffin; and finally Mrs. Jarley, the owner of the waxwork. In the context of a narrative populated by such curiosities, it is little wonder that Nell ends up forming a spectacle herself. Realizing Nell's potential for attracting visitors to the exhibition, Mrs. Jarley sends her out in the advertising cart where she becomes "the chief attraction" (29). Then, "lest Nell should become too cheap," Mrs. Jarley has her remain in the exhibition room to describe the figures to admiring audiences. In the village which becomes her final resting place, Nell is employed to replace the old person "who kept the keys of the church, opened and closed it for the services, and showed it to strangers" (52). However, she quickly comes to form part of the attraction herself: "Parties, too, would come to see the church; and those who came, speaking to others of the child, sent more; so that even at that season of the year they had visitors almost daily" (55).

The Old Curiosity Shop is a novel in which people and things are constantly put on show.[10] Nell watches the Edwards sisters together, following them at a distance on their evening walks and yearning for a similar companionship (32), and even the visit of the single gentleman to the town where the waxwork had been exhibited is "looked upon as an exciting and attractive spectacle" by the locals, "which could scarcely be enough admired" (48). Nell is perplexed to feel herself under surveillance when she pays the landlord of the Valiant Soldier for their "entertainment" in chapter 30, and as she returns to the room where she had passed the evening with her grandfather, she fancies seeing a figure go before her: "being very certain that no person had passed in or out while she stood there, the thought struck her that she had been watched." This preoccupation with watching or being put on show is part of a narrative focus upon the surface of experience in which the relationship between interior and exterior, between private and public life, is put into question. Instead of confining spectatorship to the stage, the narrative finds it in so-called private life, turning the inside outside, as it were, so that the protective space supposed to be provided by the interiorized ideal of the middle-class family – that haven in a heartless world – no longer exists.

As part of his study of popular entertainment in the novel, Paul Schlicke has noted the contrast between the portrayal of the itinerant showfolk, who appear primarily when they are "off-duty," and the presentation of Astley's – visited by Kit on his holiday in chapter 39 – whose actors are seen only in performance.[11] With the exception of the account of Astley's, the narrator goes behind the scenes, focusing upon the showfolk in private life. When

Nell and her grandfather come upon the Punch and Judy showmen in chapter 16, Short explains that they undertake repairs in a place removed from the town because "'it wouldn't do to let 'em see the present company undergoing repair'. . . . 'Would you care a ha'penny for the Lord Chancellor if you know'd him in private and without his wig? – certainly not.'" Similarly, Nell and her grandfather hear from Mr. Vuffin about problems in the trade. They share the domestic accommodation of Mrs. Jarley for a time and learn of the ease with which a waxwork figure of "a murderess of great renown" can be transformed into a likeness of Mrs. Hannah More (29). By going off-stage in its presentation of the showfolk, while at the same time putting Nell on public display, the narrative draws upon the ideology of separate spheres to accentuate Nell's plight as vulnerable and out of place.

A number of critics have commented upon Dickens's dual conception of Nell as a child and as a young woman. Almost at the age of fourteen, she is ambiguously poised between childhood and womanhood since she could have been legally married at the age of twelve. But this ambiguity is entirely in keeping with the ideal of the domestic angel as outlined by John Ruskin, for example, in what has become a *locus classicus* in accounts of domestic ideology – his essay, "Of Queens' Gardens" – where he praises the "majestic childishness" of the ideal woman as a measure of her distance from the tainting effects of the public sphere.[12] Nell's face reflects the beneficent influence of an ancestral line of domestic angels, as her grandfather's brother explains:

> "If you have seen the picture-gallery of any one old family, you will remember how the same face and figure – often the fairest and slightest of them all – come upon you in different generations; and how you trace the same sweet girl through a long line of portraits – never growing old or changing – the Good Angel of the race – abiding by them in all reverses – redeeming all their sins –
> In this daughter, the mother lived again." (69)

Generational difference disappears here just as the distinction between childhood and womanhood is made ambiguous in Nell's characterization. The everpresence of the Good Angel, the constancy of "the same sweet girl" in her ministry of domestic devotion, implies a transcendence of social vicissitudes that is in keeping with the presentation of Nell's story as a journey toward the heavenly city, as Alexander Welsh has shown.[13] But the pathos associated with this idea of a timeless female principle that transcends history is ironically and comically qualified by the inclusion of another example of such "everpresence" in the novel: the waxwork figures of Mrs. Jarley, whose identities can be transformed in a remarkably easy manner with a slight alteration of costume. Moreover, the idea of a persistent family type transcending other forms of difference is satirized in the figure of Sally Brass, who bears such "a striking resemblance to her brother, Sampson" (33) that it is only their clothes which make them distinguishable. And while Nell's early death ensures that she will never lose her youthful innocence, Dickens provides a parodic double for her in the figure of that "old-fashioned child" (34), the Marchioness.[14] Where Nell is appalled by her grandfather's gambling, the Marchioness proves a dab hand at cribbage played for sixpences with Dick Swiveller. The function of the Marchioness as a counterpart for Little Nell was recognized in burlesque dramatizations of the 1870s and 1880s in which actresses such as Lotta Crabtree doubled the roles. Despite his overt dedication to the apotheosis of Little Nell and the domestic virtue she represents, Dickens's comic imagination subverts the sentimentality and sobriety of the ideal he otherwise purveys.

While Quilp may appear to be the most obvious source of threat to Nell's happiness and security in *The Old Curiosity Shop*, the greatest evil is shown to arise from within the family itself: initially, from Fred's machinations, but later, and more disturbingly, from her grandfather's theft of the money Nell has hidden in her dress. At the end of chapter 30, having lost all his money gambling at cards, the grandfather enters Nell's bedroom to steal the funds she has kept hidden for emergencies. The sensational effects of the scene are created through Dickens's use of Nell's limited point of view to register the invasion of her room as a threat of sexual violation while she remains paralyzed by fear. But the greatest horror of all is the discovery that the unrecognizable invader is her grandfather himself. As the sensation novelists were to demonstrate in the 1860s, it is the secrets which lurk within the home – "the mysteries which are at our own doors"[15] – which prove to be the most terrifying and yet the most compelling. External sources of threat, such as that posed by Quilp, prove to be less powerful than the demon that emerges from within the family itself. The sensational effect – with its suggestion of secret crimes flourishing within the seclusion of the home – depends upon the logic associated with a separation between private and public spheres. As with his depiction of the itinerant players "off-stage" and of Nell's adventures with Mrs. Jarley and final occupation as church guide, in the novel's central scene of violation Dickens invokes and transgresses the boundary between private and public, betraying an imaginative investment in the fracturing of the family even as he affirms the domestic ideal.

Dickens's use of fractured familial relations to explore wider issues of social and economic conflict is particularly evident in the more intricately plotted novels that he wrote from *Dombey and Son* onward. Moving away from the episodic structure of *Martin Chuzzlewit*, *Dombey and Son* marks the beginning of Dickens's engagement with the family as a complex cultural construct, exploring the connections between familial and economic relations, and tracing the triumph of that form of family which values domestic affection rather than the pride of lineage. As in *The Old Curiosity Shop*, the narrative presents a variety of distorted relationships, but focuses principally upon father–daughter, mother–daughter, and brother–sister combinations. The lack or inadequacy of these familial ties is shown in the remarkable prevalence of surrogate relationships in the novel: Paul's tenuous hold upon life is fostered by a series of substitute mothers, including Polly Toodle, Florence, and Mrs. Pipchin; Sol Gills and Captain Cuttle act as surrogate fathers to Walter and Florence respectively; Walter is a surrogate brother for Florence and so on. The prominence given to these substitute relationships reveals gaps or failures in the family; but it also attests to the dominance of domestic ideology in the narrative by defining the gender roles and homemaking values of the middle-class ideal as a form of family that is available to everyone.

But while Dickens's extension of the domestic model to surrogate relationships demonstrates the dominance of domestic ideology, the instability of this ideology is also revealed in the ways in which his narratives join the domains of private and public life. His novels contain a number of examples of "threshold figures"[16] – like Mr. Carker, Mr. Dombey's business manager, who is "employed" as a go-between to demand Edith's submission to her husband's imperious will: figures who threaten the privacy of the home with intrusions from the world outside. In *Bleak House*, as D. A. Miller has shown, the police detective, Mr. Bucket, questions the nature of private, familial space by insinuating himself easily into the bosom of the Bagnet family in order to arrest their friend and guest, Mr. George.[17] But Mr. Bucket's seemingly omnipresent powers of surveillance are shown to be limited when it comes to finding Lady Dedlock, and the threat to familial privacy posed by his infiltration of the Bagnet home is reduced in his transition from public servant to private investigator for Sir Leicester Dedlock.[18] Mr. Bucket in effect takes over from Mr. Tulkinghorn – that "retainer-like . . . steward of the legal mysteries, the butler of the legal cellar, of the Dedlocks" (2), who has his own turret chamber at Chesney Wold – in serving the family interests of Sir Leicester. While he assumes the role of public servant in his arrest of George for the murder of Mr. Tulkinghorn, Mr. Bucket's pursuit of Lady Dedlock is carried out as a private employee of Sir Leicester, hired "'to follow her and find her – to save her, and take her his forgiveness'" (56). His appearance as a Dedlock retainer serves to contain the threat to the family. Moreover, his earlier infiltration of the Bagnet family to accomplish the arrest of George is neatly reversed in the deployment of his own home to keep Hortense under surveillance. His partnership with

Mrs. Bucket – "a lady of natural detective genius" (53) – gives a new meaning to the rhetorical question he had put to the Bagnets in making himself "at home" with them: "what is public life without private ties?" (49). But despite his apparent ability "'to be everywhere, and cognisant of everything'" (47) – indeed, despite his resemblance to the omniscient narrator – Mr. Bucket is unable to outwit Lady Dedlock in her final escape. She evades his detection just at the point where her identity is publicly redefined as a "fallen woman."

Along with its hearthside angels, Dickens's fiction contains a number of more complex female figures who are ambiguously poised as part of a simultaneous confirmation and critique of domestic ideology. If the Court of Chancery serves in *Bleak House* as a sign of the family's failure to regulate itself, the story of Lady Dedlock's fall is another exemplary instance of familial breakdown. The representation of the fallen woman in Victorian fiction helped to shape ideas of normal and deviant behavior as part of the formation of the middle-class family and feminine ideal.[19] So too did those representations of aristocratic women, which focused upon the surface qualities of mien or dress held to signify their social and economic value. In his portrayal of Lady Dedlock, Dickens registers a cultural shift in the definition of female identity away from the "external" attributes of class to focus on the "inner" qualities of gender. In the early chapters of the novel, the omniscient narrator maintains a respectful distance from this character, always acknowledging her rank with the polite title, "my Lady," and never penetrating her consciousness to reveal the passionate thoughts at work within. By overtly eschewing some of the power of his omniscience in this way and observing her from without, the narrator establishes Lady Dedlock's social position in formal terms (as well as maintaining her hidden past). But with the gradual revelation of her sexual transgression, Lady Dedlock's icy and inscrutable surface is shown to cover hidden depths of guilt and passion. Instead of owing her identity to her fashionable status, she acquires a new kind of subjectivity as she is progressively defined by her fallen female "nature." Gender ostensibly comes to displace class as the basis for identity in the representation of Lady Dedlock, thereby accounting for the success with which she deceives Mr. Bucket in her final flight. When she had earlier attempted to impersonate a servant by dressing in the clothes of Hortense, the ruse was unsuccessful: even Jo was not fooled. But the indomitable Inspector Bucket is duped by her disguise in the clothes of Jenny, the brickmaker's wife and mother of the dead child. The loss of motherhood establishes an identification between these two women that apparently obliterates the traces of class distinction – a gender identification that is assumed by a middle-class view of family and the feminine ideal. The transformation of

Lady Dedlock into the mother of an illegitimate child enacts a red[...]
of female identity according to the requirements of domestic ideolog[...]

While the deviant figure of the fallen woman often works to es[...]
domestic ideology as normative, Dickens's fiction also contains a num[...]
more disruptive female figures who help to expose the limitations of the
domestic ideal. The sequestration and sanctification of the Victorian middle-
class home stereotypically depend upon an opposition between "angel" and
"whore"; but Dickens exposes this logic of the demonized "other" through
the depiction of women who are "in between," who cannot be normalized
in this way. In *David Copperfield*, for example, Dickens presents the passionate Rosa Dartle, whose smoldering anger as a result of her sexual
betrayal by Steerforth (symbolized by the throbbing scar on her lip) remains
unassimilated at the end of David's narrative. She aggressively refuses to
endorse the middle-class ideal of womanhood against which David wishes
to measure her, scorning his "kind" interpretation of her vengeful wish for
Emily's death in chapter 46 – "'To wish her dead,' said I, 'may be the kindest
wish that one of her own sex could bestow upon her'" – as providing any
affirmation of a "natural" sisterhood among women. A similar challenge to
David's point of view is provided in the disturbing scene where he overhears
Rosa's attack on Emily from an adjoining room in chapter 50. Emily appeals
to the commonality of "sex" in begging Rosa to "spare" her, and to a shared
conception of the family as defined by the domestic ideal. But Rosa violently
repudiates her assumptions, insisting upon the irreducible difference of class
in determining the meaning of "family." While Emily asserts a form of
upbringing in which female virtue transcends the specificities of class – "'I
had been brought up as virtuous as you or any lady'" – Rosa refuses to
endorse this assimilation of class into gender difference, just as she rejected
David's earlier appeal to female "nature."

Neither clearly fallen nor unfallen herself, Rosa makes visible the ideological work involved in David's narrative of middle-class self-making.
Introduced by David in chapter 20 with the callous comment that "she was
a little dilapidated – like a house – with having been so long to let" – Rosa
exposes the limitations of David's middle-class, male perspective and his
unwitting complicity with Steerforth, who functions as a dark double in his
narrative. When David enters his bedroom at Steerforth's house he is made
anxious by a portrait of Rosa above the chimney-piece: "The painter hadn't
made the scar," he says, "but *I* made it; and there it was, coming and going"
(20). David's repeated emphasis upon Rosa's "lurking" manner, "searching
brow," "lynx-like scrutiny," and "piercing look" (29), reveals the disingen-
uousness of his description; for Rosa is not so much the subject who looks,
as she is the object David looks at. "Eager," "thin," consumed by a "wasting

fire within her, which found a vent in her gaunt eyes" (20), Rosa's body betrays her innermost thoughts and feelings. As she scorns the affliction of Mr. Peggotty in chapter 32, David remarks the passion "which made itself articulate in her whole figure." The legibility of her desire serves to reinforce David's male authority as narrator; but at the same time, his inability to read the sexual tension at work between Rosa and Steerforth, or to comprehend her foreshadowing of a violent rupture between Steerforth and his mother in chapter 29, helps to preserve his own "innocence." David's emphasis upon the candor of his narrative – "I write what I sincerely believe" (50) – contrasts with the insinuating manner of Rosa, who "never said anything she wanted to say, outright; but hinted it, and made a great deal of it by this practice" (20). But Rosa's oblique and evasive conversation, full of questions, leading remarks, and unfinished sentences, is a sign of her marginalization as an orphan, raised merely to be a female companion, and as the victim of male sexual violence. A perpetual adjunct to someone else's family, her angry presence challenges David's reassuring domestic ideology.

Orphanhood and illegitimacy are central preoccupations in Dickens's fiction, from *Oliver Twist*'s opening in a foundling home through to the mystery of Edwin Drood's murder by his jealous uncle. While Dickens deeply identified with the lonely plight of the orphan from his own sense of early abandonment, his so-called "darker" novels, from *Bleak House* onward, also reveal a remarkable self-consciousness in his deployment of this trope to express key anxieties and discontinuities of his age. In *Hard Times*, Dickens explores the failure of social paternalism through the exposure of a fraudulent orphan, Josiah Bounderby, and by means of a widely noted link between the situation of the Gradgrind children and that of the Coketown workers.[20] Early nineteenth-century social paternalist ideology saw the family's benevolent hierarchy as providing a model for social reform. Based upon a genealogical imperative, or what Sir Henry Maine described as "the assumption that kinship in blood is the sole possible ground of community in political functions,"[21] this view of social organization derives from the theory of political right known as patriarchalism, in which the authority of the father as family head is held to be the model for all power relations. Dickens's exposure of social paternalism's failure is especially evident in the portrayal of those characters who adhere to earlier, aristocratic conceptions of family as "kinship in blood": such as Mr. James Harthouse, and, more surprisingly, Mr. Bounderby.

Upon his first meeting with Harthouse, Mr. Bounderby characteristically boasts of the contrast in their upbringing: "'You are a man of family. Don't deceive yourself by supposing for a moment that I am a man of family. I am a dirty bit of riff-raff and a genuine scrap of tag, rag, and bobtail'" (2.2).

Dickens creates in Mr. Bounderby a "Bully of humility" whose repeated invocation of the middle-class myth of the self-made man is ironically subverted by his dependence upon an aristocratic conception of the family as "kinship in blood." As the narrator notes, Mr. Bounderby "could never sufficiently vaunt himself a self-made man" (1.4) and he literalizes the trope by inventing the story of his birth in a ditch and abandonment by his mother: "'Here I am, Mrs. Gradgrind, anyhow, and nobody to thank for my being here, but myself'" (1.4). "'Nobody threw me a rope,'" he boasts, "'Vagabond, errand-boy, vagabond, laborer, porter, clerk, chief manager, small partner, Josiah Bounderby of Coketown. Those are the antecedents, and the culmination'" (1.4). Bounderby conceals the existence of his respectable, self-sacrificing mother, Mrs. Pegler, in order to preserve his story of deprivation and isolation. But in vaunting his orphanhood, he remains oblivious to the way in which this preoccupation with origins ironically depends upon a notion of family shared by the Scadgerses, Powlers, and Harthouses, from whom he boastfully distinguishes himself. Note his self-description as "'a *genuine* scrap of tag, rag, and bobtail'" (my emphasis) in his conversation with Harthouse quoted above. As Chris R. Vanden Bossche has argued, "only within the notion of the aristocratic family does origin matter because this family defines itself in terms of lineage."[22] Thus Dickens reveals the hypocrisy of Mr. Bounderby's tale of birth in the lowest ranks of society not only by exposing its falsehood when the mother returns, but by disclosing its ideological indebtedness to a notion of family as lineage that belies the class mobility being proclaimed. When the identity of Mrs. Pegler as Mr. Bounderby's mother is disclosed in Book the Third, chapter 5, the narrator observes that the son's "boastfulness had put the honest truth as far away from him as if he had advanced the mean claim (there is no meaner) to tack himself on to a pedigree." The comparison tellingly points to the aristocratic notion of family that has underpinned Mr. Bounderby's rhetoric throughout. Middle-class self-making is here shown to harbor an anxiety about familial origins that Dickens will explore more fully in *Great Expectations*.

Mr. Bounderby's exploitation of the trope of orphanhood to aggrandize himself is revealed in a moment of unmasking that parallels the exposure of Christopher Casby as a hypocrite and renegade paternalist in *Little Dorrit*. Dickens delights in the denunciation of such humbugs, exposing their manipulation of familial ideology for self-serving ends. Silas Wegg, balladmonger and keeper of a fruit-stall in *Our Mutual Friend*, is another imposter, who "had not only settled it with himself in the course of time, that he was errand-goer by appointment to the house at the corner . . ., but also that he was one of the house's retainers and owed vassalage to it and was bound to leal and loyal interest in it" (1.5). He maintains the fiction of his position as retainer with the invention of familial names for the inmates of the house – such as "Miss Elizabeth," "Master George," "Aunt Jane," and "Uncle Parker" – and mentions the property to Mr. Boffin (who seeks an Eminently Aristocratic Mansion to let) as one to which he has "'a sort of a family tie'" (1.15). He impresses Mr. Boffin with the recitation of a stanza from "The Soldier's Tear," claiming it was written to commemorate the departure of his eldest brother to enlist in the army (1.5), just as he attempts to propitiate Mr. Venus by complimenting him on the homely surroundings of his shop in the epigraph to this chapter. The relationship between the "Friendly Movers," Wegg and Venus, provides a comic focus for the novel's interest in the profit to be made from recycling waste, as well as its investment in domestic ideology; for their cozy interviews beside Mr. Venus's hearth are rendered tragicomic by the love-lorn state of the "Articulator of human bones," who is unable to separate his private identity from his public occupation in the eyes of his beloved. Despite his overt dedication to the supposedly harmonizing virtues of domesticity, Dickens is imaginatively drawn toward the dissociation of masculine identity required by industrial capitalism. Such ambivalence is finally the hallmark of his fictional engagement with the family. In his depiction of orphans, bachelors, spinsters, and families made memorable by their failure to exemplify the domestic ideal, Dickens exposes the instability of the ideology he otherwise seeks to affirm. That his writing manifests such a tension is hardly surprising, given the widespread critical recognition of his divided imagination. But a focus on the complex ways in which Dickens interweaves the "public" issues of politics and economics with "private" family affairs helps us to understand the nature of dominant ideologies in the nineteenth century and the patriarchal structures they helped to sustain. By examining the discursive power of gender, family, and domestic ideology in Dickens's novels, we discover a new political force in his fiction, and a new way of thinking about its dynamic function within the Victorian social economy.

NOTES

1 "Charles Dickens and *David Copperfield*," *Fraser's Magazine* 42 (December 1850), 698–710. Reprinted in *Dickens: The Critical Heritage*, ed. Philip Collins (Routledge and Barnes and Noble, 1971), p. 244.

2 George Newlin, *Everyone in Dickens: A Taxonomy*, vol. III, *Characteristics and Commentaries, Tables and Tabulations* (Greenwood Press, 1995), p. 285.

3 Margaret Oliphant, "Charles Dickens," reprinted in Collins, *Critical Heritage*, p. 559.

4 J. W. T. Ley, "The Apostle of Christmas," *The Dickensian* 2 (1906), 324.

5 Quoted by Deborah Thomas, *Dickens and the Short Story* (Batsford, 1982), p. 38.

6 "Charles Dickens in Relation to Christmas," *The Graphic*, 25 December 1870, reprinted in *The Dickensian* 5 (1909), 314.

7 Raymond Williams, *Keywords: A Vocabulary of Culture and Society* (Oxford University Press, 1977), pp. 131–34.

8 *Sketches of Young Couples* can be found in the Oxford Illustrated edition of *Sketches by Boz* (Oxford University Press, 1987), pp. 549–603. "The Nice Little Couple" runs from pp. 584–87.

9 John Ruskin, "Of Queens' Gardens," *"Sesame and Lilies," "Unto This Last," and "The Political Economy of Art"* (1865; Cassell and Company, 1909), p. 74.

10 Patricia McKee discusses the novel's "surfacing of experience that cuts [the characters] off from both temporal and spatial depths" as part of an argument about the production of public knowledge and the emptying of subjectivity in *Public and Private: Gender, Class, and the British Novel (1764–1878)* (University of Minnesota Press, 1997), p. 94.

11 Paul Schlicke, *Dickens and Popular Entertainment* (Allen and Unwin, 1985), p. 120.

12 Ruskin, "Of Queens' Gardens," p. 76.

13 Alexander Welsh, *The City of Dickens* (Clarendon Press, 1971), p. 157.

14 I thank Robert Dingley for drawing my attention to this parallel.

15 Henry James, *"Aurora Floyd," The Nation*, 9 November 1865. Reprinted in Henry James, *Essays on Literature, American Writers, English Writers*, ed. Leon Edel (Library of America, 1984), p. 742.

16 Anthea Trodd uses this term to refer to those characters who "transact negotiations between the home and the external world" in *Domestic Crime in the Victorian Novel* (Macmillan, 1989), p. 6.

17 D. A. Miller, *The Novel and the Police* (University of California Press, 1988), p. 80.

18 Anthea Trodd notes Mr. Bucket's private employment and outwitting by Lady Dedlock in *Domestic Crime*, p. 32.

19 See Lynda Nead, *Myths of Sexuality: Representations of Women in Victorian Britain* (Basil Blackwell, 1988).

20 See Catherine Gallagher's influential discussion of *Hard Times* in *The Industrial Reformation of English Fiction: Social Discourse and Narrative Form 1832–1867* (University of Chicago Press, 1985).

21 Sir Henry Maine, *Ancient Law* (1861; Dorset Press, 1986), p. 141.

22 Chris R. Vanden Bossche, "Cookery, not Rookery: Family and Class in *David Copperfield*," *Dickens Studies Annual* 15 (1986), 87–109, at 88.

FURTHER READING

Andrews, Malcolm. *Dickens and the Grown-Up Child*. University of Iowa Press, 1994.

Clark, Robert. "Riddling the Family Firm: the Sexual Economy in *Dombey and Son*." *English Literary History* 51 (1984), 69–84.

Davidoff, Leonore, and Catherine Hall. *Family Fortunes: Men and Women of the English Middle Class, 1780–1850*. Hutchinson, 1987.

Gallagher, Catherine. *The Industrial Reformation of English Fiction: Social Discourse and Narrative Form 1832–1867*. University of Chicago Press, 1985.

Miller, D. A. *The Novel and the Police*. University of California Press, 1988.

Poovey, Mary. *Uneven Developments: The Ideological Work of Gender in Mid-Victorian England*. University of Chicago Press, 1989.

Sadrin, Anny. *Parentage and Inheritance in the Novels of Charles Dickens*. Cambridge University Press, 1994.

Trodd, Anthea. *Domestic Crime in the Victorian Novel*. Macmillan, 1989.

Vanden Bossche, Chris R. "Cookery, not Rookery: Family and Class in *David Copperfield*." *Dickens Studies Annual* 15 (1986), 87–109.

Waters, Catherine. *Dickens and the Politics of the Family*. Cambridge University Press, 1997.

Welsh, Alexander. *The City of Dickens*. Clarendon Press, 1971.

10

GARRETT STEWART

Dickens and language

Dickens and language: one of the great love-matches of literary history, with a bottomless dowry to boot. It often seems as if the untapped reserves of the English vernacular were simply lying waiting for Dickens to inherit them – by marrying their riches to his story-teller's instinct. No one ever wrote prose that way before. And at the same time few writers have ever sprung their manner from such outright imitation. The style of Dickens's novelistic career begins in pure derivation, a sustained send-up not only of the Johnsonian high style of journalistic and parliamentary claptrap in the eighteenth-century Age of Rhetoric but of Sir Walter Scott's editorial aliases and their prefatory paraphernalia – and then finds its true quasi-oratorical tone amid the cleared debris of tradition. Here is the launching sentence of his debut novel:

> The first ray of light which illumines the gloom, and converts into a dazzling brilliancy that obscurity in which the earlier history of the public career of the immortal Pickwick would appear to be involved, is derived from the perusal of the following entry in the Transactions of the Pickwick Club, which the editor of these papers feels the highest pleasure in laying before his readers as a proof of the careful attention, indefatigable assiduity, and nice discrimination with which his search among the multifarious documents confided to him has been conducted.

After Dickens, no one could write that way again and be taken seriously.

By the last paragraph of *Pickwick Papers*, months of serialized success later, the vestiges of the orotund high style, more relaxed and buoyant now, feel less like overkill than like understatement, as Pickwick enlivens his leisure "in hearing Sam Weller read aloud, with such remarks as suggested themselves to his mind, which never failed to afford Mr. Pickwick the greatest amusement." The moderated wordiness of an idiomatic litotes (or double negative) and the light trappings of alliteration in the "never *failed* to a*fford*" have by this point an almost vernacular lilt rather than a pedantic thud, and the narrative wording of "such remarks as suggested themselves to his mind" is less an evasive circumlocution than a personification allegory of comic asides, where even the language of parenthetical suggestion does indeed have a life of its own. The novel thus closes in the envisioned recurrent scene of its own reception: the oral recitation of popular prose, jauntily glossed at the domestic hearth.

In like fashion, mock-heaviness dissipates into its own levity from here on out in Dickens's career. In the opening of *Oliver Twist*, the labors of bureaucratic circumlocution – the pompous exertions of adult discourse – counterpoint a birth scene to suggest the human struggle which the newborn hero is slow to accept, for there was "considerable difficulty in inducing Oliver to take upon himself the office of respiration, – a troublesome practice, but one which custom has rendered necessary to our easy existence" (1). But it is not just archly elevated diction and swollen syntax that must submit to Dickens's tongue-in-cheek verbal lampoons. Even the purer literary mode of metaphor can be warped into the strained and mechanical, tactically so. When more than one metaphor is tried out at the same time, they can seem overdone and undersold. Examples again from *Pickwick* and *Oliver Twist*, in the move from comic picaresque to the more abiding forms of Dickensian melodrama: though the seething genius of Pickwick has just solved a major scientific mystery by tracing the origin of tittlebats to the local ponds of Hampstead, there sat the man "as calm and unmoved as the deep waters of the one on a frosty day or as a solitary specimen of the other in the inmost recesses of an earthen jar" (1). By contrast, such metaphoric overkill, when stripped of farce, can become genuinely incremental in *Oliver Twist*, a shift in the registers of simile so rapid as to communicate the fleeting events of Bill Sikes's accidental death by hanging: "The noose was on his neck. It ran up with his weight, tight as a bow-string, and swift as the arrow it speeds" (50). Taut cause and lethal effect snap shut upon each other in the figurative "transfer" (the etymological sense of *meta-forein*) from the living to the dead.

Pickwickian bombast marks one fork in Dickens's multiple paths as a stylist, Twistian melodrama another. And as his verbal irony gains confidence, even his stylistic comedy becomes both darker and more targeted. Gradgrind in *Hard Times* is so full of pedagogic emphasis that the rigidity of his own person seems a *pointed* affront, including the spiked bristles of his hair: "a plantation of firs to keep the wind from its bald head," where the sound-play on "firs" (with its anagrammatic twist in "*surf*ace") seems at once to summon and rule out the softness and comforting animality of "fur." In making his points, Gradgrind is insistence personified: "The speaker's obstinate carriage, square coat, square legs, square shoulders – nay, his very neckcloth, trained to take him by the throat with an unaccommodating grasp, like a stubborn fact, as it was – all helped the emphasis" (1). In such a grinding-in of the point about Gradgrind, we have moved well beyond the habitual Dickensian way in which language asserts the vitality of character from within the name itself, from Weller and Swiveller through Dedlock to Headstone, including, most unmistakably of all, Mr. Gradgrind's own associate, the schoolmaster M'Choakumchild. Names aside, Gradgrind's epitome of the utilitarian bureaucrat requires that his very necktie be "trained" rather than "tied," the constrictive revenge of his whole system. Best of all, there is the dodging of the expected formulaic apology for a simile in "as it were," ordinarily indicating a flight of fancy as contrary-to-fact. Not here. The tie may well seem ("as [indeed] it was") only one more among many facts or itemized data, any of which, when given the upper hand, may carry the threat of strangulation to the living organism. Not all characters in Dickens are embodied rhetorical strategies – or at least not in this overt way. But all of them tap for their essence the contours of the language that generates them.

Heavy-handed comparison, strident parallelism, deliberate contortions of idiom, rampant neologism, extended metaphor, phantom puns and phonetic undertones, these effects and countless others – including all the manipulated tics of dialogue, from Cockney slang to the stuffy argot of the shabby genteel – work to turn the Dickensian sentence into a histrionic scenario all its own, with grammatical subjects battling with objects for priority, adjectives choking the life out of nouns before they can manifest a verb, adverbs riding on the coattails of remorseless verb chains, and, everywhere in dialogue, slips of the tongue hitting home. "Joe, how are you, Joe?" (27) splutters Pip the former blacksmith in *Great Expectations*, now idle gentleman, when surprised by his servant with the introduction of his old friend from the forge. As so often in this novel of ironically echoing dialogue, the words are thrown back in his face with a difference – here by the broken parallelism of Joe's lower-class pronunciation: "Pip, and how AIR you, Pip?"[1] Joe puts into accidental circulation the high-toned "air" that Pip usually puts on.

Language, then, isn't just something Dickens mobilized or remodelled. Language *per se* is a way of reading him, a way of staying with him through the farthest stretches of invention – and of confronting there his unique place in Victorian letters. Consider, for comparison, two pieces of novelistic travel writing powerfully subordinated to drama and psychology from the two greatest writers of Victorian prose fiction. In each case a young woman is displaced from the native domestic life she has known and plunged into the luxuriant decay of fabled Italy. The first gives us Dorothea Brooke in Rome, a single sentence from the famous wedding journey of George Eliot's

Middlemarch. The second concerns Amy Dorrit on the way south to Venice, from the Grand Tour of *Little Dorrit*. Each is a complex example of what narrative theory would call "focalization," where external description is filtered through the singular consciousness of a character.

Eliot first, sampled by one calculatedly overwhelming sentence:

> Ruins and basilicas, palaces and colossi, set in the midst of a sordid present, where all that was living and warm-blooded seemed sunk in the deep degeneracy of a superstition divorced from reverence; the dimmer but yet eager Titanic life gazing and struggling on walls and ceilings; the long vistas of white forms whose marble eyes seemed to hold the monotonous light of an alien world: all this vast wreck of ambitious ideals, sensuous and spiritual, mixed confusedly with the signs of breathing forgetfulness and degradation, at first jarred her as with an electric shock, and then urged themselves on her with that ache belonging to a glut of confused ideas which check the flow of emotion.[2]

The cadence and the burden are deliberate, along with the delayed syntactic detonation. In a distended grammatical mimesis, the whole numbing weight of splendid, empty impressions comes pressing down on the consciousness of the heroine, the novel's ethical lightning rod. Amid the sensory overload, the discriminating mind is still sorting, weighing the antitheses, even if coming up short.

By contrast, the kaleidoscopic barrage of the Dickens passage is more unreflective and nightmarish, a dizzy unfurling of contradictory impressions without any of the perspective tacitly achieved by rhetorical balance in Eliot. The whole headlong tourist trek seems, from Amy Dorrit's assaulted perspective, like a delirious dream in its senseless, expensive repetitions, so that the subjunctive verb form "would" that governs the passage is not wishful or "contrary-to-fact" but rather the sign of a willfully "iterative" or "frequentive" tense. This is what they *would* do, day in and day out: "Among the day's unrealities would be roads" leading on to "vast piles of building mouldering to dust; hanging gardens where the weeds had grown so strong that their stems, like wedges driven home, had split the arch and rent the wall" (2.3). Compared to Eliot's almost clichéd "like an electric shock," here is a subsidiary metaphor that arrests us with a violence inherent in the scene: untended nature's revenge against the neglected remnants of culture. And note the minuscule but devastating effect of the singular "building" rather than "buildings," as if it named the undifferentiated labor and waste of the whole ancient mass, thus serving to reduce "piles" from the idiomatic term for mansions to mere mountains of stone.

Onward: "Again there would be places where they stayed the week together, in splendid rooms, had banquets every day, rode out among heaps of wonders, walked through miles of palaces, and rested in dark corners of great churches" (2.3) – so that "places" seems to dilate into "palaces" (with their own "miles" of internal tramping) under the repetitive pressure of the interchangeable. The principle of aimless iteration seems to invade even the phonetic texture of the prose as well, in a jangling association of unwanted stimuli. No sooner has Dickens's ear picked out a shadowy cause-and-effect nexus in the "mist and *scent* of in*cense*" in deserted churches (2.3) than, a clause later, his description latches onto the entwined aural knotting of "by the roads of vines and *olives*, through sq*uali*d villages." These are sites where idle luxury has reversed its terms to impoverished ennui and where, in the numbing counterplay of transitive and intransitive verbs, there "seemed to be nothing to support life, nothing to eat, nothing to make, nothing to grow, nothing to hope, nothing to do but die" (2.3).

Unlike Eliot's passage, Dickens's nauseating panorama is all drive and thrust and mounting critique: rhetorical through and through rather than weightily meditative, and honed to the straightforward vocabulary of the mind's eye. So with his famous set pieces in novel after novel, where some oddity of grammar or diction regularly offers the key to an overarching effect. There is the famous second paragraph of *Bleak House* beginning with "Fog everywhere" (1), followed by eight more freestanding verbless phrases headed by "Fog" ("Fog up the river . . . Fog creeping . . .") and mired in the continuous present of this same grammatical impasse – all prepared for by the layerings or "deposits" of mud in the opening paragraph, whose seemingly neutral choice of diction triggers the caustic metaphor (and fiscal send-up), "accumulating at compound interest." Strung out over a comparable parallelism early in *Our Mutual Friend*, and again in a perpetual present tense of inalterable routine, there are the eleven nounless verb phrases depending from the main clause: "The great looking-glass above the sideboard, reflects the table and the company" (1.2). This is the company gathered at one of the endless *nouveau riche* banquets given by the aptly named Veneerings, whose polish is only a thin layer of applied substance, not even skin deep, and so who seem to deserve no company but superficial reflections.

Sampling this syntactic format directs us as well to a related – and characteristic – adjectival device of Dickensian prose: "Reflects Veneering; forty, wavy-haired, dark, tending to corpulence, sly, mysterious, filmy." Three flatly descriptive adjectives pile up, followed by a participial (-ing) phrase that turns out to be a momentary stopgap against another threesome of denigrating attributes, the last of them, "filmy," aptly suggesting that an imperfect reflection in the glass would in fact best seize upon the shadowy essence of the man. The subject of all these reflections, the mirror, has long ago dropped away (into the freestanding verb "Reflects") so as to offer up the existence of the invited nonentities in a hovering limbo of their own artifice: "Reflects Twemlow; grey, dry, polite, susceptible to east wind" (1.2), and so forth. Again the discrete, stiffening trio of adjectives setting his attributes off from each other in their frailty and desiccation, and then another stunning run of adjectives, this time elongated and unpunctuated in imitation of all manner of optical and spiritual distortion: "Reflects charming old Lady Tippins on Veneering's right; with an immense obtuse drab oblong face, like a face in a tablespoon" (1.2). An anamorphic warping or merely the accurate, unflattering image of misshapen age? Superbly, there is no way to tell. By this point in the passage, reflection and reality have disappeared into each other, and only the glimpsed attribute haunts (via the disembodied hovering of modification) the place of a withdrawn reality.

I will be coming back to the enchainment and bunching of adjectives in Dickens, as this "minor" descriptive device can end up inflecting our sense of an entire novel. For now, the dismantling phrase about the aged coquette in *Our Mutual Friend* perfectly exemplifies, and twice over (as inanimate reflection and as dehumanizing simile), a longstanding truism of Dickensian stylistics: the collapsing of boundaries between people and things. Besides all the metaphors that bestow animation (often hostile) on houses and boots and neckties, or steal it from suddenly spoon-like human visages, there is, however, another stylistic habit, more specifically indebted to Dickens's literary precursors, that perhaps best captures – or further erodes – the blurred border between personality and objecthood. It is worth dwelling over this most narrowly delimited of rhetorical (or figurative) effects – usually revolving around the witty discrepancy between literal and metaphoric senses – as it can offer a test case for the reading of Dickensian narrative from the stylistic ground up.

As Dickens would have practiced it if not recognized its name, syllepsis (or zeugma – there is considerable terminological debate) is a device that, in its most recognized form, predicates in two different senses of its main verb. Take Pope's textbook example from *The Rape of the Lock*: "to stain her honour, or her new brocade." It isn't that "stain" *might* be figurative as well as literal when it is collocated at one and the same time with spirit and facade, honor and costume. It must be. The incompatibles are copresent at the same level of grammatical realization. At one point, for instance, the prose of *Pickwick Papers* forces upon the idiom "fell asleep" a recognition of its latent dead metaphor. Literalizing the verb in one of its paired usages and heightening the semantic fissure with a comma, Dickens calls attention to the way Mr. Pickwick "fell into the barrow, and fast asleep, simultaneously" (19), so that corporeality and consciousness, objectivity and subjectivity, are fused in the same plunge. When a related comic device is delegated to a character's own wit later in the novel, we get Sam Weller satirizing legal proclamations by noting, "There ain't a magistrate goin' as don't commit himself, twice as often as he commits other people" (25). Or there is the forlorn mastiff in *Bleak House*, discontent with his melancholy solitude and, in another gnawing confusion of materiality and spirit, "very much wanting something to worry, besides himself and his chain" (7).

Physical and emotional conditions turn in *Little Dorrit* on the merest flick of a prepositional shift, as when Amy finds a milliner "in tears and in bed" (1.7); or when in the same novel, across an internal/external (physiological/fiscal) divide, Tite Barnacle is said to be "more flush of blood than money" (1.10). The effects can be more prolonged and baroque, too. Quintessence of a reductive doubling between the external and internal – across the collapsed distinction between an integral self and its public reputation – is the image of the swindling financier spaced out across a looser but related grammatical format: "Mr. Merdle's right hand was filled with the evening paper, and the evening paper was full of Mr. Merdle" (2.12). The less showy versions of such sylleptic clefts in reference, however, remain the more unsettling – grammatically and conceptually. Confronted in later years with the file that had been associated with the convict on the marshes in the opening sequence of *Great Expectations*, Pip is "stupefied by this turning up of my old misdeed and old acquaintance" (10). The old acquaintance is only there by proxy, in the man presenting the file, and the former misdeed (in aiding the criminal) has been turned up not in the sense of uncovered at last. Rather, the act returns only in the mode of a repressed memory teased to the surface of consciousness. That the same verb could navigate these discordant zones of association seems, in effect, to miniaturize the psychological allegory of the novel as a whole, with its obsessive shadowing of present by past. At the opposite pole from traumatic memory is the eroticized nostalgia of a character in no way given to witty contradictions. Thus the softened sylleptic shift of Little Dorrit's letter, with its conflation of self and other in a displaced amorous testament to her eventual husband: "So dearly do I love the scene of my poverty and your kindness" (2.11). Again the sylleptic turn of phrase offers a microcosm of the novel's whole psychological structure – and moral: the self's past always intimately entwined with the action upon it of remembered others.

The laminated grammar of syllepsis goes even more to the heart of *Dombey and Son*. The device is repeatedly a manner of yoking unlike things together by a logic somewhere between metonymy (association) and metaphor (equivalence). Once the spiritual collapse of outer world upon inner life in the throes of a consuming ego has been diagnosed in an alliterative skewed parallelism like "the beadle of our business and our bosoms" (5) to describe Mr. Dombey, the syndrome can be read in the least insignia of Dombey's costume or demeanor, as in "stiff with starch and arrogance" (8). This is the depersonalizing flip-side of the Dickensian animism that bestows sentient energy upon lifeless objects, so that a human attitude is reduced to the rigidities of costume. The sylleptic phrasings continue apace in this novel. In Dombey's first separation from his son after the mother's inconvenient death in childbirth, the boy is given out to wet-nursing "borne by Fate and Richards" (6), where a laboring woman's embrace is ominously linked to the failed self-sufficiency of Dombey's bourgeois world. As with the forking between "starch" and "arrogance," the corporeal (bodily removal) again emblemizes the spiritual (human destiny) across a single grammatical frame.

This shifting between literal and figurative is the deepest common denominator of the sylleptic trope, in *Dombey and Son* and elsewhere. In another sartorial metonymy just barely avoiding the repressed cliché of "stout-hearted," Captain Cuttle is put before us as "one of those timber-looking men, suits of oak as well as hearts" (9). Enough tiny syntactic wrinkles of this sort accrue to a pleated pattern. Once the sylleptic paradigm – call it divided consciousness grammatically instantiated – has been established in the early chapters, across the "high" and "low" strands of the plot, it can be proliferated at will. There is the exit of Major Bagstock, who "took his lobster-eyes and his apoplexy to the club" (40) as if such eyes were a synecdoche as well as a medical symptom of his bulging and convulsive self-importance. Later, when Mr. Toots laments Florence's announced marriage, he bemoans the "banns which consign her to Lieutenant Walters, and me to – to Gloom, you know" (56). Revealed here again, in a comic key, is the cleaving between novelistic fate and its embodied nemesis in character. Or in a typifying implosion of outer reality upon inner ego so extreme as to question any grounding for that ego except the contingencies of fame or shame, there is Mr. Dombey confronting his wife-to-be "with a lofty gallantry adapted to his dignity and the occasion" (30). In yet another sylleptic microcosm of a novel's whole design, even marital encounter is here referred back to a shift in perspective within the devouring self-absorption of the central subject.

As already noticed, the two-ply phrasings that accumulate around a world-swallowing pride in *Dombey and Son* return in *Little Dorrit* as well, where they cooperate in their effects with the novel's habit of threefold modification. Dickens's fondness for adjectival triads sometimes sends the modifiers off in such different directions that they end up satirizing the very notion of a center, subjective or otherwise, in what amounts to a variant of sylleptic forking. Take Flora Finching, always at loose ends with herself, punished by description in the same key: "Flora, always tall, had grown to be very broad too, and short of breath" (1.13). The two initial axes of extremity, vertical and horizontal, yield to an inner dimension of breathless giddiness – and panting babble – whose way of being "short" is not a matter of spatial measure at all. In keeping with the novel's prison motif, the rhetorically adept villain Rigaud mocks the defiant Clennam, during his detention in the Marshalsea, with being "more free of speech than body" (2.18). And the ailing, jail-bound Frederick Dorrit admits his own exhaustion in an unravelling grammar of a related sort: "Late hours, and a heated atmosphere, and years, I suppose," said Frederick, "weaken me" (1.19), where time and place get counterpoised to that inward belatedness that comes with wasted age. There, of course, we get three (rather than two) explanatory nouns, jarring with and overdetermining the admission of intractable debility.

Beyond the paradigm of sylleptic splintering, human constriction is a curse usually borne in *Little Dorrit* on the backs of its congested adjectives, stalled in incremental reiteration upon a physical or psychic impasse. That such language should stutter – or gasp for air – under the onus of an asphyxiating society and its literal imprisonments is to be expected in a novel whose chief symbol of political stultification is named for a notorious figure of speech. This is the "Circumlocution" Office, denominating not only the civil bureaucracy by that name but a degenerate habit of language as well. Wordiness is an epidemic bias of mind whose virus can attack anywhere. Though long a mainstay of Dickens's comic resources (since *Pickwick* on, as we know), the roundabout phrase has in *Little Dorrit* been rigorously assimilated to thematic purpose. At times, what is leaden and misleading about such turns of phrase is made to confront its antithesis in the deflected pithy saying or the wordy unpacking of a maxim or two. The loathsome slumlord Casby, not content with wringing blood from the proverbial single stone, is known "to get a good quantity of blood out of the stones of several unpromising courts and alleys" (1.13). It is in this capacity that he is familiar to many "in whom familiarity had bred its proverbial result perhaps" (1.13) – the last clause ladling on over twice as many words as occasion demands. An even more laughably oblique dodge of the forthright, again swamping a proverb at its core, comes with the introduction of the rakish Henry Gowan, "whose genius, during his earlier manhood, was of that exclusively agricultural character which applies itself to the cultivation of wild oats" (1.17).

A squandering of words in evasion, chicanery, or self-promotion: these are the hallmarks of Circumlocution, both as institution and as a social discourse. Even an innocent euphemism can take the taint of the procedures its user despises, for just after Arthur leaves the Circumlocution Office for the first time, he meets Mr. Meagles, hot under the collar from his own rage at the office's red tape, who says "I only wish you had come upon me in a more prepossessing condition as to coolness" (1.10). The tendency to expatiate needlessly, to make oratorical mountains out of clerical molehills, is perhaps best distilled in the habit of the chief bureaucrat, that inextricable Barnacle on the ship of state, to bestow prolongation even on a single noun, giving the very word circumlocution "the air of a word of about five-and-twenty [not even twenty-five!] syllables" (1.10). But it is Dickens's further ingenuity with the name "Circumlocution" that turns wordiness *per se* into something like a mock-epic conceit. So tortuous is the labyrinthine gobbledegook of the Office that it becomes torturing. In the process, Dickensian prose reactivates, through etymological wordplay and pun, the ubiquitous prison motif in the novel, a prison sequestered this time at the heart of legalism itself. This is because applicants to the Circumlocution Office's patent department, in their inventive *conviction*, are immobilized as "troublesome Convicts who were under sentence to be broken alive on that wheel" (2.10), a wheel whose *circum*ference is that of punitive circularity itself. Varying the metaphor with a trivializing allusion to *Don Quixote*, another Barnacle later explains that Circumlocution is "not a Wicked Giant to be charged at full tilt; but, only a windmill showing you, as it grinds huge quantities of chaff, which way the country wind blows" (2.28). Spewing out "chaff," that reanimated dead metaphor in British English for useless verbiage or humbug, the grinding nonsense of the Office serves merely as a weather vane for the clichéd winds of change.

From the vortex of an officiating circumlocution in *Little Dorrit*, words in search of any meaning whatever must sometimes struggle free of their own ordained syntax, edging over into separate emphases, isolated into authenticity. Adjectives always come fast and furious in Dickens, but in *Little Dorrit* they come consistently bunched in threes, compressed, oppressive, bereft. The syntax of constraint sets in early. "It was a Sunday evening in London, gloomy, close, and stale" (1.3) when the hero comes home to his unloving mother's house after twenty years. The adjectives crowd tight upon each other, airless and constrained. This is often the effect of these tripled clusters: no breathing-room. So with the Clennam house itself, which is later thought by him to be, as always, "wrathful, mysterious, and sad" (2.10). So with its immediate environs on a deserted Sunday: "Nothing to see but streets, streets, streets. Nothing to breathe but streets, streets, streets" (1.3). The double assonance of the long *e*'s in these fragmentary glimpses (like cinematic quick-cuts) serves to bond constricted organic functions like "*see*ing" and "*brea*thing" to their unwanted objects in those numberless disjoint "streets." In turn, this labyrinth of aimless crisscrosses and blind alleys is further captured by that interlocking nexus of *s* sounds in the multiplied "street(s), street(s), streets," where singular and plural fuse into a shapeless disjunct totality of street, street, and nothing but street. No surprise that the motto for rent-collecting deployed by the hypocritical slumlord Casby, who patrols the network of thoroughfares and blind alleys in Bleeding Heart Yard, is "squeeze, squeeze, squeeze" (2.32), a clenched obsession crushing the life out of his tenants.

Some tenancy, however, collapses under its own weight. When the Clennam house comes crashing down from dry rot in the end, past participles take up the familiar threefold burden of a fatal refrain, with the onlookers "stifled, choked, and blinded by the dust" (2.31). Sometimes the adjectives in *Little Dorrit* are welded together so tightly that they seem to shear off from adjacent grammar altogether, as in the description of the implacable Miss Wade's uninviting anteroom, such as is "always to be found in such a house. Cool, dull, and dark" (2.20). At other times the swell of modification may in itself offer a pantomime of puffed-up self-importance. The petticoated Mrs. General expands in pomposity across her very description as "ample, rustling, gravely voluminous" (2.2). Elsewhere the adjectival triad can infect the surrounding grammar, so that "a moist, hot, misty" day – where the consonant bracket may seem to put the "*mist*" back in "*moist*" as cause to effect – can then go on to contaminate in its threefold clamminess the noun series of the next sentence: "It seemed as though the prison's poverty, and shabbiness, and dirt, were growing in the sultry atmosphere" (2.29). That's the Marshalsea, the debtors' prison in London, and its pounding description feels anticipated by the threefold similes that caught the unrelenting essence of the opening prison at Marseilles: "Like a well, like a vault, like a tomb, the prison had no knowledge of the brightness outside . . ." (1.1). Unlike the twofold similes in *Pickwick* or *Oliver*, here the figurative effort at variation seems locked into the inescapable despite itself. The metaphors alone incarcerate. This effect is close kin to the adjectival entrapments of the novel. Right through to the end, the threefold downbeat of delayed epithets (arriving after the name or noun) registers as emotional or environmental deadlock. Among other effects, this triadic modification is used to usher out, in adjacent sentences from the penultimate chapter, two of the least heroic characters of the book, Amy's sister and brother: "Here was Fanny, proud, fitful, whimsical . . . Here was her brother, a weak, proud, tipsy, young old man" (2.33). As always, the very form of the modifiers is symptomatic. It is Fanny's fitfulness, the intermittence of her motives, that fractures her attributes into a jagged taxonomy rather than consolidating them into a focused personality, just as her brother's character is disintegrated from within by the idle clash of his waistrel traits: three failings in adhesive contamination, then the paradoxical implosion of the last pair ("young old"), the whole lifeline in collapse.

Given the recurrent triadic device of adjectival pile-up in *Little Dorrit*, with its choke hold on both human identity and its smothering urban ambience, the recuperative finale of the novel would be well advised to moderate and rectify rather than simply to escape such a pattern. So it does. The grooves of threefold formulation seem relaxed at last to various triplings less rigid, more emotionally capacious. When Amy puts from her own mind, and keeps from Arthur's knowledge, her having been financially cheated by his mother, indirect discourse inhabits her gentle intent in triplicate. But it does so in such a way that for once we get a falling rhythm of release rather than the grip of insistence: "That was all passed, all forgiven, all forgotten" (2.33). Nearing their marriage, indirect discourse again projects the heroine's own emotional tonality, for she "never came to the Marshalsea now and went away without seeing him. No, no, no" (2.34). What in another context might come off as a forced, meretricious affirmation reads here as a curative tripling, like the magic words of an exorcism.

Within a few pages, just as Amy and Arthur have signed the wedding register in the church next-door to the prison, the last sentence of the novel's second-to-last paragraph sets up the fragmentary grammar of the closing one: "They paused for a moment on the steps of the portico, looking at the fresh perspective of the street . . ." (2.34). Though there is the sense of "new prospects" as well as of mere "view" in the pictorial metaphor of "fresh perspective," the underlying connotation of draftsmanship in the phrase picks up on a more extended earlier figure. I have in mind one of Dickens's few grammatical lapses (a dangling participle with no proper antecedent), yet one that seems turned to canny advantage. "Looking back upon his own poor story, she was its vanishing-point. Everything in its perspective led to her innocent figure" (2.27). It is as if the sentence had meant to say in indirect discourse: "Looking back upon his own poor story, he realizes [as we do] that she has always been its vanishing-point." Instead, the grammar has undergone its own foreshortening, bringing forward the object of desire in the very effacement of an anchoring subject other than our own free-floating identification with his (and so her) "story." Even in a laxity of grammar, that is, Dickens can rescue – and resecure – the very nature of readerly identification as the true cornerstone of his narrative aesthetic.

At the novel's close, the cadenced fall of the prose has the new married couple hovering momentarily "in the autumn morning sun's bright rays" (2.34) before they "went down." As if building on, or lifting off from, all the compartmentalized adjectival modules of the novel, this run-up of evocation transfigures three nouns in a row into adjectival modifiers on the way to the fourth and finally descriptive "bright." The process is soon to be reversed in the nominalization of three adjectives. As the next paragraph opens upon its parallel syntactic fragments, three more predicates, punctuated as whole sentences, take up the dying fall of "Went down" as they sketch out the future lives of the couple: varied from "went down into" the modesty of their life together to "went down to" (2.34) their various earthly service.

After which the grammar collects itself for what is perhaps the most "stylish" (and stylized) sentence Dickens ever wrote: "They went quietly down into the roaring streets, inseparable and blessed; and as they passed along in sunshine and in shade, the noisy and the eager, and the arrogant and the froward and the vain, fretted, and chafed, and made their usual uproar" (2.34). After all the novel's impacted triadic adjectives, "inseparable and blessed," in its lattice-work of internal chiming, is the hard-won phrasing of parity and union, of reciprocated and interknit mutuality. With the loosening prepositional cadence of "in sunshine and in shade" recalling (and appeasing) the Marseilles prison setting of the novel's first chapter, with its starkly dichotomized title, "Sun and Shadow," the couple now accepts the world's duality in the again duplex form of "the noisy and the eager," to which is appended the last threefold modification in the book. Amid a frictional jostling of assonance and alliteration (including the "fricative" *f–v* sounds capped off in "*f*retted and cha*f*ed"), the married pair must now enter among "the *arrogant* and the *froward* and the *vain*," including that final if neutralized hint of circumlocution – last vestige of the world's nonsense – in the faint semantic twinning of the near synonyms "arrogant" and "vain." In any case, threefold adjectives have by now hardened to substantives, attitudes grown personified, though somewhat shadowy and insubstantial for all that. Then at last, after five clauses depending from "went down," like a precinematic "loop" effect (one of the countless anticipations of cinematic editing in the very syntax of Dickensian prose), we come upon the tacit antithesis of the last word, "*up*roar" (my emphasis on Dickens's harbored syllabic twist), which meets the descending couple halfway – and on the world's terms. But on language's own terms as well. The least word in Dickens can have a directionality, a dynamism, a suppressed etymology all its own.

Endings often call upon unprecedented reserves of Dickensian ingenuity in this way. *David Copperfield* winds down with a simplicity of diction so extreme as to be flamboyant in its own right, when the autobiographical narrator, playing on the double meaning of "life" as both biographical and biological, closes off the former with "O Agnes, O *my soul*, so *m*ay thy face be by me when I *close* my life indeed" (64). Despite the clipped and simple diction, its segregated forms begin to suffuse each other under the pressure not only of feeling but of sheer phonetic proximity. Among the echoes sent rippling across the ridged surface of these decisive single words is precisely the pivotal linkage that seems to generate alike the "so" of both mortal analogy and its redemptive final prospect, with "soul" taken up in "*close*."

There is an even more famous and debated closural passage in Dickens, of course, having also to do with a first-person narrator's conjugal prospects. It occasions, in fact, one of Dickens's rare comments on the quality of his own language. Notoriously ceding to the suggestions of his friend Bulwer-Lytton to soften the ending of *Great Expectations* by reuniting Pip and Estella, Dickens wrote in a letter to his friend Forster, about a coda both tempered and embellished at once, that "I have put in as pretty a little piece of writing as I could."[3] But how might this self-styled prettiness connive to qualify reunion by keeping before us the unhealed scars of the past, as many have suspected about the passage from less stylistic evidence? The interpolated material begins with Pip's lingering approach to the demolished Satis house, a place yet again of pure projection, but this time the projection (at least at first) of memory rather than fantasy. "There was no house now, no brewery, no building whatever left, but the wall of the old garden" (59). Grammar negates the tripled shapes of the past even before the incremental syntax attaches "whatever left" as a kind of afterthought. The approached "place" is all "clear space" now, walled and evacuated. Again a loosened, bidirectional syntax adjusts the ensuing "passage" of Pip into his own decimated past: "A gate in the fence standing ajar, I pushed it open, and went in." As the freestanding clausal grammar (a rare format for Dickens) half insinuates by ghostly apposition, Pip alone can offer his own and only access to a past scene on which he has always kept, as it were, a door open.

This same stress on nostalgic subjectivity, with the "I" still "ajar" to desire, is carried through to the end of the novel by the complicities of diction and syntax. A metaphor of writing or drawing ("trace out") is immediately called upon to suggest the etching of memory, all while an emphatic parallel syntax seems fading away into the deletions of ellipsis: "I could trace out where every part of the old house had been, and where the brewery had been, and where the gates, and where the casks." Dickensian sentence structure has never been (and this is saying something) more sure of itself. So long gone, these last features of desolation have been deprived of all being (and its predicative grammar of "had been") save that of the mind's phantom tracery. Into this tenuous delineation of the passed and the absent, a "solitary figure" shows itself. Or not quite. Rather than "revealed itself," the "figure showed itself aware of me," checked in full disclosure by the predicate adjective ("aware") of the sentence's reflexive construction. Across seven more repetitions of the neuter pronoun ("it" for "figure" rather than person), Pip's language must slowly and tentatively retrieve the eroticized body of Estella: a figment of residual desire before it is an incarnate intention. "As I drew nearer it," for example, "it was about to turn away, when it stopped, and let me come up with it" – both catch up to it, of course, and also "come up with it" in the other sense by virtually engendering its manifestation: surfacing it from repressed desire, conjuring its renewed promise.

Such is the doubleness, slippage, and reversion that layers this closing scene even before arriving at the novel's voluminously debated last sentence, where it is grammar once more, every bit as much as the semantic evasion discussed by critics, that continues to equivocate the straightforwardness of romantic uplift – and again by pivoting around the shifting valence of the verb "show," hovering still in a syntactic limbo between self-revelation and external disclosure. This whole ameliorative finale is conditioned, of course, by the novel's recurrent symbolic "mists," rising momentarily now, lifting their ban on vision, so that "in all the broad expanse of tranquil light they showed to me" (59) we might well expect "showed" as a verb of disclosure or prophecy – awaiting its object rather than already closed round on it. Not so. What we are likely to have read as an adverbial phrase ("in all the . . . light," taking "they" as subject) is unfolded instead as the beginning of a fuller subordinate clause, awaiting the subsequent main syntax of the sentence. The passage has immediately moved, that is, to activate its inversion of subject/object relations across the delayed logic of its transitive grammar, laying further stress on the continuing subjectivity of desire's double negation. Yet again Dickensian sentence structure has turned upon its heels, so that "in all the . . . light [which] they showed to me, I saw no shadow of another parting from her."

In this self-displacing grammar across the phonetic dilation of "show" into "*shadow*," the dissipated mists show forth nothing but the light they otherwise occlude, from within whose ambient gleam the squint of prediction reveals no silhouette of loss. The eighteenth-century inflections of *Pickwick Papers* are now decades behind us. The litotes ("not un-") of Dickensian comic style has been mellowed – and complicated – to the suspended disbelief of hedged confidence (the negated negativity of the echoic "no shadow"). The point isn't that Pip finally sees the light. Rather the opposite. Flooded by a suddenly uncurtained field of brightness, bedazzled once more by the figure of expectancy (in Dickens sustained irony), the long-enthralled subject of desire sees for a moment, at least, no darkening nonlight. All we can locate for sure in this closing moment is respite rather than repair. Transfiguring his own original intent for the passage with such "pretty" revision, Dickens develops its true beauty in the unravelling tug of elegy at the thinly stitched hem of restitution. Language for Dickens is once more the very medium of nontranslucence, elastic, volatile, and elusive, a language whose writing – delegated to his invested narrator as Pip's own "tracing out" – frays the very assurances it seems to bind. Dickens and language: the deepest pact of his genius sealed yet again in one of its most exacting and exquisite tests.

NOTES

1 The capped word is actually botched by a typo, normalized to "ARE," in the otherwise scrupulous new Norton Critical edition of the novel, ed. Edgar Rosenberg (Norton, 1999), p. 169. As a check on this misprint, see for example (following all other previous editions) *Great Expectations*, ed. Angus Calder (Harmondsworth: Penguin, 1980), p. 241.

2 George Eliot, *Middlemarch*, ed. Bert G. Hornback (Norton, 1977), p. 134.

3 *Great Expectations*, ed. Rosenberg, p. 536, quoting Dickens's letter to John Forster, 1 July 1861. This is an emendation in the novel's conclusion that has brought forth, according to Rosenberg, some "hundred-odd commentators (hyphen optional)," through whose claims and counterclaims he wittily sorts in his giant afterpiece, "Putting an End to *Great Expectations*," pp. 491–527.

FURTHER READING

Alter, Robert. "Reading Style in Dickens." *Philosophy and Literature* 20:2 (April 1996), 130–37.

Brook, G. L. *The Language of Dickens*. Andre Deutsch, 1970.

Newsom, Robert. "Style of Dickens." In *Oxford Reader's Companion to Dickens*, edited by Paul Schlicke. Oxford University Press, 1999, pp. 541–45.

Sorensen, Knud. "Charles Dickens: Linguistic Innovator." *English Studies* 65 (June 1984), 237–47.

Stewart, Garrett. *Dickens and the Trials of Imagination*. Harvard University Press, 1974.

11

NICOLA BRADBURY

Dickens and the form of the novel

By accident and by design, Dickens effectively determined the shape, pace, structure, and texture of his own novel form, and developed both professional and aesthetic expectations of the writer and reader in the production and reception of his work.[1] He made the novel what it was for the Victorians, creating and managing an appetite for fictions that would in turn make both imaginative and social demands. Throughout his career, the arts of the storyteller, the deferral tactics of the *Arabian Nights*, the capacity of the journalist to observe and report, the power of the satirist for reform and of the clown or tragedian to move an audience were brought into play, not despite the constraints of part-publication, but actually by exploiting serial form.

Novels in parts, whether separate volumes or shorter units, were not unknown in the eighteenth century, but it was Dickens with *Pickwick Papers* in 1836 who brought part-publication to such success that it became the dominant pattern for the novel through most of the Victorian period.[2] This was Dickens's first novel, but not his first work. He was a practiced writer, the author of *Sketches by Boz*, when Chapman and Hall asked him to supply the text for a publication in monthly numbers to accompany a series of etchings by Robert Seymour. This artist, in fact, committed suicide before the second monthly issue came out; his replacement was unsatisfactory, and Dickens, now the senior member of a creative partnership, proposed Hablot K. Browne as illustrator. Their collaboration was successful: *Pickwick* achieved phenomenal popularity, with monthly sales rising from 400 to 40,000 once Sam Weller entered the story; Dickens's career as a professional novelist took off, and Browne, as "Phiz," continued as his principal illustrator from *Pickwick* to *Little Dorrit*. All Dickens's novels appeared in parts,[3] whether separately published in paper-bound pamphlets with illustrated covers and advertisements, or as part of the journals he both contributed to and edited throughout his working life. This system of publication became a part of "that mysterious paper currency which circulates in London"

(*OMF* 12) of Victorian literature, with complex cultural, economic, and aesthetic implications for the novel form.[4]

Serial publication,[5] either in weekly or more generally twenty monthly numbers at a shilling a time (the last a double-issue with Part 19, and costing two shillings), brought novels within the budget of many who could not afford one and a half guineas for a three-volume work. The evidence of audience response in sales figures, like the visible output of the author, engendered an economy of production and consumption: a measure of the dialog between the novelist and his public. Such close correspondence extended from the financial to aesthetic spheres of influence. Part-publication enabled Dickens to generate and sustain levels of curiosity, suspense, audience manipulation, over the ungovernable pace of reading. It also exposed the author to the pressure of public demands in the development of character and plot. Serialization, in a sense, foreshadows the dramatic rapport which Dickens later developed with live audiences in his hugely popular public readings.[6]

The first signs of this process appear in *Pickwick* as structural features of fictive form. Those two great standbys of the storyteller, the traveler's tale and the true romance, each in their comically deflected mode, its humorous variant on the form, compete to organize an innocently belated exercise in the picaresque: in effect, commenting through form on fiction itself, the pleasures and dangers of nostalgia. Dickens's first novel recalls the eighteenth-century models of Fielding and Smollett, with extravagant entertainment, variety of incident, character, and tone. In *Pickwick* those shifts are accentuated by incidental stories in deviant modes: the ghost story, the debtor's, the madman's tale, which echo the themes of the main plot but in a different emotional register. Here shock tactics modulate into complex form, and the beginnings of what the Russian theorist Bakhtin has called dialogism,[7] where mixed modes (Pickwick's gentlemanly assumptions, Sam Weller's comic grotesque) jostle in counterpoint with competing ideologies (one nostalgic for eighteenth-century rationalism, the other engaging a new realism with entrepreneurial extravagance). But Dickens might have found a source for such formal play in fiction, with the great *Ür*-text of novelistic fabrication, Cervantes's *Don Quixote* (1604–14). The Knight of the Sad Countenance and Sancho Panza stand behind Mr. Pickwick and Sam Weller, while Quixote's romantic delusion over the lady Dulcinea del Toboso is comically inverted in Pickwick's misunderstandings with his landlady Mrs. Bardell.

In *Pickwick*, the skill of the story-teller is often ventriloquized into surrogate narrators such as Alfred Jingle, "the man with the brown paper parcel." His tales, and others, share certain characteristics. Narrative economy, often through grammatical elision, acts as a dramatic device of emphasis. Counterpointing this, however, runs a tendency to figurative or alliterative elaboration supported by sharp graphic detail and macabre material. Sometimes the imagery takes over. Jingle's preposterous "romance" of Donna Christina illustrates this:

> "[S]plendid creature – loved me to distraction – jealous father – high-souled daughter – handsome Englishman – Donna Christina in despair – prussic acid – stomach pump in my portmanteau – operation performed – old Bolero in ecstasies – consent to our union – join hands and floods of tears – romantic story – very."
>
> (PP 2)

The tale skips in and out of absurdity along a brilliantly alliterative line of imaginative logic, from "despair" and "prussic acid" to the "stomach pump." The action-packed sequel, veering into the criminal mode, emerges with all the aplomb of detective fiction. Donna Christina dies, while as for her father:

> "Remorse and misery," replied the stranger. "Sudden disappearance – talk of the whole city – search made everywhere – without success – public fountain in the great square suddenly ceased playing – weeks elapsed – still a stoppage – workmen employed to clean it – water drawn off – father-in-law discovered sticking head first in the main pipe, with a full confession in his right boot – took him out, and the fountain played away again, as well as ever."

The argument by images leads inexorably from floods of tears to the stopped fountain. The romance matter of love, despair, and death stands in macabre counterpoint to the forensic diction, as the professional impersonality of "search made everywhere" gives way to a triumphant whodunnit. Jingle's tall tale exhibits in brief the construction and transgression of norms of narrative decorum. It is outrageously entertaining, but has further narrative functions. Dickens also uses it economically to expose the teller and reveal his audience. Their responses vary from the gravely mistaken Pickwick's "Evidently a travel-ler in many countries, and a close observer of men and things" to the roman-tic Tupman: "Mr. Tupman said nothing; but he thought of Donna Christina, the stomach pump, and the fountain; and his eyes filled with tears." The nar-rative is virtually rewritten in their reactions; but the novelist draws it neatly to a close in Mr. Tupman's prolongation of the play on words in the Spanish tale. Stylistic extravagance and structural economy vie for dominance. The part must compete with the whole, demand and reward instant attention, yet con-tribute to the cumulative effect as the novel grows. Indeed, Jingle's manic, improvisational style, characteristic of the chaotic circumstances of *Pickwick's* origin, gives way to a more sustained, though still varied, structural develop-ment when Sam Weller arrives and the novel discovers its direction.

The subsidiary stories of *Pickwick* develop some thematic coherence while permitting variety of pace and effect, which works indirectly to enhance the innocent Pickwick's stature. He acquires experience, as it were, by proxy: not in terms of plot, but of the whole reading process of the work which grows up around him. In *Oliver Twist* Dickens exploits the productive economy of serial form in a more disciplined and daring way. The dramatic principle of contrast is marshaled through the model of melodrama. Indeed, the text proclaims: "It is the custom on the stage, in all good murderous melodramas, to present the tragic and the comic scenes, in as regular alternation, as the layers of red and white in a side of streaky well-cured bacon" (*OT* 17). Dickens develops this crude device, not merely for effect, but as both structural principle and thematic schema, since in all melodrama, good struggles with evil. *Oliver Twist* is organized, not quite like streaky bacon, but through the polarities of country and city, youth and age, innocence and experience, poverty and riches, light and dark, magistrate and criminal, female and male: some thematic, some symbolic pairs. So the novel presents two contrasting worlds, but poses the question, how are they contingent? The physical movement of the boy conducts readers through giddy textual oscillations between shifting modes and tones: comic and terrible, sensation novel, Newgate, and pastoral. While the plot veers spectacularly, melodramatically, from mystery and suspense to crisis and catastrophe, with sensational reversals in every line of development, both character and symbol develop in ways which combine melodramatic alternation with novelistic progression.

The tendency is for the plot to mark differences, while symbolism unites the diverse areas of the novel world. But Dickens's use of coincidence subverts this function of the plot, and his use of interwoven storylines and repeated motifs suggests that action itself may have a symbolic force. The novel moves from opposition toward reverberation. Observation, recognition, and repetition operate structurally in the reader's shifting engagement with the work. Melodrama and coincidence contribute to this expressive modulation, while symbolism competes with plot in the organization of the novel. The novel form actually expresses the balance and conflict which lie at the heart of its themes and which also control its workings: the active and passive aspects of experience itself. Finally, however, these two strains move apart. There are two quite distinct endings. Melodrama for Fagin, Bill Sikes, and for Nancy, all obliterated in blood as the dark side of the novel is consumed in symbolic gloom; a neat plot resolution for Oliver, finally secured with Rose Maylie and Mr. Brownlow in comic romance. Such a pattern of "multiple endings" is one aspect of form Dickens developed through his career, and it significantly modifies the commonly recognized motif of "closure."

Dickens was already at work on his next novel while publishing *Oliver Twist*. *Nicholas Nickleby* relishes the diverse possibilities of the form: melodrama, oppression, pantomime, romance; an intricate plot, a sustaining myth of origins, a startling deployment of coincidence. The novel under Dickens's management can take the strain of proliferating modes, extreme characterization, and episodic development – can sell itself, indeed, to an enthusiastic public.[8] The Victorian novel is not a single formal category but compounded of diverse modes.[9] Besides the eighteenth-century picaresque or rogue novel in comic or satiric mode, episodically constructed on the adventures of a hero's journey, there was also the psychological tradition growing through romance and sensation novels and through gothic extravagance. Sir Walter Scott indicated the historical scope of the form. Newgate novels, dealing with the sensational world of violent crime and Newgate prison, and "silver fork" romances of upper-class manners offered contrasting approaches to contemporary low and high society. Dickens's work as a journalist in both streets and law courts and as House of Commons reporter added to his range, practiced in capturing attention, with an eye for detail and an ear for speech patterns. And he never forgot the importance of his earliest narrative experience as a child enthralled and terrified by his nurse's stories. Fairy-tale and fantasy stirred deep responses. So did Dickens's "artistic" heritage, both visual and literary. Hogarth pointed social satire through pictorial narrative, scene and sequence, the management of detail and design. Shakespeare, above all, was a great precursor, echoed thoughout Dickens's work, and contributing perhaps most importantly to his development of complex form.

Control, balance, and design, always tested by contrary effects of chaotic proliferation and disorder, are the two forces at work in Dickens's development of the novel form. Inevitably his experience and professionalism grow with success. "Boz" entitles himself "the Inimitable," an intriguing variant on serial form. He is an actor, a manager, an artist, an editor. He publishes other Victorian novelists. He is a paterfamilias and clubbable literary friend. Professionally he works toward legal copyright in England and America. Socially alert, he campaigns against notorious abuses. Dickens is progressing toward that figure of the Establishment who will be buried in Westminster Abbey, to strikingly public and international shows of grief. But his creative energy issues in challenges, to literature, his audience, himself, exploring an increasingly complex sense of the self within society. Dickens's is a highly conscious and provocative exploitation of the range and power of the novel form. From the episodic picaresque of *Pickwick* and the crude if well-cured melodrama of *Oliver Twist*, his work evolves in a dialogic sequence whose style and structure are deeply connected with his themes.

Dickens's powers in creation of character and as satirist of social evils have always been acknowledged but often supposed to be superficial, a matter of an eye and ear for idiosyncracies. It is his formal development of chaotic and productive tensions in the novel through what may be diagnosed as sympathetic, inductive, corrective, and affective structures that harnesses such immediate effects to deeper understanding.

Dombey and Son illustrates this. Dickens now develops a tighter form. With *Dombey* he began a practice that he would maintain throughout the rest of his writing career: the writing out of copious notes (known as number plans or "mems") as a guide to future chapters, timing and pacing of plot incidents, characters, names, titles, etc. The composition of the mems before the actual composition of the book is a major reason for the tighter organization of *Dombey and Son* and the novels that followed (in contrast to the "looseness" of Dickens's earlier novels).[10] Instead of episodic journey narrative the story is organized around a single location, though one with many levels of meaning: the House of Dombey. Authorial negotiation with subject and audience and readerly consumption are brought into line with business practice by the full title: *DEALINGS WITH THE FIRM OF DOMBEY AND SON Wholesale, Retail and for Exportation BY Charles Dickens*. This ambitious transaction foregrounds the mercantile motif which governs both the economic and social worlds of the novel, but it also alerts us to the strategies of the novelist. From the title page, each element works, however outlandishly, toward a complex whole, which is both in some sense an analog of Dombey himself, a compound of conflicting desires awaiting reconciliation, and also an investigation of the individual in relation to his world that mediates author, reader, and text, and questions issues of identity and values. The business world ties in with the private through ambition, fantasy, desire, expressed through structure and style. The interaction of different dynamics provides the machinery and the texture of the novel. Chapters, parts, and monthly numbers function structurally and rhetorically as well as contributing to the narrative, and the 19/20 part serialization is "architecturally" constructed in four equal sections, with critical turning points at the end of number 5 (Paul's death), 10 (Dombey's remarriage), 15 (Edith's departure), and 18 (the death of Carker), resolving in the final double number.[11]

The first number not only introduces the main characters of the novel, opens the story, and indicates the main themes, but also through a kind of accordion effect between the four chapters it articulates the dynamic rhythms of the work and the conjunction of a working world, a financial, social, historical context, with the inner workings of the individual, so that both are actually felt in reading. Here the ground is laid for what Dickens designated in a letter to John Forster "the struggle with himself, which goes on in all such obstinate natures" (25–26 July 1846, Pilgrim 4.590) that will provide both the vital thread and twist between the Dombey of the opening and the close, and the dynamic of the novel. The birth of Dombey's son and the death of his wife, all in chapter 1, enact in narrative and symbolic terms two possible courses for his central conflict. The assertions of chapter 1 are reinforced in chapter 3 with the treatment of the dismal house of Dombey and the theme of identity inscribed in the name at Paul's christening. But chapter 2 turns aside to Miss Tox, the Chicks, and the Toodles, to life after death; while chapter 4 brings in Walter Gay, a future "son." Dark and light strands of the work run side by side, analogs challenging unitary development.

These seeming shifts of subject, theme, and tone continue to stretch the reader. While Dombey is the focus of Part 1, attention shifts to Florence in Part 2, then to Paul in Part 3. Both Dombey and Florence are bound up with Paul until his death in Part 5. In Part 6 both are given up to mourning and frustrated love. And so it goes on. The rivalry between the Carker brothers acts as a subplot to Dombey's inner struggles, while the story of Alice and Mrs. Brown opens out the history of Mrs. Dombey and glances at Florence's crisis of love and duty. Multiple narrative lines, plot complications, and different styles make reading the novel increasingly strenuous, yet this directly inducts readers into the experience of the work, which involves exploring the energies of a damaged and damaging personality through the rhetorical polyphony of modes within the novel form.

One example of this multivalent functioning of parts and aspects of the novel within the whole is chapter 6. After the first number setting out Dombey's ambitions and hinting too at the contrary thrust of the narrative, chapter 5 opens the second part with Paul's christening. But the day is more funereal than celebratory. And chapter 6, though it appears to be on a different subject, can also be read as an extended ironic comment on Dombey's expectations, and the course of the novel as a whole. It describes Staggs's Gardens – a place in which Dombey could have no interest, but which is the home of little Paul's nurse, and where she is taking the child, contrary to Mr. Dombey's orders. The strange place-name acts as a sly dig at Dombey's recent christening. Worse, the whole neighbourhood has just felt "The first shock of a great earthquake": in literal terms, the approach of the railroad, but a foreshadowing of the disruption Dombey is to suffer. Images of destruction and construction are elaborated with Dickensian relish, and they actually constitute an obstruction in the narrative; yet they carry symbolic significance as psychological figures "unintelligible as any dream."

Long and short paragraphs alternate, with images of location and displacement. But on the way home, "wild confusion" strikes the party, for "surprises, like misfortunes, rarely come alone." The comical rush of improbabilities here, from the assault on Polly's boy to the narrow escape from a carriage accident, from the runaway mad bull to Florence's getting lost and kidnapped by the witch-like Mrs. Brown, shows narrative plausibility overrun by incident, defying the sensible reader's disbelief. Fairy-tale displaces realism. Florence's new shoe is replaced by young Walter "as the Prince in the story might have fitted Cinderella's slipper on." Her rescuer is like Dick Whittington and Saint George. Yet fairy-tale, myth, and legend rhetorically assert a fictional world opposed to Dombey's calculations, and in this way narrative mode contributes to the oblique attack made throughout chapter 6 on his assumptions.

Despite its surface confusion, this episode is far from extraneous to the development of the work. The chapter has its own shape and growth. The image of Florence lost in London takes color from the confusion attributed to the streets themselves, and it can be linked with the loss of her mother at the opening of the novel, and the death of little Paul which will come soon. But the incident also foreshadows her later flight from the House of Dombey, while her rescue now introduces her future husband. Florence's escape will follow on Edith's elopement, a catastrophe which also has links with Mrs. Brown, through her daughter's alliance with Carker. Besides these intricacies of plot and theme the chapter provides a pattern for the novel in terms of structure and style. The variety of subject, theme, and fictional mode, moving into the city, the world, into other homes, and out of the claustrophobia of the opening chapters into fantastic versions of insecurity, suffering, and loss – and of redemption too: these extraordinary deviations from the course set by Mr. Dombey accurately predicate the novel as a whole. *Dombey and Son* will swerve away from him and his world and its mode of naturalism, and will indulge in highly plotted and fantastical excursions; but only to return, with Florence, and with the conclusion that all such escapades are in effect comments on the central experience, and that resolution lies in reconciliation with him.

Because, however, we are not allowed to focus on single stories or individual characters, or to relax into one fictional mode, by the time Dombey himself faces ruin there is a kind of relief. Our readerly exhaustion corresponds to Dombey's collapse. Then, in a brilliant fusion of symbol and image, the reflections of Dombey and his daughter are framed in a mirror, united in mutual recognition;[12] the perfect, fragile figure of return, of restoration, not least in its quality of repetition. What Dombey sees, and we see with him, is what he might already have known. The narrative union between characters corresponds in plot terms to the psychological drama creating integrity within the individual. This momentary and still imperfect apprehension of wholeness comes with a sense of relief, rather than triumph, recognition rather than new perception. It is the conclusion of a work in which imaginative unity contends throughout with disjunctive or dialogic tactics: where the reader's textual experience mirrors the protagonist's psychological processes.

The personal and cultural crisis of *Dombey and Son* is reflected in a proliferation of novelistic effects which amounts to a multiple-personality disorder of the form: except that this is orchestrated chaos. Later novels demonstrate further developments in affective form, including both inductive and corrective effects, leading the reader "By experience," as Mr. Bumble wished the Law would learn (*OT* 51), toward fuller participation in the work, both through sympathy and conversely in necessary distrust. While familiar myths and fairy-tale motifs entice the imagination to anticipate certain rewards, the novel form can also frustrate and redirect expectations. Dickens uses this pattern of temptation and surprise to stimulate and investigate reader response. Take the old topos of romance, adulterous love. *Dombey and Son*, *David Copperfield*, and *Bleak House* betray a fascination with this subject, but they also explore its allure in a deconstructive way. The supposed signs of adultery appeal to readerly knowingness. The mere suspicion of illicit passion tempts the reader with its telltale signs to construe a hidden narrative, which is yet to be condemned, and not least for its deceptions. Here is a paradox, an exercise in readerly complicity, which Dickens conducts with both cunning and delicacy through a series of works in which the supposition of guilt rebounds on the overactive imagination when the novels prove to require a deeper and more charitable kind of understanding. Edith Dombey does not yield herself to Carker. Annie Strong, for all her disordered dress and lost cherry ribbon, which David Copperfield reluctantly interprets as infallible signals of a fall, is better known in loving innocence through the simple trust of the guileless Mr. Dick. Esther Summerson's censorious godmother is herself felled by a stroke when reading the story of the woman taken in sin. Through Dickens's manipulation of the novel form and its interpretive conspiracy, the fable of adultery is revealed as a shameful fabrication, its guilt displaced into a narratological drama of betrayal in which the reader is directly implicated. Discovering the "true" fiction is a heuristic process, yet this *éducation sentimentale* is also a violation of innocence, which can never fully be recuperated.

Half-hinting at the unspeakable or working through refraction and reflection to constitute a narrative of indirect revelation, Dickens's novel form flirts with shadow texts and potential tales, inviting interpretive energy even in excess, but not without reckoning. In *Bleak House* Dickens makes an important contribution to the development of detective fiction, and he implicates the reader in its processes; but he also exposes the form to serious questioning. A controlled structure, the selective deployment of a double narrative technique, interwoven plots moving between locations and groups of characters, shifting chronological shape, style, and fictive mode, lead to the readerly imperative of interpretation. Offering and withholding information, the novel moves fitfully, and the effect is to depute to the reader the function of detective which is thematically essential to the work but ethically dubious.

Chapter 22, introducing detective officer Bucket, demonstrates how this narrative entrapment works. The reader is limited to the view of the bewildered law stationer Mr. Snagsby, repeatedly surprised by the revelations in Tulkinghorn's secretive chambers and appalled at the spectacle of the streets outside. Moving through description, narrative, dialog, and dramatic action, this chapter has every kind of storytelling, stimulating curiosity within a fine circle of mystery, leaving everyone but the lawyer and detective just as much in the dark while telling them just what they think they need to know. Yet throughout the chapter there are hints that this surface level of interest is not the whole story. What Bucket can find out, what Tulkinghorn can tell, is not enough. Bucket can operate within the maze of London, and Tulkinghorn can pay him for results, but neither of them can foresee the consequences. The murder of Tulkinghorn by his agent Mademoiselle Hortense is directly motivated by their business deal here. Their tool Jo will die of the disease caught from those he is trying to help. Esther will be disfigured by his illness. Her mother will be discovered, and she too will die. All these plot events work as symptoms, not of a narrative line, but the symbolic setting of the story. It is only the thoroughly mystified, horrified Mr. Snagsby who sees that "infernal gulf" for what it is: hell. It is by sharing Mr. Snagsby's confusion, not Bucket's professionalism or Tulkinghorn's control, that the reader is reduced to a kind of helplessness more open to experience than the knowing detective.

Dickens extends the scope and gravity of this structural technique working through induction and correction to a complex affective involvement for the reader with the novel form. More than the lure of mystery, tension, surprise, the mechanisms required for successful serialization sustain prolonged and profound enquiries into the conditions and values of imaginative life. Opening *Little Dorrit*, Dickens wrote to Forster: "It struck me that it would be a new thing to shew people coming together, in a chance way, as fellow-travellers, and being in the same place ignorant of one another, as happens in life; and to connect them afterwards, and to make the waiting for that connection a part of the interest" (19 August 1855, Pilgrim 7.692–3). And this "new" fictional technique dependent on ignorance, chance, and deferral develops into an oblique endorsement of the heroine's quiet patience.

There is one theme unifying this text: imprisonment, which provides plot, location, and imagery, and inescapably binds the constrictions of social institutions with the habitual constraints of the individual psyche. Dickens told Forster that "Society, the Circumlocution Office and Gowan, are of course three parts of the one idea and design" (Forster, 8.1). Yet for each structural or symbolic element of *Little Dorrit* inscribing imprisonment, another aspect of the novel can be found working against that doom. Due order of law, for example, is countered by chronological disruption in the narrative, which throws up good fortune as well as punishment. The twists of plot argue against inevitability. The division of the novel into two books entitled "Poverty" and "Riches" allows for a see-saw effect; this is further varied by every kind of textural multiplicity within each volume. The thematic balance of poverty and riches, prison and liberty, old and young, and so on, is disconcerted by the urge toward narrative resolution in the developing story-line. Deep confusion dissolves rigid boundaries between the fictive and reading experience. Disparate idioms, foreign words and phrases, and bizarre variations on native speech help orchestrate a fictional cacophony which has ideological, ethical, and even spiritual implications: the biblical model of Babel is invoked on the first page of the text. Finally, there are within the work both episodes and characters conveying notes of unresolved protest, while the "happy ending" is presented with a restraint inimical to fairy-tale conclusion.

Little Dorrit's displacement of the protagonist as overt center of interest in narrative, plot, and theme can be seen as part of a larger development in Dickens. Here, as in *Dombey and Son* and *Bleak House*, the dislocation or marginalization of the protagonist may be read as a narrative version of social disorder, expressing the imbalance of a political, economic, and ethical hegemony, and its destructive effects on the individual. Yet however powerless, Little Dorrit shifts the dynamic axis of the work. She is more than a victim of injustice or type of the oppressed: she has her own kind of strength, which is conveyed through the interest she quietly sustains. Rather than depicting utterly hopeless confusion, corruption, and constraint, the "prison" of Victorian realist determinism, Dickens demonstrates through different aspects of the novel form the contention, however unequal, of two sets of values and two forces: coercion and acceptance, activity and patience.

The chaotic effects of earlier Dickens are marshaled in the two books of *Little Dorrit* into a monumental narrative of the struggle between two models of social existence, two kinds of novel, two qualities of being: the active and realistic, or the responsive, interiorized, and imaginative. Both are subject to chance but seek out a larger pattern, whether spiritual or secular, destiny or determinism, shaping experience. The dynamic key to these works lies in the way that Dickens harnesses the tensions and pleasures of the novel form with the experience it addresses. However panoramic the social picture or extravagant the emotional register, they are conveyed in reading not discursively but formally through the fluctuating responses required and rewarded by the text.

Nowhere is this more fascinating than in *Great Expectations*. Dickens's most tautly condensed novel is brief by Victorian standards, but complex. The novel form is used to express both the range and the painful constrictions of Pip's human experience, in fortune, in love, in time, in being itself. How? First, through elements of myth, folk, and fairy-tale.[13] However pertinent to Victorian social structures of class and gender, the novel invokes deeper fantasies. The orphan child, wicked stepmother, ice maiden, and fairy godmother; the testing encounter with a frightful stranger; sudden riches, snatched away: this is a tale of familiar anxieties and longing. The effect of recognition is intensified by selecting Pip as first-person narrator, at once the helpless subject and powerful agent of the text, caught between memory and desire. The sense of experience in process lying behind a narrative in construction is evoked, not related. Pip's story is shadowed and illuminated through echoes and reflections in situations, characters, ambitions, repressions, throughout the text. While Magwitch makes his very own gentleman, Pip creates the Frankenstein's monster of the boy in top boots. If Orlick is Pip's secret demon, Trabb's boy flaunts his self-importance in open burlesque. Even Wopsle as Waldengarver stages lessons in pretension; while Shakespeare's *Hamlet* haunts the novel like a father's ghost.

Serial form accentuates the sense of process, movement in time, in this articulate structure of comparisons and contrasts, just as in the manipulation of plot.[14] Working with the reader's own expectations, anticipation, and disappointments, *Great Expectations* makes imaginative use of the divisions and delays of part-publication. The shorter interval between issues resulting from the novel's weekly serialization accentuates the sense of rapid fluctuations in Pip's experience, which also shifts suddenly in the text between interior and exterior scenes, and between Pip's imagination and the dramatic world. The phases of Pip's experience are structured in three "stages" as if they were discrete, from childhood longing to the "gay fiction" of enjoyment and its aftermath; but the irony is that they follow inevitably in sequence. The catastrophe concluding stage 2 which takes Pip by surprise is actually implicit in the sudden turn of his fortunes at the end of stage 1; and both derive from the moment recorded on the first page of the novel, when Pip meets Magwitch just as he begins to make out "the identity of things." But this strong pattern of Pip's fortunes is overlaid by the shadow plot of his desires. The novel has two "openings": first in the graveyard, then again when Pip goes to Satis House, the moment selective memory prefers to suppose the real beginning of his adventures. Strangely, there are also two endings. Not simply because Dickens was persuaded to alter the original, where Pip, walking with little Pip in London, met Estella, now widowed but remarried. In the published conclusion, Dickens found a form which perfectly balances closure against an open ending. Pip "saw no shadow of another parting" from Estella; the ambiguous phrase allows two distinct, even competing, readings: romance or realism.

Doubling, persistent throughout Dickens, is the dominant motif of his last complete novel, *Our Mutual Friend*. Here he returns to themes, situations, devices he has used before, and exploits the elements of the novel form with baroque extravagance. Even the Postscript reads like a more assured version of the design announced to Forster as "a new thing" in *Little Dorrit*; for now Dickens knows what he is doing, and proclaims that he knows it, and that we, his readers, can take pleasure in that certainty: "To keep for a long time unsuspected, yet always working itself out, another purpose originating in that leading incident, and turning it to a pleasant and useful account at last, was at once the most interesting and the most difficult part of my design."

Exploring the issue of identity, the text both proffers and obstructs the problem through two conflicting techniques: on the one hand concealment (the unidentified corpse, the hidden history), but on the other hand, doubling, leading to an information overload. As the novel develops, John Harmon, alias Rokesmith, alias Julius Handford, conceals his first identity by assuming a number of others, taking a string of pseudonyms; yet his purpose is not to disguise but reveal the truth of his real relations with those whose values are confused by worldly fortune. Unlike Pip's first-person tale, caught between memory and desire in quest of its own integrity, this apparently "omniscient" narrative is effectively made up of its characters' misapprehensions and concealed designs. The confusions of a complex multiplot form work to destabilize security, and indirectly to create the conditions for a more philosophical or spiritual understanding. Amid the novel's varying levels of consciousness and purpose even life and death are rendered provisional states, not absolute categories. Then, as the Harmon plot begins to resolve and his identity is established, the thematic shadow plot of Wrayburn and Headstone (refracted further through Rogue Riderhood) grows increasingly troubled.

It is in Wrayburn himself, and the knot of characters surrounding him, rather than in Harmon, who engineers so much of the plot, that the dynamic of *Our Mutual Friend* works itself out most energetically. What remains romance for Harmon, always mere pretence, and always liable to be unveiled, has all the dangerous immediacy of psychological realism in Wrayburn's case, where the doubling and deceits are obsessive, involuntary, externalized in dramatic action, and always threatening further complications. Wrayburn, Headstone, and Riderhood are all three figures of desire: an appetite implicitly without end, and by its nature therefore self-contradictory. The antagonism between these disturbingly interchangeable figures dramatizes this contradiction. There is also an internal conflict. The object of desire, for all its necessary otherness, can also be seen as a projection of selfish need. And this appears in both the disparity and the congruence of ambitions between the three men. The distinctions between characters and plots dissolve in their mutual obsessions; the dramatic plot both literally and symbolically engulfs both Wrayburn and eventually Headstone and Riderhood too in the waters flowing to the Lock. Their immersion, more critical than Harmon's imagined drowning, has the potential to extinguish or to change their being.

Dickens's development of the novel form invites quite distinct critical and theoretical approaches. A historian of publishing might note his remarkable expansion of the market, stylistic "branding" by the Inimitable, and attention to consumer demand. Analyses allied to structuralism and its heirs might emphasize patterns of binary opposition and the inevitable breakdown of such patterns in the face of Dickensian multiplicity. Dickens's manipulation of story displays the ancient and effective patterns of plot and subplot, peripeteia or reversal, crisis and catastrophe, together with a peculiarly Victorian interest in the temptations and problems of coincidence and closure: devices which might overstretch readerly credulity. Here poetics verges on reader-response criticism, together with generic recognition of the various modes in play in the Victorian novel besides realism: from melodrama to crime fiction, and such traditions as myth and fairy-tale, or even popular ballad, which Dickens incorporated into his work. Bakhtinian dialogism offers an ideological as well as an aesthetic interpretation of such carnivalesque displacement of a single tone by obstreperous polyphony. Bakhtin indeed allows celebration of both Dickens's comedy and sentiment: the great selling points to his early readers, which have since been obscured by solemn analyses. While Dickens, like all notable writers, may seem to have anticipated all subsequent critical approaches, his strength is still, as it always was, in his wide popular appeal.

NOTES

1 See Grahame Smith, *Charles Dickens: A Literary Life* (Macmillan, 1996).
2 See John L. Sutherland, *Victorian Novelists and Publishers* (University of Chicago Press and Athlone Press, 1976).
3 See Robert L. Patten, *Charles Dickens and his Publishers* (Clarendon Press, 1978).

4 Kathleen Tillotson, *Novels of the 1840s* (Oxford University Press, 1954) was among the first to discuss this critically.

5 See J. Don Vann, *Victorian Novels in Serial* (Modern Language Association of America, 1985), pp. 1–17.

6 See Philip Collins, *Charles Dickens: The Public Readings* (Clarendon Press, 1975).

7 Mikhail Bakhtin, *The Dialogic Imagination: Four Essays*, ed. Michael Holquist, trans. Caryl Emerson and Michael Holquist (University of Texas Press, 1981).

8 See Paul Schlicke, *Dickens and Popular Entertainment* (Allen and Unwin, 1985).

9 Helpfully summarized by Michael Wheeler, *English Fiction of the Victorian Period 1830–1890* (Longman, 1985).

10 See Harry Stone's invaluable *Dickens's Working Notes for his Novels* (University of Chicago Press, 1987), which provides a detailed history of the "pre-life" of Dickens's novels, as well as facsimiles of all of Dickens's number plan manuscripts.

11 See William Axton, "'Keystone' Structure in Dickens' Serial Novels," *University of Toronto Quarterly* 37 (October 1967), 31–50.

12 See Terence Cave, *Recognitions: A Study in Poetics* (Clarendon Press, 1988).

13 See Harry Stone, *Dickens and the Invisible World: Fairy-Tales, Fantasy, and Novel Making* (University of Chicago Press, 1979).

14 Peter Brooks, *Reading for the Plot: Design and Intention in Narrative* (Knopf, 1984) gives a deconstructionist reading.

FURTHER READING

Axton, William. "'Keystone' Structure in Dickens' Serial Novels." *University of Toronto Quarterly* 37 (October 1967), pp. 31–50.

Bakhtin, Mikhail. *The Dialogic Imagination: Four Essays.* Edited by Michael Holquist, translated by Caryl Emerson and Michael Holquist. University of Texas Press, 1981.

Brooks, Peter. *Reading for the Plot: Design and Intention in Narrative.* Knopf, 1984.

Brown, James M. *Dickens: Novelist in the Market-Place.* Macmillan, 1982.

Patten, Robert L. *Charles Dickens and his Publishers.* Clarendon Press, 1978.

Schlicke, Paul. *Dickens and Popular Entertainment.* Allen and Unwin, 1985.

Stone, Harry (ed.). *Dickens's Working Notes for his Novels.* University of Chicago Press, 1987.

Sutherland, John L. *Victorian Novelists and Publishers.* University of Chicago Press and Athlone Press 1976.

Tillotson, Kathleen. *Novels of the 1840s.* Oxford University Press, 1954.

Vann, J. Don. *Victorian Novels in Serial.* Modern Language Association of America, 1985.

12

RICHARD L. STEIN

Dickens and illustration

Two early examples suggest the importance of visual art in Dickens's conception of his own role. One is the title of his first book, *Sketches by Boz and Cuts by Cruikshank*, which doubly insists (the parallel of the two artists, the author as sketcher) upon the similarities of writing and drawing. The other is the first image in the last number of *Nicholas Nickleby*, Daniel Maclise's portrait of Dickens, subsequently incorporated as the frontispiece to the first edition (figure 1), a formal representation of the writer and the fact of his literary success. Replacing the fourth illustration of the final number, in some sense this image also illustrates; but rather than picturing some portion of the text, the portrait refers beyond it and beyond the writer's mere textual presence to his life as a public figure. We see Charles Dickens supplanting Boz, a personage emerging from a pseudonym, his face rather than his prose the guarantor of identity, as if visuality has replaced the uncertainty of a mere name, mere words, with a self both recognizable and authentic ("Faithfully yours," as the valediction over his signature declares). With this new public image attached to his writing, Dickens complicates the very conception of his "identity" (a term that can refer to the singular essence of some thing or person as well as to its equivalence to something or someone else): to know the writer we must see his face – see it, that is, formally rendered by a major contemporary painter. Presenting the "real" Dickens with a picture, illustrating the author, the portrait locates both the writer and his fiction within Victorian visual culture.

Illustration, then, is a complex category, one in which Dickens took special interest. The term does not always refer to pictorial imagery, nor even (as the example of the *Nickleby* portrait suggests) to visual representation of prior written texts. Our sense of the word as primarily visual was only becoming widespread in the first decades of the nineteenth century, as illustrated books (which had appeared frequently in the eighteenth century) began to proliferate. According to Martin Meisel, "the pictorial sense of 'illustration' came to speak for itself" by 1844, when the *Quarterly* printed a review of

"Illustrated Books."[1] The *OED* explains that to "illustrate" first denoted verbal elucidation; its first example of "illustration" in the sense of "an illustrative picture . . . illustrating or embellishing a literary article, a book, etc.," comes from an 1816 volume called *A Cabinet Illustration of Great Britain*. John Harvey cites Lady Blessington's invitation to Harrison Ainsworth to provide accompanying text for a plate in her *Book of Beauties* (1834); the writer promised his "best efforts . . . to make my illustration of the engraving" worthy of the rest of the book.[2] In the early nineteenth century the word commonly denoted verbal explanation or exemplification, as in Harriet Martineau's *Illustrations of Political Economy* (1832–34), which elucidated economic theories as simple, fictional narratives. All the more reason why Dickens as a young, ambitious writer in the 1830s might have insisted on a parity of roles in the title of his first book. The writer also illustrates, as the subtitle of *Sketches by Boz* reminds us – *Illustrative of Every-Day Life and Every-Day People* (one section is labeled simply "Scenes"). But the changing conception of such terms, and of the respective roles of different kinds of artists, also may inform Dickens's letters directing Cruikshank and the other illustrators who made drawings for his books.

Most of Dickens's fiction was published serially, in monthly "parts" or "numbers," each typically including thirty-two pages of letter press and two illustrations.[3] Of eighteen original illustrators, some provided all the illustrations for one or more individual works, some collaborated on particular books, and some supplied only a few drawings (for instance, Edwin Landseer's only contribution was a single illustration to *The Cricket on the Hearth*).[4] This essay will focus on two illustrators, each significant in different ways. The first, Hablot K. Browne, who called himself "Phiz" (for physiognomy), illustrated ten of the fifteen novels (including collaboration with George Cattermole on *Master Humphrey's Clock*), most of Dickens's work from 1836 to 1860, and therefore is usually referred to as Dickens's principal illustrator. The other, George Cruikshank, who illustrated only two of Dickens's works – *Sketches by Boz* and *Oliver Twist* – still remains Dickens's best-known illustrator, particularly for such powerful images as "Fagin in the Condemned Cell." And since Cruikshank is also remembered for his claim (notably after the novelist's death but first made much earlier) to have originated some of the characters and situations of *Oliver Twist*, Dickens's correspondence with him may be the best place to begin considering the writer's sense of the relation between those two creative roles, between (to use the nineteenth-century terms for these practices) the work of the writer's "pen" and the illustrator's "pencil."

However we finally regard Cruikshank's claim of creative priority (Robert L. Patten's biography of Cruikshank documents its history and notes ways in which it may be partly valid), Dickens's letters of advice on particular illustrations for *Oliver Twist* suggest that a struggle for creative authority already had begun. One to "My Dear Cruikshank" from early 1838 concerns the drawing of "Mr. Bumble and Mrs. Corney Taking Tea": "I have described a *small* kettle for one on the fire – a *small* black teapot on the table with a little tray & so forth – and a two ounce tin tea cannister. Also a shawl hanging up – and the cat & kittens before the fire" (?mid-January 1838, Pilgrim 1.353). The first words encapsulate the tone and point: I have created the verbal model, your job is to provide a visual equivalent. In fact, as Patten notes, no hanging shawl appears in the passage, although Dickens may have intended to add one.[5] Not wholly accurate himself, Dickens nevertheless insists on accuracy by his illustrators – insists, that is, that they provide "faithful" rendering of details he imagined first. Jane R. Cohen observes that he "exerted unprecedented authority over everything but the actual execution of the illustrations" (Cohen, *Charles Dickens*, p. 5). His letters of instruction remind us, as they were intended to remind their recipients, that control belongs to the writer, that the "project" is his property; there is no doubt who is to understand himself as an artist, who as a mere illustrator.

Still, such letters tell only part of the story. Illustrators sometimes took a good deal of initiative, welcome or not. Dickens instructed Cruikshank not to draw "the scene of Sikes's escape." "I find, on writing it, that . . . [it] will not do for illustration. It is so very complicated, with such a multitude of figures, such violent action, and torch-light to boot, that a small plate could not take in the slightest idea of it" (?6 October 1838, Pilgrim 1.440). Ignoring this advice, Cruikshank produced one of the finest illustrations for any of the novels: narratively complex, graphically detailed, psychologically compelling, a dramatic image of a climactic scene. For Dickens, though, what counted as success in illustration may have been something simpler and more generalized. While his letters instructing artists emphasize details, he reserves fullest praise for drawings that capture a pervasive mood. In 1841 he tells George Cattermole, chosen to supply antiquarian images for *Master Humphrey's Clock*, that "this is *the very first time* any designs for what I have written have touched and moved me, and caused me to feel that they expressed the idea I had in my mind." Significantly, he also terms this "a pleasure I cannot describe to you in words" (30 January 1841, Pilgrim 2.199).[6] If visual pleasure cannot be specified verbally, perhaps the most important narrative facts are those that resist picturing. In instructions to Hablot Browne for one of the designs to *Martin Chuzzlewit*, Dickens ends a list of significant details (trees "in every stage of decay," "miserable log-houses," "a pair of rusty compasses," "Martin in shirt sleeves," etc.) emphasizing a more elusive emotional content: "Mark the only redeeming feature.

2 Hablot K. Browne ("Phiz"), "Paul and Mrs Pipchin," from *Dombey and Son* (1846–48).

Everything else dull, miserable, squalid, unhealthy, and utterly devoid of hope: diseased, starved, and abject" (?15–18 August 1843, Pilgrim 3.542–43). Is this the mood he wants Browne to capture or a reminder of what only novelists can create? Dickens acknowledges his tendency to ask too much of pictures in a letter to Forster about a John Leech illustration for *The Battle of Life*: "You know how I build up temples in my mind that are not made with hands (or expressed with pen and ink, I am afraid), and how liable I am to be disappointed in these things" (?12 December 1846, Pilgrim 4.679–80).

One disappointment concerned Browne's drawing of "Paul and Mrs. Pipchin" (figure 2). Some of the uneasiness may be related to its position, near the beginning of *Dombey and Son* (in the third number). These are sections where ". . . First Appearances are Made . . ." as the fourth chapter's title notes. Dickens seems concerned that things appear as he has designed them, that the writer rather than the illustrator shape our response. His remarks stress accuracy and the need for visual acknowledgment of the illustrator's subordinate role:

> I am really *distressed* by the illustration of Mrs. Pipchin and Paul. It is so frightfully and wildly wide of the mark. Good Heaven! in the commonest and most literal construction of the text, it is all wrong. She is described as an old lady, and Paul's "miniature arm-chair" is mentioned more than once. He ought to be sitting in a little arm-chair down in a corner of the fireplace, staring up at her. I can't say what pain and vexation it is to be so utterly misrepresented. I would cheerfully have given a hundred pounds to have kept this illustration out of the book. He never could have got that idea of Mrs. Pipchin if he had attended to the text. Indeed I think he does better without the text; for then the notion is made easy to him in short description, and he can't help taking it in.
>
> (?November–December 1846, Pilgrim 4.671)

The editors of Dickens's letters, acknowledging that "CD is hardly fair to Browne," speculate that the "real trouble no doubt was that CD had a clear picture in his memory of Mrs. Roylance" (the model for Mrs. Pipchin) (Pilgrim 4.671n.). But some of the "trouble" may come from Browne's ability to construct his own "clear picture," an illustration that remains faithful to details of the writer's text while achieving a haunting power of its own.[7] It is not the work of someone who merely "attended to" instructions. Perhaps it is the writer who is at risk of being "misrepresented" here – not by inaccuracy but by a kind of artistic rivalry, by Browne's refusal to limit his job (Dickens's language is heavily inflected by a sense of social and artistic status) to "the commonest and most literal construction of the text."

Even when illustrations seem closest to "literal construction" they make us aware of the reconstruction it necessarily involves, description redescribed from the perspective of a second medium and a second imagination. Cruikshank's drawing of "Oliver's Reception by Fagin and the Boys" (figure 3) includes numerous narrative details: Oliver's new clothes and books, the candle Charley Bates holds "so close . . . as to nearly set him on fire," the Artful Dodger picking Oliver's pocket, Fagin's "mock humility," the intimidating presence of Bill Sikes and his dog, Nancy in the background. Cruikshank's touch is in gestures and expressions, Nancy's odd smile and ambiguous placement just outside the group around Oliver, and a pervasive darkness (illuminated by that single candle) that produces two special

3 George Cruikshank, "Oliver's Reception by Fagin and the Boys," from *Oliver Twist* (1837–39), *Bentley's Miscellany*, November 1837.

effects: Bill's enormous shadow, almost his double, which heightens his nightmarish power; the dog's grotesque white eyes, which we see almost apart from the rest of its body, suggesting a ghostly rather than simply animalistic threat. Are these shadow effects foreshadowings? Could Cruikshank have known the role those eyes would play in the account of Sikes's death? One wonders if Dickens had planned that scene yet, if the drawing might have influenced it by heightening this element of the text. My point is not to reopen arguments over Cruikshank's role in the novel's creation but to suggest his gift for visualizing its areas of dramatic potential, for transforming its darkness into a feature of his own style.

Browne achieves something similar in the "dark plates" for *Bleak House* and *Little Dorrit*.[8] In the rest of this essay I will focus on the former, his subtlest collaboration with Dickens and a special case for both men. Harvey explains that Browne developed his technique illustrating Charles Lever's *Roland Cashel* (1848–49) but only in *Bleak House* could make the somber etched backgrounds a "center of interest" (Harvey, *Victorian Novelists*, pp. 151–52). As Michael Steig puts it, "the illustrator employs the dark plate technique to convey graphically what is for the Dickens novels a new intensity of darkness."[9] And they convey more: the narrative's intense self-consciousness, its heightened attention to the limits of knowledge and representation. Browne's illustrations move beyond plot and character to depict the very conditions of seeing and knowing, the limits of our access to truth. The dark plates represent only the most conspicuous example of a consistent effort to picture the novel's thought – the way Dickens thinks in narrative, the way the narrative requires a reader to think and perceive.

By some standards, Browne's *Bleak House* drawings may seem disappointing, as they did to some contemporaries (Steig, *Dickens and Phiz*, p. 58). Illustrations typically supply relevant details: the arrangement of a crucial scene, the appearance of characters, telling gestures, emblematic reminders of moral significance. Hence the crowded appearance of many Dickens illustrations, as artists attempt to keep up with the sheer quantity of narrative information – as in "Florence Parts from a Very Old Friend" (*Dombey and Son*), which includes eight characters in dramatic poses, an equally expressive dog, and a good deal of significant decor. But if readers of Dickens came to expect this density in illustrations, it is conspicuously missing in most of those for *Bleak House*. Browne often depicts figures in near or complete isolation (as in the drawing of Jo that also appears on the first edition's title page). Several scenes contain no human figures at all – "Tom all alone's" and four drawings (including the frontispiece) of Chesney Wold. Other images withhold crucial information or leave it obscure – e.g. Lady Dedlock's face hidden or shadowed by her bonnet in the encounters with Jo and Esther ("Consecrated Ground" and "Lady Dedlock in the Wood"). John Harvey argues that Browne's "change of style was radical and sudden" in moving to the dark-plate technique in the twelfth part (with "The Ghost's Walk") (Harvey, *Victorian Novelists*, p. 152.) Yet the use of spare, suggestive outline is visible as early as the novel's first illustration ("The Little Old Lady," showing Miss Flite meeting the Wards in Chancery), where hints of weather (heavy clothing, buttoned collars) and atmosphere (the dim background through which a coach and buildings vaguely appear) subtly evoke the foggy, claustrophobic world of the novel's opening paragraphs (figure 4). Furthermore, as in the other illustration for the first number ("Miss Jellyby"), Esther's face is averted, hidden by her bonnet, suggesting the obscurity of her birth and what will increasingly be the importance of

4 Hablot K. Browne, "The Little Old Lady," from *Bleak House* (1852–53).

her features; by the time we reach the illustration of "Lady Dedlock in the Wood," the face concealed by a bonnet reminds us of the unpictured but textually stressed resemblance of mother and daughter. But this is a suggestion only, an understated visual allusion. Such illustrations make us strain to see what cannot be seen, to penetrate darkness, to unravel secrets; they make us aware of their limits, the limits of both images and sight. Picturing things seen and the conditions of seeing, they evoke the novel's methods, creating visual parallels to the demands of the text.

Browne's visual methodology is particularly apparent in the pairs of illustrations that accompanied each monthly number (the last double number included four), inserted before the text (and after the advertising supplement, which also continued after the end of the final chapter of each number).

Individually, illustrations preview the text, supplying images by which readers could anticipate (or later reassess) plot, characters, or the novel's developing concerns. Paired illustrations do this and more, since they also express a novel's distinctions, its internal differences, the poles between which a particular number moves. The monthly companion illustrations to *Bleak House* are particularly effective in illuminating this crucial dimension of the novel – its oscillations, its emotional and representational range. The very order of successive drawings structures our developing sense of the novel – its world, its perspective. This procedure begins almost systematically as the first number presents images focusing on characters ("The Little Old Lady," "Miss Jellyby"), the second illustrations concerned more specifically with plot ("The Lord Chancellor copies from memory" and "Coavinses"); the third number then introduces the novel's first topical drawing, "The visit at the Brickmaker's." The conventionality of the earlier images sets that last one apart, as do the figures of the genteel visitors standing just inside the Brickmaker's doorway: we see the novel and its characters entering foreign territory. Our response is also shaped by the unlikely companion image: "In Re Guppy. Extraordinary proceedings." The pair's distinct tones (and their titles, which always help define an illustration's textual function) further stress the point of the contrast: the extraordinariness of ordinary poverty (figures 5 and 6). Later images juxtapose London poverty with the polite world of companion illustrations – for instance, "The Dancing-School" and "Consecrated ground" (v), or "Sir Leicester Dedlock" and "Tom all alone's" (xiv). The effect is both to map the novel's social extremes and to evoke its process of social analysis, its method. As in the contrasting pairs near the end of the novel – "Light" and "Shadow" (xvi) and "The Night" and "The Morning" (xviii) – Browne depicts the patterns underlying the novel's shifting perspective: its structure, its developing dialectic.

In these terms, the final pair of illustrations may seem anticlimactic; it is, in a literal sense. Dickens novels typically end with summation, tying up loose ends of plot in a last, sweeping glance at the future of central characters – a final tableau, to use the language of contemporary theatrical practice. Martin Meisel has traced the debts of Victorian fiction to "pictorial dramaturgy which substituted situation for action as the constituting unit of the play" (Meisel, *Realizations*, p. 56). This "art of effect," as he terms it, often reaches a climax when narrative arranges itself into frozen, pictorial scenes, which in turn provide prime material for illustrators. If the practice is evident throughout Dickens's novels and their illustrations, the melodramatic peak is likely to come in the closing numbers, where last words and last images render poetic justice, predict moral continuity, and arrange

5   Hablot K. Browne, "The Visit at the Brickmaker's," from *Bleak House* (1852–53).

6 Hablot K. Browne, "In Re Guppy. Extraordinary Proceedings," from *Bleak House* (1852–53).

characters into scenes of satisfying, stable order. There are successive versions of this pictorial dramaturgy in the final double number of *Nicholas Nickleby*, illustrated by not only the Maclise portrait of Dickens, but (in order) "The Breaking Up of Dotheboys Hall," "Reduced Circumstances of Mr. Mantalini," and "The Children at their Cousin's Grave." It is as if the author's watchful presence allows the action to progressively slow and consolidate in preparation for a final, frozen effect: figures disposed in a peaceful, expressive group, collectively portraying happiness, faith, moral instruction, family unity, and narrative completion (figure 7). But if this is the standard by which nineteenth-century audiences judged them, the last illustrations for *Bleak House* fall short. Even as a unit, "The Magnanimous

7 Hablot K. Browne, "The Children at their Cousin's Grave," from *Nicholas Nickleby* (1838–39).

conduct of Mr. Guppy" (figure 8) and "The Mausoleum at Chesney Wold" portray too little of the closing pages, refuse too much of the task of concluding. Yet what they do supply may be equally important in Browne's progressive imaging of the novel's perspective: a final juxtaposition of private and institutional worlds, grave and comic tones. Hence the final illustration of Guppy (he is pictured in six of the novel's nineteen parts), stressing this minor figure's major role. Alongside the drawing of the mausoleum that in the text turns out to contain Lady Dedlock, this illustration balances moral seriousness with comic detachment. Even before we begin this number, the image reassures us; in spite of a last glance at death, *Bleak House* will not end on a bleak note. Here as elsewhere, illustration shapes our approach to narrative; it suggests what we should read and how.

In doing so, illustration still illustrates. For the text similarly concerns itself with what and how we see, with visual images and the culture in which they circulate. Architecture provides the first object of this attention to visuality. *Bleak House*, after all, is named after an ancient house and organized around an antiquated institution that itself is imagined as a kind of structure; on her first visit to legal London, Esther notes the church-like entrance to Kenge and Carboy's, with "a steep, broad flight of stairs" and a surrounding "colonnade" (*BH* 3, pictured in the first illustration of the meeting with "The Little Old Lady"). Many other images take central roles in the novel – from the portrait of Lady Dedlock that helps Guppy uncover the secret of Esther's parentage to the painted Roman figure of Allegory pointing from Mr. Tulkinghorn's ceiling. J. Hillis Miller observes that the visual motif of pointing recurs throughout illustrations and text, figuring the "procedure of indication which is the basic structural principle of *Bleak House*" and on which the novel's "labyrinth of . . . connections" depends.[10] But the very idea of that connected world has a background in pictorial tradition, particularly (as John Dixon Hunt shows) in Hogarth's practice of creating a single, interrelated environment through the resemblances of apparently disparate parts.[11] Yet for all the novel's linked social detail (its "point"), it also illuminates an insistent indeterminacy, an absence of visible significance at precisely the places where traditional iconography would lead us to expect meaning clearly pictured. Browne draws our attention to the paradox. For example in the illustration titled "Consecrated Ground," where Jo points through the churchyard gate to Nemo's grave, the boy's gesture directs our eyes past the edge of the image, toward an invisible world of death that resists imaging and interpretation. In the related text, Jo avoids the same "grave" reality, first confused by Lady Dedlock's questions and then distracted by a rat. Is the place consecrated? "'I don't know nothink of consequential ground,' says Jo, still staring." Is it blessed? "'I'm blest if I know,' says Jo. staring more than ever . . . 'Blest?' repeats Jo, something troubled in his mind. 'It ain't done it much good if it is'"(*BH* 16). So much for conventional pointers, conventional markers of meaning, at least for one ordinary observer.

We encounter the most dramatic example of such iconographic failure in the novel's best-known image, the pointing allegorical painting in

8 Hablot K. Browne, "The Magnanimous conduct of Mr. Guppy," from *Bleak House* (1852–53).

Tulkinghorn's chambers. Indeed, the whole building announces a decay of traditional signification: "a large house, formerly a house of state . . . let off in sets of chambers now; and in those shrunken fragments of its greatness lawyers lie like maggots in nuts." Its "painted ceilings" have lost all legibility save that conferred by Dickens's parody: "Allegory, in Roman helmet and celestial linen, sprawls among balustrades and pillars, flowers, clouds, and big-legged boys, and makes the head ache – as would seem to be Allegory's object always, more or less" (*BH* 10). From the first, then, this allegory of Allegory depicts little more than the genre's decline from the sublime to the ridiculous, and exhibits what Leonée Ormond calls Dickens's "unease about allegorizing high art."[12] What the painting fails to represent is suggested in a second account, in the chapter on "Tom-all-Alone's," where "Allegory, in the person of one impossible Roman upside down, points with the arm of Samson (out of joint, and an odd one) obtrusively towards the window" (*BH* 16). It points, that is, toward a world outside traditional iconography altogether, where Lady Dedlock coincidentally passes by in disguise, unseen by the usually vigilant Tulkinghorn, on her way to find Jo and the graveyard.

When Dickens introduces the painting for the last time it points to another dead body, but this in itself suggests that "A new meaning in the Roman" (as Browne's illustration is titled) must come from outside its original allegorical scheme. The scene of Tulkinghorn's murder remains hauntingly ambiguous, described in suggestive but equivocal images toward which the Roman gestures: "He is pointing at a table, with a bottle (nearly full of wine) and a glass upon it, and two candles that were blown out suddenly, soon after being lighted. He is pointing at an empty chair, and at a stain upon the ground before it that might be almost covered with a hand . . ." (*BH* 48). That final detail encapsulates the paradox of iconographic collapse. An intervening hand would interrupt our view, for no apparent reason beyond an impulse to disturb the alleged fixity of a visual mark. Whose hand is it? Dead or living? Why "might" it try to cover this stain? We are reminded of children touching wet paint. Or is this the "hand" of writing, of a narrative that nearly (but only nearly) obliterates all traces of the visual? In fact, the passage juxtaposes three distinct kinds of visual signification: the formality of traditional allegory, the articulate evidence of everyday objects, the suggestiveness of random marks (as in the stained walls Leonardo found so fascinating). Conventional iconography gives way to more varied visual information. Browne's illustration emphasizes the blankness of the formal surroundings, pierced by shafts of light that cross "the empty chair" to illuminate the stain below it (figure 9).[13] The Roman (along with the conventional decor) is absorbed in the darkness of the upper half of the image; the only possibilities of significance reside in the ordinary objects beneath, bathed in a light from

9 Hablot K. Browne, "A New Meaning in the Roman," from *Bleak House* (1852–53).

outside the ancient building. As in the text, emphasis falls on contrasted signifying modes: allegory has been socialized, traditional iconography supplanted by a more diffuse and complex visuality. Tulkinghorn's death chamber is represented through a pictorial grammar constructed out of ordinary objects, a new Victorian iconography of everyday detail.

Miller calls *Bleak House* "a document about the interpretation of documents" (Miller, "Introduction," p. 11). It makes equal sense to think of it as a study of the adequacy of a much wider range of representations – legal, political, historical, personal, familial, documentary, and not least of all aesthetic. Dickens's account of "Roman" allegory explores the limits of formal iconography, much as the interplay of the novel's narrative voices (perhaps like the paired illustrations of the monthly numbers) contrasts different forms of knowledge. Yet Esther herself represents not only a certain way of thinking but a certain way of seeing, an aesthetic: she is drawn to particular sights, views them in her own way. The novel returns to these matters in its last pages: Esther meditates on "her old looks" and what she sees as she studies her face in a mirror while conversing with her husband in a specific part of their new home – "the porch of all places, that dearly memorable porch" of the home John Jarndyce has prepared for her new life. In a novel named after one building we cannot avoid paying attention to this other one, a modern, miniature replica of the first, New Bleak House, as we might call it in the language of the contemporary Victorian building boom. Why might Dickens turn to such matters?

Architecture was in the air at mid-century, especially after the 1851 opening of the Crystal Palace, a building Dickens regarded with some ambivalence.[14] John Ruskin, the most influential architectural critic of the day, was more hostile, for he assessed the industrial modernism of Joseph Paxton's oversized greenhouse against the traditions embodied in gothic naturalism. His study of *The Stones of Venice*, which appeared in the years of *Bleak House* and the Great Exhibition (1851–53), pays tribute to medieval architecture's almost literal vitality: "Undefined in its slope of roof, height of shaft, breadth of arch, or disposition of ground plan, it can shrink into a turret, expand into a hall, coil into a staircase, or spring into a spire, with undegraded grace and unexhausted energy . . ."[15] Such organic flexibility demonstrates gothic's enduring human content, an unlimited ("living," Ruskin would say) adaptability to the widest possible range of needs and uses; this is an important part of what makes medieval architecture "memorable," to use Esther's term. And although New Bleak House is not gothic, the "rustic cottage of doll's rooms" has been fitted to mirror many traditional qualities Esther admired in the original. The porch is "dearly memorable," then, in several respects: as the place where Jarndyce announced her future as Mrs. Woodcourt, as a site of architectural allusion, as one of many parts of the house (re)designed to evoke Esther's fondness for the past.

Esther, in fact, understands that architectural details can be arranged as what she calls "aids to memory" (*BH* 51). And memorability is likely to increase when buildings are designed to suit special needs, with the impulsive disregard of rules that Ruskin associates with gothic naturalism (and that Dickens might have called spontaneous construction). The Woodcourts have followed this model with their new home: "With the first money we saved at home we added to our pretty house by throwing out a little Growlery expressly for my guardian" (*BH* 67). The emphasis falls equally on domesticity and *domus*, homelife constructed in and by the physical environment. "Beginning the world" (to use another of the novel's phrases) apparently involves building the world, or rebuilding it; Ruskin would have agreed. How better to conclude a novel of ruined structures, unstable institutions, uncertain images, antiquated iconographies, unmemorable artifacts that seem to promote a more general social forgetting – a survey of aesthetics that begins with the title house itself, illustrated at the center of the wrapper design, or with the ancient form of Chesney Wold pictured in the frontispiece? The novel in effect ends where it began, locating its personal, moral, and institutional concerns (and foreseeing their resolution) within the material forms of a visual culture.

I have been tracing the novel's discourse on the visual, one that spills out of the text and into the illustrations and beyond, into (or is it out of – where does such a discourse begin or end?) the illustrated advertising supplements to the monthly parts. The *Bleak House Advertiser*, a varied assemblage of texts and images (there are similar collections in "Advertisers" for all the novels issued in monthly parts) was not, of course, controlled by Dickens or Browne, although Dickens did block Chapman and Hall's advertisements for his forthcoming work when they ran counter to his schedule (30 November 1840, Pilgrim 2.160). Yet the jumble of random ads oddly fits this narrative of objects, documents, images, and struggles for success and information. The *Bleak House Advertiser* provides a kind of reader's guide to the novel's place in mass society. It lists books (many illustrated), magazines, newspapers, maps, and printing presses; furniture and cutlery; medicines, clothing, jewelry, parasols, wigs, false teeth; ironwork, locks, fountains, water-purifiers; banks and insurance companies; cotton; beer; opera glasses; and more. Some ads directly or indirectly echo the novel (see Altick, *The Presence of the Present*, pp. 64–67, 236–39). One six-page series of ads for *Lloyd's Weekly London Newspaper* promises a Dickensian range of current information: "The Parliamentary Debates, Law Intelligence, Police Reports, Sporting Intelligence of all Kinds, Trials at the Old Bailey and Assizes,

THE LATEST INTELLIGENCE

10 Anonymous, ad for *Lloyd's Weekly Newspaper* from the *Bleak House Advertiser*.

Foreign News, Movements of the Army and Navy, . . ." and so forth. Not incidentally, this series, like many entries in the "Advertiser," is illustrated.

One of the *Lloyd's* drawings suggests another way to consider the relation of Dickens, illustration, and visual culture in *Bleak House*. It depicts two fashionable ladies riding in a carriage through Hyde Park, the Crystal Palace in the background (figure 10). The darker and more alert of the pair (are we meant to think of Esther?), her head turned toward the viewer, holds *Lloyd's*, which she apparently has been reading to her fairer, more abstracted companion (Ada?), while their African footman leans forward to peer (possibly to read) over their shoulders. The caption, "The Latest Intelligence," may refer to the newspaper, to the building, or even, if we view the image as reactionary satire, to the fact that women, servants, and blacks might take an interest in these matters at all. It also may refer to vision as the most powerful contemporary form of cognition. An image of the contemporary world, the "topics of the day" in Richard Altick's phrase, the drawing mimics the universal preoccupation with current knowledge in *Bleak House*. It also appeals to our own hunger for information (compare the announcement in the same *Advertiser* for the eighth edition of the *Encyclopedia Britannica*, that "great repository of human knowledge"). But this is information in a modern, multidiscursive sense, raw data that overflows the boundaries between disciplines, forms of expertise, and modes of representation. Here the diverse worlds of politics, law, sport, fashion, and more, rub against one another, crossing lines of class, race, and gender – and verbal and visual art as well: high culture next to popular culture (though it would be difficult to place *Bleak House* or the Great Exhibition in either category), print alongside visual culture, the world of art next to the world of advertisements, genteel society immersed in the society of the spectacle. It is not clear if *Lloyd's* promises to stabilize, ridicule, or merely record this modern intersection of institutions, disciplines, and roles, this messy blurring of separate spheres. And while the ad implies that it is precisely at moments like this that writing is most needed, it paradoxically (like Dickens using the Maclise portrait to announce his authorship) makes the claim with pictures.

In one sense, though, this claim is not as paradoxical as it seems, nor the paradox as unprecedented. W. J. T. Mitchell observes that "all arts are 'composite' arts (both text and image); all media are mixed media, combining different codes, discursive conventions, channels, sensory and cognitive modes."[16] And whether or not such mixing is always equally true of all the arts, the interaction of arts and discursive codes intensifies with the emergence of Victorian visual culture. It is, in effect, an emerging modernity, marked by the increasing importance of visual media and visual technologies,[17] by the first forms of the culture industry (perhaps best represented in *Bleak House* by the Woodcourts' modest home improvements). Dickens responds and contributes to this proliferating Victorian visuality throughout his career; *Bleak House* is not so much a special case as a particularly rich example. This may explain why he dedicated the novel "As a Remembrance of our Friendly Union To my Companions In the Guild of Literature and Art." It may also explain why he ends it as he does. After so much attention to aesthetics, visual experience, and the limits of conventional iconography, it seems fitting that Esther's survey of her own face concludes alluding to words that cannot be spoken about appearances that cannot be recovered – to her own lost "looks." Yet the ellipsis with which her narrative ends suggests that this looking, like this speaking, is interrupted only temporarily, that it will continue beyond the sentence, beyond the moment, beyond the ending, beyond the text or textuality in general. And beyond Esther's agency. For by now her beauty is not merely contained in a reflected image for private consumption but available in the form of a more general cultural property. Her image, like her mother's, now circulates in an extensive visual economy. The narrative stops precisely as she senses this, as she recognizes the indeterminacy of her appearance, the extent to which her image and her self-image – her identity – have passed beyond her control. *Bleak House*, that is, ends at the point its principal subject recognizes herself as an object in visual culture, at the moment narrative acknowledges its own inescapable place in a world of images.

NOTES

1 *Quarterly Review* 74 (June, 1844). Cited in Martin Meisel, *Realizations: Narrative, Pictorial, and Theatrical Arts in Nineteenth-Century England* (Princeton University Press, 1983), pp. 30–31.
2 *Victorian Novelists and their Illustrators* (New York University Press, 1971), p. 11.
3 See Robert L. Patten's entries on "Publishing, Printing, Bookselling: Modes of Production," and "Serial Literature," in *The Oxford Reader's Companion to Dickens*, ed. Paul Schlicke (Oxford University Press, 1999).
4 See Jane R. Cohen, *Charles Dickens and His Original Illustrators* (Ohio State University Press, 1980) and Robert L. Patten's entries on "Illustrators and Book Illustration" and various individual artists in *The Oxford Reader's Companion*.
5 Robert L. Patten, *George Cruikshank's Life, Times, and Art* (Rutgers University Press, 1996), vol. 11, p. 72.
6 Patten observes that Dickens treats Cattermole "with a reverence and deference rarely accorded to any other of Dickens's collaborators." "George Cattermole," *The Oxford Reader's Companion*, p. 68.
7 Q. D. Leavis echoes Dickens's view of Browne's "treachery." F. R. and Q. D. Leavis, "The Dickens Illustrations: their Function," *Dickens the Novelist* (Chatto and Windus, 1970), p. 353.
8 On Browne's illustrations to *Little Dorrit*, see Meisel's on "Dickens' Roman Daughter," *Realizations*, pp. 302–21.
9 Michael Steig, *Dickens and Phiz* (Indiana University Press, 1978), p. 131.
10 "Introduction" to the Penguin edition of *Bleak House* (Penguin, 1971), pp. 16–17.
11 "Dickens and the traditions of graphic satire," *Encounters: Essays on Literature and the Visual Arts*, ed. John Dixon Hunt (Norton, 1971), p. 136.
12 "Dickens and Painting: The Old Masters," *The Dickensian* 401 (Autumn, 1983), 93–146 at 145.
13 Luke Fildes, who was illustrating *The Mystery of Edwin Drood* at the time of Dickens's death, drew a memorial watercolor of the writer's study titled "The Empty Chair" for Wilkie Collins's essay on "Charles Dickens's Study" in *The Graphic* (25 December 1870). The image and title may allude to the scene of Tulkinghorn's death.
14 Philip Landon argues that the novel's encyclopedic replication of the natural and human world mirrors the Great Exhibition: "Great Exhibitions: Representations of the Crystal Palace in Mayhew, Dickens, and Dostoevsky," *Nineteenth-Century Contexts* 20:1 (1997), 27–59. On the relation of the *Bleak House Advertiser* to the novel's social topics see Landon and Richard Altick, *The Presence of the Present: Topics of the Day in the Victorian Novel* (Ohio State University Press, 1991), p. 70. For the Great Exhibition and commodity culture see Thomas Richards, *The Commodity Culture of Victorian England: Advertising and Spectacle, 1851–1914* (Stanford University Press, 1990).
15 *The Library Edition of the Works of John Ruskin*, ed. Cook and Wedderburn (Allen, 1903–12), 39 vols., vol. x, p. 212.
16 *Picture Theory* (University of Chicago Press, 1994), pp. 94–95.
17 For the most important recent survey of such matters, see Jonathan Crary, *Techniques of the Observer: On Vision and Modernity in the Nineteenth Century* (MIT Press, 1990).

FURTHER READING

Christ, Carol T. and John O. Jordan (eds.). *Victorian Literature and the Victorian Visual Imagination*. University of California Press, 1995.

Cohen, Jane R. *Charles Dickens and His Original Illustrators*. Ohio State University Press, 1980.

Crary, Jonathan. *Techniques of the Observer: On Vision and Modernity in the Nineteenth Century*. MIT Press, 1990.

Hunt, John Dixon. "Dickens and the traditions of graphic satire." In *Encounters: Essays on Literature and the Visual Arts*, edited by John Dixon Hunt. Norton, 1971, pp. 124–55.

Jaffe, Audrey. "Spectacular Sympathy: Visuality and Ideology in Dickens's *A Christmas Carol*." *PMLA* (1994), 254–65.

Landon, Philip. "Great Exhibitions: Representations of the Crystal Palace in Mayhew, Dickens, and Dostoevsky." *Nineteenth-Century Contexts* 20:1 (1997), 27–59.

Meisel, Martin. *Realizations: Narrative, Pictorial, and Theatrical Arts in Nineteenth-Century England*. Princeton University Press, 1983.

Miller, J. Hillis. "The Fiction of Realism: *Sketchs by Boz*, *Oliver Twist*, and Cruikshank's Illustrations." In *Charles Dickens and George Cruikshank*. W. A. Clark Memorial Library, University of California Press, 1971, pp. 1–69.

Mitchell, W. J. T. *Picture Theory*. University of Chicago Press, 1994.

Ormond, Leonée. "Dickens and Painting: Contemporary Art." *The Dickensian* 402 (Spring, 1984), 93–146.

"Dickens and Painting: The Old Masters." *The Dickensian* 401 (Autumn, 1983), 130–51.

Patten, Robert L. *George Cruikshank's Life, Times, and Art*. 2 volumes. Rutgers University Press, 1992–96.

"Hablot Knight Browne," "George Cruikshank," and "Illustrators and Book Illustration." *The Oxford Reader's Companion to Dickens*, edited by Paul Schlicke. Oxford University Press, 1999.

Steig, Michael. *Dickens and Phiz*. Indiana University Press, 1978.

Stein, Richard L. *Victoria's Year: English Literature and Culture, 1837–1838*. Oxford University Press, 1987.

13

JOHN GLAVIN

Dickens and theatre

Dickens and theatre? It comes down to what you might mean by "and." If you mean something like: could Dickens come into the theater as a participant, I'd say, certainly not. Oh yes, he tried. But early on he found he couln't. And thereafter he didn't.

That may seem surprising. Dickens is by every standard account the most theatrical of Victorian novelists. This *Companion* would be thought considerably less companionable if it lacked a chapter on Dickens and theatre (though perhaps not this chapter on Dickens and theatre). All his life Dickens paid fierce, unremitting attention to other people's plays and to other people's performances. What he saw he regularly purloined, and then transformed into fiction. He probably knew as much about the practical work of theaters as anyone working on a nineteenth-century stage. (Here I should point out that, following the practice in theatre studies, I am spelling as theatre anything like a playhouse, particularly a professional playhouse, and as theater, the practice or theory of performance.) Acting obsessed him. He supported actors experiencing financial hard times and even dreamed of the great actor Macready as his desirable double. His novels were quickly adapted to the stage, not just as they appeared, but, through the vagaries of serial publication, often even before they appeared (in book form). And, ever since, both his plots and his characters have provided a sturdy resource for stage and screen, both large screen and small, up to and including the present moment. In addition to which, as everyone knows, his characters, at least all the memorable ones, seem far more like performers than persons, self-conscious, hyperbolic, and, well, just plain theatrical.

Not to mention the fact that his long liaison with the actress Ellen Ternan literally transformed not only the final years of his life but each of his final heroines, the ones with all those variations on her name: Estella, Bella, Helena.

Yes, that is the standard view. And every word of it is true. However, it's just as true, and far more advantageous, to say something far less standard.

Dickens wrote a few early and relatively successful pieces for theatre. Then he stopped. After that, he spent most of his subsequent and splendid career watching plays rather than producing or performing them. Which makes the standard view sound a lot like Jane Austen's Lady Catherine De Bourgh describing her musical talents: "If I had ever learnt, I should have been a great proficient" (*Pride and Prejudice*, chapter 31).

Dickens, too, never learnt – to act in plays or to make plays. But even if he had, and here my nonstandard view dips into heresy, I doubt he'd have been a great proficient. Or even merely proficient. As a young man, he took acting lessons. The lessons led to a Covent Garden audition. But, and this is a very big but, he ducked the audition, said he was sick, never rescheduled it, and never did anything more with all those costly lessons. Yes, by all accounts, all his life he was a terrific reader and an inimitable mime, an amateur performer and a constant show-off. But neither a beautiful voice nor a gift for mime is acting. Nor is narcissism necessarily talent. Later in life, successful and prosperous, he produced amateur theatricals, conspicuously in the 1850s a series of Twelfth Night performances for his growing family at Tavistock House. And on occasion he assisted his younger colleagues to carpenter longer scripts, notably *Mr. Nightingale's Diary* with Mark Lemon (1851), and *The Frozen Deep* with Wilkie Collins (1857). But amateur theatricals are only by a sort of courtesy title theatre. And, in any case, virtually everybody in non-dissenting England dabbled in amateur theatricals. What else do you call the Victorian Parliament?

Moreover, and most compelling, throughout his novels, theaters invariably represent sites and rituals of degradation, for both men and women, but especially for men.

This is my starting point, then: Dickens both loathed and longed for the playhouse. He turned, reluctantly, from stage to page, because the action-prone stage demands from its protagonists a degree of agency Dickens found literally unimaginable. Paradoxically, however, his fiction chimed more closely with the theatre of his age than with its fiction. Pretty much everyone agrees Dickens's fiction is spectacular. I'm going to literalize that claim to say that in an era of Spectacular Theatre Dickens wrote a comparably Spectacular Fiction, where Spectacular, on both stage and page, meant something like realism eradicated.

To follow up these claims, the remainder of this chapter focuses on two Dickensian sports (to use a Darwinian term): his first published play and his last published novel. The play: his early, extremely successful foray into the world of professional theatre, the *burletta*, *The Village Coquettes* (1836). The novel: the late, unfinished *Mystery of Edwin Drood* (1870: unfinished because, of course, Dickens died before he could complete it). With the *bur-*

letta Dickens enters the theater, but doesn't stay for long. With the second, for the last but by now means for the first time, theatre enters Dickens, resoundingly.

The distinction I draw between theater and theatre permits me now to claim that the first part of what follows, the *Coquettes* section, concentrates on Dickens and theater, that is on Dickens's relation to professionally staged performance. And the second part, the *Drood* part, focuses on something not at all the same, theatre and Dickens, or, to be more precise, Spectacular Theatre and Dickensian Spectacle.

Dickens and theater

In his early twenties, Dickens wanted desperately to succeed in the theater. He did not follow up on his acting ambitions. But he did try hard to make it as a playwright. He began with a very successful two-act farce, *The Strange Gentleman*, which ran for almost sixty performances after its debut in September, 1836, and was then revived for a shorter run in 1837. He continued with the longer, richer *The Village Coquettes*, for which he wrote both book and lyrics, with music by John Hullah. This, his second written but first published play, opened at the splendid St. James's Theatre on 6 December 1836 (with *Strange Gentleman* heading the bill). It featured a first-rate cast of contemporary musical stars, notably John Braham and John Pritt Harley, virtually forgotten now but just about the biggest performers Dickens could have hoped for at the time. Though not well received by the critics, *Coquettes* seems to have been quite popular with audiences. It ran for nineteen nights, was withdrawn over the Christmas season, but revived in 1837. It was being remounted slightly later in Edinburgh when the theater burned down, destroying not only the costumes and scenery but the musical score and all the parts. Meanwhile, in March 1837, Dickens's latest theatre piece, a one-act burletta, *Is She His Wife?* opened, again with John Pritt Harley in the lead. This time, however, there was no long run.

But notice the dates. September 1836–March 1837. The First Series of *Sketches by Boz* had appeared in February 1836. *Pickwick* commenced at the end of March. The Second Series of the *Sketches* came out on 17 December, nine days after *Coquettes* debuted. *Bentley's Miscellany* began in January 1837. And in its pages *Oliver Twist* started to run in February. Those twelve months, February 1836 to February 1837, constitute Dickens's *annus mirabilis*, a year in which he was not only inventing himself as a writer of published fiction but also as a writer of staged plays. He was in effect starting two parallel careers. Or perhaps it's better to say he was testing both himself and the marketplace to see which would reward him. And in that marketplace the new and lavish St. James's Theatre packed a lot more cultural heft than those struggling new publishers, Richard Bentley and Chapman and Hall. Yes, from the start, Dickens made more money by writing for publication. But also from the start he was clearly thrilled to mingle as one of themselves among theatre professionals and to merge with the green-room crowd. Indeed, he got himself rebuked in print by no less a figure than his later editor, John Forster, for insistently thrusting himself forward at the final curtain of *Coquettes*, a custom then considered vulgar and unworthy seriously literary authors.

What's more, he could have kept it up. Remember: this is Dickens. If he could produce three pieces for the stage, two of them quite successful, in the same period in which he was writing both *Pickwick* and *Oliver*, and editing the *Miscellany*, he could certainly have maintained a later career (like Bulwer Lytton) writing for both stage and page. And, in a sense, that is exactly what he did do by creating a shadow or surrogate theatricality through his subsequent regular, at times heavy, involvement in amateur theatricals.

But professional involvement in the professional stage he had all but abandoned by the end of 1837. We might even read *Nicholas Nickleby* (1838) as a kind of formal renunciation of professional theatre. At a pivotal moment in the novel Nicholas sternly denounces the theater, fleeing Portsmouth and the Crummles Company for London and a life of writing (accounts in a warehouse, but writing nonetheless). Nicholas is in so many ways Dickens's surrogate that it is hard not to read this renunciation *à clef* as the author's own, a public putting behind himself of any further theatrical "fooling here" (30).

But why? Why would the playhouse seem *fooling* to the Dickens then transforming himself from Boz to the author of *Nickleby*? The most obvious answer would doubtless speak about language. Here, then, is a tempting claim. The theater failed Dickens primarily because its conventions could not accommodate his most enduring and fundamental need: to play with and against language. Theatrical language indicates. It relentlessly points to, points out, names what it needs its audience to know. It cannot pause, detour, delay, because theatre's primary demand, and reward, is continuous, suspenseful, interesting action. In the theater we want to know what's happening, and we're impatient with anything that blurs our view. (In the contemporary American theatre, interestingly, the actors' highest praise for a script is to call it *crisp*.) And this indicative burden is particularly striking in the early nineteenth-century stage, assigned by culture to restore, reinforce, amplify, consolidate, stabilize. Victorian theatre summed up and re-presented meaning to its audiences gap-free, reliable spokesmen reciting reliable landscapes. But Dickens's language delights to, indeed depends upon, detour and delay, continually pointing away from its ostensible subject, refusing the demand for stable reference.

And yet, surely, the man who transformed the language of the novel could also have transformed the language of the stage. Why could Dickens not do for his time and theatre what Shakespeare did for his?

Pondering that question suggests there must be something else about theaters, something beyond but also enclosing language, that closes Dickens out. That something begins to emerge when we turn from active language to action itself. Unfortunately, this means that – since you're as likely to have hummed as to have read *The Village Coquettes* – I have to produce a slight summary of its slim plot.[1]

Set in the English countryside in the early eighteenth century, the play depends on a parallel between class-crossing triangles. Lucy Benson, the daughter of a prosperous farmer, is engaged to Edmunds, a man of her own class. But Lucy is also being beguiled into a liaison by the local landowner, Squire Norton. In the other, more *déclassé* triangle, Lucy's fatherless cousin, Rose, is courted by an eminently respectable yeoman, John Maddox, while being seduced by an entirely unrespectable dandy, the Hon. Sparkins Flam, Norton's best friend down from London on a visit. However, both entrapments get revealed before they go very far or do much harm. Nevertheless, Old Benson, Lucy's father, manages to insult his landlord, who, in reprisal, orders him off the farm despite generations of faithful tillage. Almost immediately thereafter, however, the Squire repents of both his anger and his lust. Flam's double-dealing is easily exposed, and things end with the greatest happiness of the greatest number as everyone delights in exiling Flam from the restored idyll, where both true love and loyal service are finally and richly rewarded.

Obviously, that plot operates within the broadly melodramatic genre so ably defined by Peter Brooks. Into an idyllic setting, an unscrupulous outsider, here Flam, inserts himself. He poisons the relations among the denizens of the idyll, bringing it to the verge of collapse. But his misprision gets unmasked in the nick of time and he is expelled from the restored and renewed ideal. In its mixture of farcical action and sentimental song, *Coquettes* also seems indebted to the venerable English tradition of the ballad opera, supremely epitomized in Gay's *Beggar's Opera*. Nevertheless, I'd rather stress the ways in which the play seems engaged by Shakespeare's late romance, *The Winter's Tale*, specifically by the fourth act, the inimitable Bohemian pastoral. That contrast, between a dramatic masterpiece and a Dickensian – well, why be unkind, let's just say *burletta*, tells us a great deal about why Dickens could not enter the theater. Even after he got there.

I'm also happy to make this connection because by a nice coincidence

Winter's Tale happens also to undergird as *Ür*-text the other Dickens title in this chapter, *The Mystery of Edwin Drood*.

Winter's Tale Act IV, itself a kind of one-act ballad opera, takes place largely at a sheep shearing, very much like *The Village Coquettes*'s harvest home. Both depend heavily on the rituals, comic and lyric, of these supreme autumnal spectacles. And their plots are also highly alike. Both center on a heroine (Perdita/Lucy, shadowed by Rose) dishonestly courted by a slumming better-born hero (Florizel/ Norton, shadowed by Flam). The exposure of this amour threatens ruin to the girl's father and brother, until in each the seduction is exposed, and partially resolved, when a cozening comic interferes: the immortal Autolycus, in Shakespeare; in Dickens, his clear avatar, the rural con man, Martin Stokes.

But there the similarities, crucially, evaporate. Shakespeare is driven by, while Dickens entirely lacks, ardor. Florizel and Perdita, smitten with each other, risk their lives to consummate that passion. But, at the first opportunity, Norton and Rose leap apart – "Who, us? In love!" – thrilled to be excused the erotic hook. Rose cares even less for Flam. And Flam claims simply to be behaving like a good houseguest. If your host seduces one of the village maidens, the experienced guest immediately seeks out her cousin. Edmunds, the appropriate lover, with no parallel in Shakespeare, does literally nothing, except moan about all the fallen leaves he sees. Young Benson, Rose's brother, ditto. In fact it's hard to avoid concluding that some characters are included only to provide a range of voice types for the ensembles.

There is action, but it comes almost entirely from Martin, the Autolycus-figure. Autolycus of course both speeds and impedes action in *Winter's Tale*. But he functions throughout as a counterforce to the principal action, the through-line that derives from the drives of the principals. Florizel risks all, country, rank, life, because he's mad about the girl. And Perdita does the same (though at the time she doesn't know she has a rank to risk). So do the other characters surrounding Act IV: Leontes and Polixenes and Paulina. Hermione doesn't, of course, but that means she's got to die a third of the way through the play and can return to the stage only as a statue. It's that way not just in Shakespeare but in all drama. The central characters, driven by desire and need, risk whatever it takes to take back from the world what it is they want – or they are beaten back trying. That is why we call them protagonists. Indeed, all genuinely dramatic characters, even those who are not protagonists, have lives, make their lives, because they determine their plots. But anything that happens to anybody in *Coquettes* happens primarily through Martin, and secondarily through Flam. Martin not only rescues the girl (from Flam!, acting he thinks for his host), he also literally rescues the plot. Yet Martin, crucially, acts always only on others' behalf, never for himself, and Flam acts only, mistakenly, on behalf of Norton. None of the principals of *Coquettes* desires to act out the plot in which they find themselves and from which they feel powerless to extricate themselves. Only the outsider, the surrogate actor and marginal performer, can do that for them. The dramatic conflict of protagonists has given way to a shadow play of surrogates.

That's my answer to the question why can't Dickens enter the theater. Dickens can imagine performance, but not drama. In fact, what he delights to imagine is the displacement of dramatic action: surrogate intervention, someone else acting on your behalf. Indeed, Martin heralds what will become Dickens's paradigm plot, the preferably disinterested outsider intervening to free a protagonist from a fundamentally false self and situation. Repeatedly that fortuitous, gratuitous intervention drives Dickens's fiction. The Cheerybles save Nicholas Nickleby. John Jarndyce saves Esther Summerson. Sydney Carton saves the Manette–Darnay menage. Dickens loves performance, acting out the self, but can't undertake drama, acting for the self.

And that also, by the way, seems to resolve the language question. To write for the stage one has to find natural the language of indication and assertion, language that strives above anything else to be effective. But Dickens writes for exactly the reverse: a world playing with words while its principals wait to be found; a world which longs not to be effective but effected; to be acted upon, not to act.

Okay. But here comes the paradox. He couldn't go into the theater because he couldn't do drama. Nevertheless, theatre came into, had to come into, Dickens, because like the theatre of his time, he required *spectacle*.

Theatre and Dickens

Through the middle third of the nineteenth century Dickens's most ambitious peers pushed fiction increasingly and impressively toward realism. Anyone who reads Thackeray, Charlotte (but not Emily) Brontë, Eliot, and Trollope feels that Dickens is in that company anomalous. In contrast to their increasingly naturalistic solidity, Dickens is, well, theatrical. And that's because he was using the novel to do work assigned in his time to the field of theatre, not fiction. What work? The work that is central to the era that produced the Great Exhibition and patented the plate-glass window, the work of spectacle, where everything that is solid can and does, as Marx said, melt into air.

Spectacular Theatre dominated the mid- and late nineteenth-century stage. (The term has been canonized by the doyen of nineteenth-century theatre historians, Michael Booth.) Since the Restoration theatre had used continuously recycled backdrops of conventional settings (castles, lakes, throne rooms), framed by narrow, flat side screens that remained in place while the drops were lowered and raised. For a new play old scenery might be repainted. For a major opening a few new drops might be commissioned. But until the middle third of the nineteenth century scenery tended to remain one-dimensional, conventional, background. With Spectacular Theatre illusion exploded. Every play became one-of-a-kind. Managers mounted scene after scene, each of three-dimensional, richly detailed, life-sized sets changing with the utmost rapidity both between and during scenes. Literally hundreds of stage hands, below, behind and above the proscenium, hauled these illusions into and out of sight; the back of the house was now a kind of gigantic, stationary sailing ship, bristling with masts and stanchions, perilous with winches and pulleys, rigging and traps. And supported by these machines and those men, theatre morphed into magic, apparently inexhaustible sequences of full, distinct, and diverse worlds. (For this reason Spectacular Theatre is rightly seen as a key predecessor of film.)

More important even than this visual richness and complexity was the demand that each scene appear and disappear effortlessly. Theatre called each new scene a "discovery," but its audiences demanded they *discover* nothing on their own. No trace of those stagehands, of dangling tackle, or about-to-be-cued performer could be glimpsed lest – and here is Dickens's own *All the Year Round* enthusiastically joining in – "we [be] rendered unbelieving . . . our young illusions rudely checked" ("A New Stage Stride," *AYR* [31 October 1863], p. 229). Because, the article went on to insist, the function of theatre is "to carry out the illusion in a manner that is truly marvelous" (p. 230).

But what "illusion"? Plainly, the illusion of dis-embodiment. Paradoxically, the principal task these solid sets performed was to dissolve. Spectacular Theatre did not ask its audience to accept the mimetic reproduction of an actual world (that would come later, with naturalism). In that sense Spectacular Theatre wasn't so much about what the scenery seemed as about what the scenery did, about the keenly ephemeral pleasure stoked by the alternating consolidation and dissipation of many merely suggested worlds. And what was happening to the stage was paralleled by what was happening on the stage. Spectacular Theatre told – delighted to tell – *spectacular* stories, stories of wreck and ruin, of second sight and haunting, stories which broke through boundaries of sense and of fact, which demanded illusion, which required dissolution. Spectacular Theatre staged not only the aesthetics of, but also the argument for, dis-embodiment.

We can recuperate that argument by looking at Charles Kean's 1856 adaptation of our base text, *Winter's Tale*.[2] Kean's tenure of London's Princess's Theatre at mid-century was a definitive moment in the history of Spectacular Theatre. And the high point of that tenure was his *Winter's Tale*, an extraordinarily lavish production running an unprecedented 102 nights. Extraordinary also because, when you think about it, *Winter's Tale* seems virtually a countertext to Spectacle, a cautionary tale about the dangers that spring from untrammeled illusion, a powerful argument for re- not dis-embodiment. And, as we're about to see, Kean had thoroughly to revise the play to make it work as Spectacle.

Those revisions bring Kean's production fascinatingly close to the Dickens of *Edwin Drood*, so close that we might almost be tempted to insist that Dickens saw and copied the production. But Dickens was the actor Macready's close friend. Macready was the sworn enemy to Kean's father, the much greater actor, Edmund Kean. And Dickens was never one to forget or forego a feud. No, in all probability Dickens never saw what Kean did. My point is, precisely, that. He didn't need to. He and Kean were after the same thing. It's not a question of influence but of parallel purpose.

But how does royal jealousy in ancient Sicily parallel provincial envy in a Regency cathedral town? Remarkably. Each tells fundamentally the same two-part story. Each first half presents a hitherto intimate male pair, in the play blood brothers, in the novel uncle and nephew. Suddenly the host member of the pair, a narcissistic man of fierce impulse, maniacally conspires the death of the other, driven by lurid and grotesque sexual jealousy. That jealousy leads both play and novel to the death of a prized boy, Edwin in the book, Mamillius on the stage, which in turn precipitates the destruction of the community he centers.

After the boy dies, the principal girl's getaway gives rise to the second half. The heroine, Rosa/Perdita, is spirited off to a rough and comic pastoral, Bohemia/Staple Inn, where she becomes infatuated with a handsome young man, Tartar/Florizel. And that's just about where Dickens stopped writing. Indeed, that's where Dickens stopped entirely. So there's no more plot to parallel.

But enough curtailed narrative remains to suggest how the novel, like the play, turns its second part over to the renewing power of nature. At their mid-points both play and novel make a big fuss about Time. Dickens called *Drood*'s fulcrum chapter "The Dawn Again." And the illustrated cover for the novel's original parts shows a crypt scene, suggesting a strong potential correlation to *Winter's Tale*'s final "awakening" of the statue–Hermione. We can conjecture – with the ending of *Drood*, we can only conjecture – the crucial parallel discovery of a live body concealed in a space of effigy.

A particularly tantalizing parallel if, as some critics suppose, the body would have been female, that of Helena Landless. And made even more tantalizing when we reconstitute the curtailed prayer from the evensong quoted at the end of the first chapter: "When the wicked man turneth away from his wickedness that he hath committed, and doeth that which is lawful and right, he shall save his soul alive." A prayer that seems to pre-figure Jasper as Leontes.

But it's not just that *Drood* is a kind of *Winter's Tale*. What matters is that it's astonishingly close to the kind of *Winter's Tale* we find in Kean's Spectacular adaptation. Beyond merely commissioning a virtual museum of antiquarian sets and costumes, Kean made the *Tale* Spectacular in three major, interlocking ways: what he did for Leontes (whom he played); what he did to Time; and what he did with bodies, specifically female bodies.

Breaking with acting tradition, and Shakespeare's text, Kean chose to make Leontes plausible. The difficulty in playing Leontes has always been the sudden violence of his inexplicable jealousy. Within a minute or two of his first entrance he turns so vehemently against the man and the woman he loves best in the world, that he can only now desire them dead. To make this about-face plausible, Kean blocked the first scene to suggest that something illicit might well be going on between Polixenes and Hermione. He then cut scores of lines, his own and others', eliminating every suggestion that the tyrant is either mad or immoral or both. Something *was*, plausibly, rotten in the state of Sicily. Everything that followed became merely the exercise of kingly craft in disarming dubious associates. Motiveless malignity flaccidly resolved into reasonable misperception.

Kean also restored Time's thirty-two-line soliloquy, dropped since the Restoration. But he didn't only restore it, he embellished and amplified it in ways that make it a scene of privileged instruction. Shakespeare wrote a single speech for a solitary figure. Kean set that speech into a Spectacular three-scene tableau. First, the moon goddess attended by star-nymphs disap-peared into the ocean, on the platforms the Victorian stage called sliding traps. These permitted stationary figures to glide from one side of the stage to the other while slowly sinking out of view. The goddesses gave way to Time, appearing from the dark as a seated, enormously winged Kronos, car-rying a paring hook. He spoke thirty of the thirty-two original lines. And finally, Time in his turn descended giving way to Phoebus in the sun chariot ascending into a brilliant blaze.

This tableau rerouted the play just as much as Kean's choice to rational-ize Leontes. Shakespeare's text insists that redemption, physical and moral, depends on the play's female trinity: virginal Perdita, maternal Hermione, and Pauline the "mankind witch" (11.3.67). But for Kean, at the crucial turning point of the play, female goddesses uncomplainingly descend and disappear, giving place to figures of unmistakably male authority. Indeed, at the last moment, the hitherto immobile Phoebus unexpectedly cracked his whip and what had seemed only figures of horses began to move.

Phoebus continues and completes what Leontes began. Leontes's initial male excess justifiably disrupts a disappointing domestic order, opening the way to that desirably illusory spectacle Phoebus's male authority now sparks into full life. In Shakespeare's text, men deal death, women bear life, and renew it. On Kean's stage, females, like the nymphs, crowd, enclose, blur. Males break through, and brighten.

Inevitably, then, Kean's Spectacle works to disperse all forms of embodied space, particularly female bodies. He regularly crosses his audience's perspective with another, more important sight line, suggesting a larger, significant space they do not occupy. The audience thus observes, supremely, a world it does not have to endure or even share. Hermione's trial they watch, as it were, from its wings while the principals face an up- and off-stage audience of extras. In the final scene, framing wings suggest an enclosure into which the audience peers but from which it is also markedly excluded. And these spaces fill repeatedly with bodies so extravagantly multiplied that any sense of an individual body dissolves in the mass. In the finale, on a relatively small stage, there were 172 performers. In the fourth act pastoral that number almost doubled to 300. Of course, in such a theatre, inevitably, the lover Florizel gets played not by a man but a woman, a Miss Leclerq, a pantomime boy not an embodiment of desire. And it's no surprise that in the crucial final scene, where the text calls for one inimitable woman, Kean supplied an entire colonnade of figures. Will the real Hermione please step forward? Will we notice her when she does?

Here's Kean's reading, then. Protagonist, a sympathetic criminal, reread as sadly but justifiably excessive, refusing the form and rule of a depleted past. Time, a complementary and encompassing male ideal, continuing but correcting male energy from disruption into discovery. Space, an improved illusion, the simulacrum that displaces the mere intricacies of body. All to stage a text which insisted that saving a single woman's warm body could redeem all time's depredation. Now that's adaptation.

And what of Dickens?

Unalike as they are in many ways, Jasper's opium addiction functions very much like Kean's rationalization of Leontes: as a justification. Just think of *Drood* without the opium. A thwarted, jealous functionary mean-spiritedly plots to destroy the marriage of two admirable lovers. Jasper as Iago. But Cloisterham and opium turn Jasper from being damned into being, merely, doomed. The suffocating routines of crypt-like Cloisterham cry out for disruption. The consolatory opium dreams, with their Brighton Pavilion faux-orientalia, affiliate him to the long line of frustrated Romantic artist heroes, goaded by a philistine world into crimes we know how to exonerate. And, indeed, the weight of critical speculation suggests that we will learn that Jasper committed the murder when, drugged, he wasn't feeling quite himself. But, as himself, he will ultimately help resolve the mystery, as a form of rehabilitation The real villain becomes then not the user but the dealer, the Princess Puffer, the malevolent mother who feeds Jasper's disease even as she plots his destruction.

And to repair the rightly broken pieces there is Tartar. Like Apollo, Tartar appears suddenly, literally out of nowhere, at the start of what would have been the book's second half. He rises, theatrically, as on a trap, seen for the first time, "on the window-sill," dangling "so much more outside than inside, as to suggest the thought that he must have come up by the water-spout instead of the stairs" (17). He's out there because Tartar lives, we learn, in a "garden in the air" (20). And he not only lives like a god, he looks like one too, to be precise just like a sculpted Apollo: "handsome . . . with a young face, but with an older figure in its robustness and its breadth of shoulder." Indeed, he's so authentically Apollonian he's even "extremely sunburnt"; his manservant, the "image of the sun in old woodcuts" (21).

What's more: not only does Tartar live, look, and move like an Apollo, he functions like one too, at least like an Apollo at the Princess's Theatre. Of course, the novel breaks off before Tartar gets to accomplish much. But what we have shows this presiding deity of Staple Inn making things stable not only for the "old 'uns" like Grewgious but also for the Perdita-like heroine. He rescues her from the enclosure of women, the Nuns' House, powerless to cloister her from harm. Indeed, harm in the dangerous form of the seductive voice teacher is by those women supportively welcomed. No surprise there, when mothers in Cloisterham must be fragile bullies, like Mrs. Crisparkle, or dead – all those orphans – or death's head: the grotesque Princess Puffer who boasts "there's land customers, and there's water customers, I'm a mother to both" (22). In a world of women like these, the muscular, nurturing male must take up the burden of bearing life. Only Tartar, like Apollo, can bring "The Dawn Again" (the title of the last chapter Dickens wrote).

Princess Puffer, thus, reversed Kean's Princess's Theatre. Both offer roughly the same sort of razzle dazzle: "cymbals crash and the Sultan goes by to his palace in long procession. Ten thousand scimitars flash in the sunlight, and thrice ten thousand dancing-girls strew flowers." Kean or Dickens? Dickens, actually (1). But Kean's spectacle makes fantasy public and respectable. The dingy opium den caters to shameful, solitary vice. The Princess's Theatre disembodies; the Princess Puffer satisfies the body's craving. Just think of all those bodies heaped on her bedstead. Which is why, unlike Kean, she finds business so "*dreful bad.*" It's not simply that her customers' bodies pay an increasingly terrible price for the illusion she mixes. Far worse is the way in which the illusions themselves (reversing Kean's) insist her clients admit themselves embodied and limited. The Cathedral tower and the bed spike inevitably thrust into the procession, forcing Jasper to recognize them as his own, and with that recognition the already chaotic, the always disappointing illusion falls entirely apart.

It's not Dickens's Princess who parallels Kean's but Dickens himself. It's Dickens who is like Kean the supreme manager of Spectacle, who offers us the viable alternative to the ruinous, moldy, airless Close. The Princess's dearly bought, insufficient interludes are Spectacle's parody. Dickens's pages sustain illusion, an extended, coherent alternative reality. The Princess's drugs offer only fantasy, scattered, imitative, unintelligible, reality's inevitably inadequate substitute. Inadequate because it works in, not against, the body. The Princess, a self-proclaimed mother, traps men in the body's unsatisfiable desire. That's this novel's, and Spectacle's, notion of true woman's work. It's "womanish love" (12) that kills. The phrase is Edwin's way of describing Jasper's pathological obsession for him. And motherly love maims: the mothers here are, after all, the Princess and Mrs. Crisparkle. The only safe haven, the Staple Inn, means putting yourself under the protection of lifelong bachelors: Bazzard, Grewgious. As to the young men: Edwin desires only to break off his engagement. His romantic replacement, the muscular Tartar, has of course a splendid body, but it's clear that body is only good to look at: watch Rosa watching him rowing.

In this novel, in every Dickens novel, the carnal is always the frustrated. That frustration is Neville Landless's entire story. And it's also Jasper's, who must concede that the endlessly fantasized seizing of his rival's body, when accomplished, "seemed not worth the doing" (22). To thrive in *Drood*, as with Kean, desire must seek not to hold but to behold. Thus, in the powerful scene of the singing-lesson, where Jasper does succeed, he mesmerizes Rose. She speaks of feeling "compelled by him," but she remains throughout untouched: "He has made a slave of me with his looks" (7). He has made her, we now understand, into Spectacular Theatre.

So that's, by way of Kean's *Tale*, Dickens's Spectacle. Refusing realism's restrictive canons of limit and embodiment, Dickens aligns his fiction with Spectacular Theatre's promise to displace the solid with new discoveries, endlessly shifting and diverse. He builds his novels as places of play, springing his audience (as his protagonists are sprung) from the feminized regime of the domestic body and domesticated space, insisting we not only accept but sanction outrageous male excess as our only route to pure pleasure. In this Spectacle ungoverned male imagination melts realism's solidities. It releases the rules, undoes the limits, freeing the rest of us for those *far, far better worlds* of apparently inexhaustible *illusion* Dickens knowingly insisted *we*, all of us, *go to the play* – or his pages – *to cultivate*. Spectacle thus retrieves its connection to specious, not merely pleasing and deceptive, but pleasing because deceptive. The (male) eye learns happily to treat the (female) other merely as the view. And in return for acceding to its access, Spectacle guarantees for all its audiences inimitable simulacra, illusions infinitely to be preferred to anything merely like life.

But if Dickens can embrace Spectacle, why can he not also enter the theater? Are we back where we started? No. Because all theatre, but especially Spectacular Theatre, is *scopophile*. And *Drood* particularly, but also Dickens generally, is profoundly *scopophobe*. (Our only jargon, and two good terms to know.) Theaters stage display and observation as the twin coordinates of pleasure, the more of both the better. But Dickens sees looking as only about power. He wants to reveal but not to act, to show but not be seen. To display the other is to dominate but to be seen is to be degraded, scrutinized, persecuted, vulnerable. Just recall how Jasper loathes the routine exposure of his professional public performance. How sedulously he works to keep himself from being under surveillance. And how insistently that defense is penetrated by the relentless search of those who see, and seeing know: the Princess and the mysterious Datchery. Thus the characteristic thrust of this Dickens plot (and so many others): to flee sight, to escape with Rosa from the power of eyes, to the hidden, the enclosed, the out-of-the-way, the unobserved.

And that's why, though theatre can come into and subsume Dickens, Dickens cannot go into the theater. He does not wish even to imagine entering the Spectacle. He longs for the rapture of illusion, of illusion projected and produced. To capture that thrill, he teaches the page to mimic the stage. He makes fiction theatre's safe reflection, inventively defending against an increasingly realist regime the aesthetics of Spectacular illusion. But at the core there also lurks the enduring anxiety and its defensive fantasy: that at the moment when one must publicly perform, some sympathetic male spirit will sweep down and snatch one from the rigors of scrutiny. Which means it's always going to be Dickens *and* Theatre, because the *and* is indispensable. For Dickens theatre must always be the other, the longed-for something to be written, safely, someplace else.

A final note, to keep the engines searching. What about all those public readings? Dickens spent a significant part of his final years and energy consumed by public, and highly profitable, readings from his fiction. In effect, performing them. Yes, indeed, but aren't those exacting public performances what, all his biographers agree, killed him?

NOTES

1 For *The Village Coquettes* I have used Christopher U. Light's edition, published by Florida Literary Foundation, Inc. in cooperation with Sarasota Music Archive, Inc. (Sarasota, Florida, 1992).
2 The data on Kean's *Winter's Tale* comes from the Folger Shakespeare Library, Washington, DC, which contains the promptbook and the original set designs.

FURTHER READING

Brannan, Robert Louis. *Under The Management of Mr. Charles Dickens.* Cornell University Press, 1966.

Booth, Michael R. *Victorian Spectacular Theatre 1850–1910.* Routledge & Kegan Paul, 1981.

Brooks, Peter. *The Melodramatic Imagination.* Columbia University Press, 1985.

Fisher, Leona Weaver. *Lemon, Dickens and "Mr. Nightingale's Diary": A Victorian Farce.* University of Victoria: English Literary Studies, 1988.

Gager, Valerie. *Shakespeare and Dickens: The Dynamics of Influence.* Cambridge University Press, 1996.

Glavin, John. *After Dickens: Reading, Adaptation and Performance.* Cambridge University Press, 1999.

MacKay, Carol Hanbery (ed.). *Dramatic Dickens.* Macmillan, 1989.

Marshall, Gail. *Actresses on the Victorian Stage: Feminine Performances and the Galatea Myth.* Cambridge University Press, 1998.

Meisel, Martin. *Realizations: Narrative, Pictorial and Theatrical Arts in the Nineteenth Century.* Princeton University Press, 1984.

Roach, Joseph. *Cities of the Dead: Circum-Atlantic Performance.* Columbia University Press, 1996.

Vlock, Deborah. *Dickens, Novel Reading and the Victorian Popular Theatre.* Cambridge University Press, 1998.

14

JOSS MARSH

Dickens and film

If cinema, born 1895, was the child of Victorian visual technology and the entrancement of the eye, then the Victorian novel stood it god-parent. Its direct ancestors were the photograph, the panorama, and the magic lantern; the circus and the melodramatic theatre; the railway, which turned the world into "moving pictures" and opened up touristic pleasures; the ghoulish waxwork and the *tableau vivant*; and the overwhelming, kinetic city. But it was from fiction that film inherited its mass audience, its social function, its plots, and its techniques of narration. And from no other author did film inherit so much as from the Victorian writer who most imaginatively absorbed the influences of those other ancestors: Charles Dickens.

Since 1897, when the Mutoscope Company put the *Death of Nancy Sykes* [sic] on the screen, more films have been made of works by Dickens than of any other author's: there are 130 Dickens films on record[1] and only *Dracula* and *Dr. Jekyll and Mr. Hyde* beat out *Oliver Twist* and *A Christmas Carol* (of which there are 30-plus versions each) for the status of most-filmed single fiction in history. Part of Dickens's lure is the childhood appeal of his fiction, along with the "Inimitable's" proto-modern celebrity status, and the sheer familiarity of the texts, reinforced by frequent theatrical adaptation; part derives from the "mythic" characters who – like the film stars of Hollywood's golden age – seem larger than the stories that contain them. The attraction is partly economic: all of Dickens's fictions were out of copyright by 1920. It speaks both of national identity and of international appeal and interpretive openness. For although Dickens figures as large in the history of Britain's cinema as he does on its ten-pound note, Dickens films have been produced in movie-making cultures as diverse as the silent-era Scandinavian (a reflective and shadowy *Little Dorrit* of 1924, for example) and the contemporary Portuguese (an updated *Hard Times* of 1988, that bares the text's social-critical agenda in documentary black and white).[2]

More broadly, in filming Dickens, as the first paragraph of this introduction indicates, film returned to its origins in Victorian spectacle: where else but in Dickens could one find such imaginative entrammelment in the panorama or the magic lantern (his pregnant image for the city); where else find such dreams (as in *Christmas Carol*) of time travel and materialization, so suggestive for the film image? Moreover, there is a more striking affinity between Dickensian modes of narration and film's developed techniques of story-telling (including editing, camerawork, and design) than exists between film and any other author.[3] The matter of Victorian spectacle lies outside the scope of this essay, but it will explore all these other factors, in a roughly chronological thematic overview that must live with two imposing historical and conceptual conditions. First, that we cannot know the whole picture: 80 percent of all feature films of the silent period (1895–1928), and an ever-increasing number of later films, have been and are being lost to corporate destruction or material decay, and Dickens films are no exception. Second, that all adaptation is interpretation, and all interpretation is time-bound.

Cinema's first decade was a time of cheap vaudeville-like shows and one-minute "attractions." But from the time that the new medium began to aspire to "art" status and narrative length, cinema looked to literature for materials, techniques, and respectability. In America, for example, the Vitagraph Company laid claim to the murdered body of Dickens's Nancy in an early long film of 1909. But the British cinema rapidly became the most literary of all. While this may have assisted in the formation of a second-rank movie-culture which is snobbishly "dedicated to an out-of-date, exhausted national ideal," it has also produced some great works and inspired directors.[4]

In 1922, 23 percent of film output in Britain, in 1935 26 percent, and in 1939 54 percent was based on novels.[5] And the urge to adapt the "Inimitable" was imperative from the first, despite the challenges his language and broad canvas offered to adaptations that were shorn of the power of words and often ran an hour or less. Now known only from stills and reputation, Hepworth Company's 1912 *Oliver Twist* (58 minutes) was only the second feature film made in Britain (the first was Shakespeare's *Henry VIII*). It was apparently no less violent than Victorian stage versions of the novel, which were frequently banned. But it started Hepworth and his director Thomas Bentley on a chain of adaptations that illuminate Dickens's appeal and conceptual importance for film and its makers. Their *David Copperfield* (1913) may have had over-long intertitles (scraps of dialogue and narration between shots) which – in their fetishization of the author's words – give away all his story's suspense, primitive camera movement, and too frontal and tableau-like a presentation to the audience, but

11 Eighteenth-century London reconstructed in "facsimile" for the Hepworth Company's landmark 1915 film of *Barnaby Rudge*.

its investment in "the actual scenes immortalised by Charles Dickens" (opening title) set British film on a long and fruitful course of preoccupation with production design.

"*Taken on the actual spots that have been made so famous by the author in his novel*": the topographical titular claim was loudly repeated in full-page advertisements for the "HEPWORTH MASTERPIECE."[6] This was a claim only a *British* company could make: through the genius of place, the already flagging industry could exploit its most valuable literary property. Hepworth and Bentley followed *Copperfield* with *The Old Curiosity Shop* (a text Bentley eventually shot three times in his career), *The Chimes* (1914), and – climactically – *Barnaby Rudge* (1915), for which the heart of Old London in 1780 was recreated in giant "facsimile" in a rural field near Walton-on-Thames (figure 11), and in the wake of which "Dickens director" Bentley became the first British talent to be head-hunted by Hollywood.

The reasons for Hepworth and Bentley's profitable fixation are not far to seek. One of the key pioneers of film form, especially continuity editing, Hepworth had been "saturated" in Dickens since childhood, when he "gloried" in his lantern-slide lecturer-father's most successful piece, "a topographical extravaganza called *The Footprints of Charles Dickens*."[7] For his part, Bentley was not only a "Dickensian" actor and Dickens impersonator, but a photographer with a passion for recording the "real" places of Dickens's fiction. Between the two of them, this unlikely pair laid the foundations for that mysterious slippage of modern culture, whereby Dickens = London = Victorian = England, a slippage which dictates, for example, that Gatwick Airport today be equipped with a "Dickens" tavern, or that armchair tourists need only pop *Oliver!* in the VCR to walk the streets of "Dickens's London." (Dickens, as author, was never once mentioned in publicity for Columbia's musical blockbuster of 1968, though "Dickens's London" was cited in every other press release. The city's recreation at "its rheumatic and choleric best" was a central object of every BBC television adaptation of the 1990s.)[8] This was not the appeal Thackeray and other Victorians made to film. "Dickensland" (the fans' coinage) anticipated Disney's empire by the best part of a century: so intensely had Dickens imagined London that he had laid the foundations for that virtual travel through time and space on which all period film is predicated.[9]

The idea brings us, of course, to the other motive force behind Hepworth and Bentley's fixation: history. *Rudge* was (as the subtitle put it) *A Story of the Gordon Riots of 1780*. In it, for one of the very first times, the fiction film assumed its paradoxical role of historical record. "It is difficult," enthused the *Star* newspaper, in terms to make a historian blink, "to believe we are not witnessing the actual historical scenes as described by Charles

Dickens." Scale and history together made *Rudge* "Britain's greatest film" (*Daily Citizen*).[10]

Those were appeals already made by *A Tale of Two Cities*, Vitagraph's 45-minute film of 1911, an obvious spur to British competition. The 1911 *Tale* was notable for its production values and occasional text-inspired experiments with point-of-view, but burdened by inartistic reliance on prior audience knowledge (introducing the Marquis's assassination, for example, with the otherwise cryptic inter-title "The face at the window") and baffled by the temporal complexities of Dickens's plot, which it straightened out to a chronological walking-pace, from an initial one-shot scene pitting angry "paupers" against the Marquis to a final dissolve that merges Carton's face into a family group with Lucy and her children, filmically fulfilling his fantasy of fatherhood at the novel's end. Film had not yet worked out the techniques of flashback, and the *Tale* proved (and remains, through a fine bilingual Anglo-French TV coproduction of 1989) a challenge to adaptation.

The *Tale*'s other challenge, one that brings vividly to mind how differently readers and viewers apprehend and identify character through the different markers of names and faces in fiction and film,[11] is its central premise of Carton and Darnay's extraordinary likeness. Vitagraph's 1911 version throws away the *Tale*'s courtroom revelation with a cursory shot of their profiles, introduced by a preemptive title; other versions downplay or play with the similarity. Herbert Wilcox's British film of 1925, however, relied on resemblance where the film medium's insistent realism denied it: *The Only Way* was not only a filmed version of the stage hit of 1899 (a late example of an old formula, made anachronistically modish by a sumptuous backdrop of high-art sets), but a vehicle for its original Carton, plump and middle-aged John Martin Harvey, preposterously paired with a slim young Darnay.

The Only Way was a national expedient. By 1925, Hollywood had taken 95 percent of the British market; home producers responded (as they still respond) to the cultural threat with no less than five adaptations of Dickens in that year. But nothing could stop American appropriation of Dickens under the studio system, and a romantic role like Sydney Carton offered obvious possibilities for a handsome matinee-idol. Ronald Colman exploited them to the full in the 1935 MGM *Tale of Two Cities*, wresting the part from Leslie Howard, for whom it had been developed at Warner's: the story was a template for every Hollywood history-drama in which (as MGM's publicity put it) a single man's love "challenged the flames of revolution!" from *Gone with the Wind* to *Dr. Zhivago*. The disjuncture between the visual style in which Colman is filmed (soft-focus close-ups and meditative reaction shots) and the documentary style of the crowd scenes of historic action was producer David O. Selznick's doing: he assigned the mob scenes to an

entirely separate second unit, as if "story" in the *Tale* could literally be separated from "history."

The visual style of Selznick's earlier Dickens venture, MGM's 1934 *David
Copperfield*, with its perfect cast and superb director (George Cukor), had a
more Dickensian source: W. C. Fields as Micawber (replacing Charles
Laughton, who had the legs but not the requisite music-hall bounce) struts
through the film in comically under-sized trousers as a result of a design decision to base all costumes on the novel's original illustrations by "Phiz."
Illustrations to Dickens had gained familiarity through Victoria's reign as
blueprints for *tableaux vivants* or "living pictures" (one of the other, less-
known ancestors of cinema), and have been obvious sources for film. In
1909, the Vitagraph *Twist* made Cruikshankian mythic moments of Oliver's
introductions to Dodger and Fagin; in 1987, for her *Little Dorrit*, Christine
Edzard drew heavily both on "Phiz's" dark plates for the novel and
Cruikshank's illustrations to *Sketches by Boz*.

Lauded for its integrity of research design – eighty-nine sets, largely based
on the period London sketches of George Scharf, dressed with artifacts
(bricks, glasses, pottery, paste jewelry, advertising posters) made in unique
purpose-built workshops at Edzard's own Docklands studios, and peopled
by 242 speaking characters (besides hand-picked extras) in authentically
dyed, hand-sewn costumes (later exhibited at the Museum of London) –
Edzard's two-part, six-hour "Dickensathon" of 1987 may be taken both as
the ultimate example of the Dickens film in its aspect of historical reconstruction and virtual tourism and as a conceptual turning point (figure 12). The
way to production of *Little Dorrit* was paved by the Royal Shakespeare
Company's eight-hour marathon *Nicholas Nickleby* (1980): Edzard's cast
were trained stage actors; and her sense of the work was essentially experi-
mental (the film's two parts took the gendered perspectives of Arthur
Clennam and Little Dorrit) and performance-oriented, allowing for the
expansion onto screen of the full "magic democracy" (as Nabokov once
called it) of Dickens's minor characters, like irascible Mr. Wobbler, briefly
seen dribbling marmalade onto documents in the Circumlocution Office
(1.10).

Television has taken Edzard's lead, since 1987, in frequently substituting
a two- (or sometimes three-) part theatrical format for the traditional serial
episodes to which Dickens's texts naturally lend themselves. But while
quality productions of the 1990s have also, like Edzard's film, foregrounded
the psychological and cultural anxieties of the works – the BBC's *Great
Expectations* of 1999, for example, became a meditation on class guilt and
(self) forgery; its *David Copperfield* of 2000 the working-out of a
Dickensian–Freudian family romance – more popular made-for-TV movies

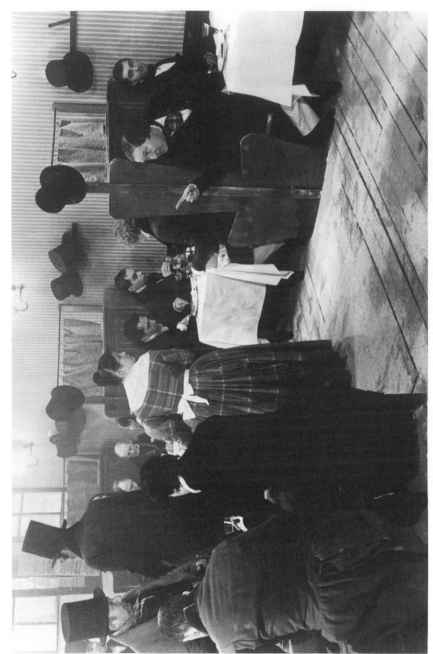

12 The "Slapbang restaurant," in Christine Edzard's evocative marathon *Little Dorrit* (1987).

and series from Disney, Hallmark, and others, have lapsed fully into the Christmas-card style of Dickensian cheer brewed up by earlier British ventures: *Scrooge* (released 1970), which turned Dickens's psychology of redemption into a recipe for "dropping out" and "turning on," and the Oscar-winner whose success it aped, *Oliver!* (1968), in which, under the film musical's generic sign of emotional plenitude, famine became excess – as in the Workhouse boys' opening chant, "Food, Glorious Food!" – and everything, even experience, had a price – as in the set-piece production number (recorded by several sixties artists, and instantly comprehensible to consumer culture), "Who Will Buy?" Of the more sentimental favorites among the novels, *A Christmas Carol* has been most seamlessly absorbed into the lifeblood of American popular culture, as Paul Davis demonstrates in his richly detailed study, *The Lives and Times of Ebenezer Scrooge*. Loose adaptations like Capra's *It's A Wonderful Life* (1946) shift emphasis to Bob Crachit (Capra's George Bailey), of whom they make an American Everyman, demonizing the big-time capitalist Scrooge; they reached their apogee of cultural integration in the 1988 media-world satire *Scrooged* (1988) and Disney's *A Muppet Christmas Carol* (1992).

No Dickens films have had more impact on film history or more importance for Dickens's popular and critical reputation, however, than two films of the 1940s. They were made in the context of a post-World War II boom in literary adaptation, fueled by voracious wartime reading of the classics, especially of Dickens, as were Cavalcanti's processional *Nicholas Nickleby* (1947) and Noel Langley's character-crammed *Pickwick Papers* (1952). And they were made by a single director: David Lean. *Great Expectations* (1946) was a rarity among screen adaptations in satisfying both literary purists and the mass audience; *Oliver Twist* (1948) was a more controversial masterpiece. And the two films' aesthetic success has a great deal to do with Lean's respect for the inherently cinematic qualities of Dickens's texts.

Dickens's Pip and Oliver were well-chosen figures for the late 1940s: like millions of British children during the war, they struggled with hardship, hunger, and separation from family; and like those children, for whom a new society was being built, they aspired to more prosperous futures. Their stories seem to have spoken directly to David Lean: here were figures who might say, with the man whose life story he later filmed as *Lawrence of Arabia*, "I'm just an ordinary man," yet whose destined extraordinariness illuminated the ordinary. Collaboration with Dickens precipitated the period of Lean's greatest achievement as a director.

Like nearly every filmmaker Dickens has profoundly influenced, however, Lean discovered him through the medium of theatre: *Great Expectations* was directly inspired by actor Alec Guinness's shoestring 1939 stage

13 Designer John Bryan with white-card model of his set for Jacob's Island, in David Lean's *Oliver Twist* (1948).

adaptation. When the Cineguild production company began casting around for subjects in 1944, Lean quickly suggested the novel, and was just as quickly confirmed in his choice. By developing a distinctive British style, in "a great cycle of Dickens films,"[12] industry commentators hoped British cinema would fend off resurgent American competition, from which wartime conditions had protected it, and perhaps break into the US market.

Nervous of the adaptation, Lean handed it to a Dickens scholar, Clemence Dane. When that produced a respectful collage of truncated snippets, he set to himself, with his producer Ronald Neame, to produce a ruthlessly selective script which nevertheless gave "full value," as Lean put it, to the most filmic Dickens scenes. "You have to savour Dickens," he explained, "you can't just skip through in shorthand."[13] The opening sequence of the finished film, a classic of visual story-telling, validated the method. Critic Julian Moynahan transcribes it: "Begins with book pages turning by themselves, the voice of John Mills speaking Pip's first words ("My father's family name being Pirrip . . . ") – boy running on dike, into graveyard, placing flowers at grave marker. INSTANTLY the convict, fearful to behold, pouncing! Abruptness, violence, pitifulness, all there just right."[14]

The shock value so vividly registered in Moynahan's memory was a product of extraordinary artistry. The visual world of Lean's *Great Expectations*, like that of his still more innovative *Twist*, was the creation of a little-known genius of cinema, designer John Bryan (figure 13). The sense of foreboding evoked as the boy runs along the dike, for example, is not a simple product of the lowering sky above him. The sky itself is the product of Bryan's imagination: a fake cloud, painted on glass, and superimposed along the top of the screen, provides a visual equivalent for the suggestions and linguistic density of Dickens's style. The scene's hyper-real, "Dickensian" quality, meanwhile, is the result of Bryan's greatest innovation, "trick" perspective. "[A]t first glance to an unskilled observer," a distorted and foreshortened set like the churchyard, with its ten-foot-high church and man-made trees in which distorted limbs and faces are almost but not quite discernable, "looks like the work of a slightly mad [wartime] camouflage artist." But through a camera lens with a dramatically longer and narrower range than normal (another innovation, by cameraman Guy Green), the forced perspective created the impression, in Bryan's words, of a "natural" yet curiously enhanced field of vision.[15] Dickens's novel asked that Lean put "ordinary human people into a fairy-tale story and background," and it was precisely this doubled effect of the stylized and brutishly real that Bryan's innovations produced.[16] The film's leap forward in representative power was even fueled by the austerities of production in the wake of the War: "cloud" glass, "trick" perspective, and miniatures (like the crystal chandeliers seen in the film's ballroom sequence, hand-carved from perspex) were cheap alternatives to full-size sets and expensive shoots. Bryan's encounter with Dickens permanently impacted the design practices of post-war cinema.[17]

Great Expectations (like Lean's *Twist*) was cut without reference to the soundtrack, like the silent films on which Lean had trained as an editor in the 1920s. "What we wanted to create," he recalled, "was the world as it seemed to Pip when his imagination was distorted with fear. That, after all, was what Dickens himself did" (Brownlow, *David Lean*, p. 211). The object of the opening sequence was to defy the great "grey," "sweet-sucking" cinema audience's impulse to comfortable lethargy, without moderating dialogue that was almost comically "over-the-top" (p. 220). The solution (planned in detail by Lean and his editor, Jack Harris) was to emphasize the shock of the convict's appearance by subliminal means: the camera pans with Pip as he turns from the frightening graveyard until he runs into the convict, to whom we cut in a shot long enough (1.4 seconds) to let us register his "horrible" figure, Harris writes, "but not sufficiently long enough to . . . be able to decide that he [is] . . . recognisably human." Meanwhile, "Pip's scream starts four frames" – the fraction of a second – "before the [next] cut, at just the precise moment that the apparition is taken away from the audience's sight."[18] This scene, and Miss Havisham's burning, were large factors in the film's being denied a "U" ("Universal") certificate, while Britain's aged chief censor, ironically, lectured Lean for tempting "thousands of boys with no education to come to London to lead a good life" (Brownlow, *David Lean*, p. 223).

The cutting and timing of *Great Expectations* were tightened by Lean's five-week research trip to the States; and an eye on the US market dictated its publicity's overemphasis on the star-power of its star-crossed lovers, Pip (John Mills) and Estella (Valerie Hobson). In fact, Lean had warned Mills, fresh (appropriately) from his lower-class roles in Lean and Coward's condescending wartime dramas *In Which We Serve* (1942) and *This Happy Breed* (1944), that the part of Pip was essentially a "coat hanger" for "all the wonderful garments that will be hung on you" (Brownlow, *David Lean*, p. 211); he very sharply restricted Hobson's performance as Estella to an emotionless blank. (Hobson thought the part "very thinly written" in the original novel [p. 219], a fact that calls to mind the apparent ease with which Estella was removed from the public reading version Dickens prepared of his text in 1861.)

Great Expectations belongs not to its "stars" but to its ensemble. The larger-than-life "Dickensian" character, sharply etched by behavior, appearance, and verbal tics, was the dream assignment of every character-actor, and a number made careers of single roles or types of role: Edna May Oliver, for example, played Betsey Trotwood in MGM's *Copperfield*, and Miss Pross in their *Tale of Two Cities*; Seymour Hicks filmed his lifelong stage role of Scrooge in 1901 (possibly), 1911, and 1935 (Pointer, *Charles Dickens*, p. 14). Lean's 1946 *Great Expectations* took two actors from Guinness's stage production, fey Martita Hunt as Miss Havisham and, as Herbert Pocket, Guinness himself, who later inhabited Fagin (Lean, 1948) and William Dorrit (Edzard, 1987); Francis L. Sullivan, Lean's corpulently assertive Jaggers, had first played the part for Universal in 1934, and embodied Lean's Bumble (still more corpulently) two years later. Young Pip's unglamorous ordinariness was conveyed by a non-actor, Anthony Wager.

The greatest impact, however, was made by seventeen-year-old, Lolita-like Jean Simmons, as young Estella. So much did she usurp the role that her name was accidentally substituted for Hobson's in American publicity; more than fifty years later, in 1989, Disney scored a coup in turning her into Miss Havisham, Estella's double. That role, of all others, demands suggestive casting: the sexualized screen persona of sixties icon Charlotte Rampling illuminated its neurotic pathos in the BBC version of 1999; two years before, an uneasy Americanized update with too focused an eye on its youth audience remodeled the role, aptly played by Anne Bancroft (the mother–temptress of Mike Nichols's classic 1967 *The Graduate*), as a caricature hag. By an act of screen incest, the update's "Miss Dinsmoor" took more after Miss Norma Desmond, has-been silent-star *femme fatale* of Billy Wilder's 1950 *Sunset Boulevard*, than Miss Havisham. But the slippage was logical, too: Wilder's masterwork is a cynical homage to the mythic power (and, in Lean's hands, Oscar-winning success) of "that Dickens novel," in which a boy first came to "play" for an aging woman's pleasure, in a decrepit mansion.

Lean's *Great Expectations* is a brighter fable than Dickens's novel (or Wilder's virtuoso adaptation). The post-war atmosphere of austerity and celebration into which it was released made its luxuriance of ballroom and costume more innocent pleasures than Dickens would have them. But other changes stir more unease. The film's "shocking" omission of Orlick, Joe's surly journeyman, Pip's "psychopathic" alter ego, is one (Moynahan, "Seeing," p. 153). Another, and greater, is the film's ending.

Dickens had toiled famously over its revision; scripting it defeated Lean and Neame. Eventually, the film's famously "unfaithful" finale was written (without credit) by Lean's wife, Kay Walsh (who also wrote, also uncredited, the opening to his *Oliver Twist*, which silently restores the experience of Oliver's mother.) We cut from Pip confiding to Biddy, as they lie companionably in the long grass near Joe's forge, that his "poor dream" of Estella "has all gone by," to a long shot of Pip outside Satis House (not ruined, but exactly as he and we have last seen it), admitting in voice-over: "I knew, as I said those words, that I intended to visit the old house again . . . " As he contemplates its rusted gates, he hears again the child-voice of Estella calling from the past – "What name?" – and follows it to Miss Havisham's room. Inside, in the dim light, all seems as before. But one thing is different: it is Estella's voice that greets him – "Pip" – not Miss Havisham's. The dialogue that follows is a radical divergence from the original novel:

> PIP Estella: . . . What are you doing here? I thought you were in Paris with your husband.
> ESTELLA I have no husband, Pip. Have you not heard?
> PIP I have been ill, Estella. I have heard nothing.
> ESTELLA When Mr. Jaggers disclosed to Bentley Drummle my true parentage he no longer wished to have me for a wife.

Estella is thus conjugally "unsoiled" and unproblematically rich, a real blunting of Dickens's "probing analysis" of Pip's "caste-ridden, ruthlessly

14 "I have come back, Miss Havisham! I have come back!" Pip precipitates the famously unfaithful ending to David Lean's *Great Expectations* (1946).

competitive, and money-grubbing society" (Moynahan, "Seeing," p. 151). But before Pip can claim the prize that Americanized romantic movie tastes now dictate he win, he must remove another obstacle – Estella's entrapment in the "dead house" of Miss Havisham, a logical development of a design latent in Dickens's text. He does so with Hollywood bravado: "I have come back, Miss Havisham," he shouts to its echoing shadows, "I have come back . . . to let in the sunlight" (figure 14). A dimly lit long shot (employing *rim* or *outline-only lighting*) now shows us Estella seated rigidly in Miss Havisham's throne-like chair. Then:

> *Medium close shot* PIP tears down a curtain.
> *Medium shot* ESTELLA suddenly backlit.
> *Long shot* PIP tearing down more curtains.
> *Medium shot* ESTELLA as *light strikes her face and breast.*

"Look at me," Pip urges her; "Come with me." And, turning slowly to each other, as romantic music swells, the two run out of the desolate house, like children released from school:

> *Medium long shot* They turn to look back at the gate.
> GREAT
> EXPECTATIONS
> is superimposed over shot as they go out into the sunlight.[19]

Anathema as it has proved to literary critics, the Lean–Walsh ending does have a Dickensian source. At the opening of chapter 29, Pip imagines Miss Havisham has reserved it for him to "admit the sunshine into the dark rooms" of the sleeping house, "tear down the cobwebs, destroy the vermin." But for Dickens, and the adult, narrating Pip, that was a piece of fairy-tale wish-fulfillment, no sooner spoken than spurned. To take it as a template for resolution is indeed "strictly movieland" (Moynahan, "Seeing," p. 151).

But all adaptations are timebound. There was no cloud on the film's original critics' near-unanimous announcement, "Britain makes her finest film,"[20] as if it were reserved always for the making of a Dickens film (*Barnaby Rudge* in 1915, *Little Dorrit* in 1987) for that patriotic encomium to be pronounced. Pip announcing his return to the Satis House shadows has more than a dash of the heroic serviceman of 1945–46, home from the front to tear down the blackout curtains and claim his bride, who (as in the fantasies of *film noir*, the dominant genre of the later forties) can be put back in her proper, submissive feminine place now that war work is over. And the film's ending has been roundly praised by film critics, in terms that may enhance our sense of the original text. Lean needed visual "guts" in *Great Expectations*, and cameraman Guy Green produced them by forcing the contrast values of his black-and-white film stock. In the final scene, Green's lighting alone bears the burden of explanation that is largely carried, in Dickens's revised final chapter, by his suggestive imagery of "shadows" and "partings." The three-step sequence of Estella's awakening – the progression from rim- to back- to frontal spot-lighting italicized above – is rightly dubbed by Alain Silver "The Illumination": the ray that warms her frozen heart as Pip lets in the sunlight falls not from the direction of the windows (which are off-screen right) but from above and to left of the shot. It is as if – catching at the imagery of photography that quietly saturates the novel, from the first-page invocation of "a time long before the days of photographs" to the very idea of Miss Havisham's time-stopped entrapment in a "dark room" – the falling beam mars the exposure, spoils the deathly portrait she sits for, of herself as Miss Havisham. Not unlike Dickens himself, juggling his audience's demands for the readmission of romance in his revised ending, Lean's film here resolves the "plotted psychological conflicts" of the narrative on a purely symbolic and graphic level.[21]

Lean's second Dickens film, *Oliver Twist* (1948) is a still more sustained response to the inherently visual qualities of Dickens's writing: *Twist*'s suggestive use of dumb show, for example, without any recourse to dialogue or authorial commentary, translates into a mutely inventive sequence of Nancy's spying upon Monks and Fagin in the "Three Cripples" pub; the novel's use of light and shadows inspires a style which has been called at once both "gothic" or "Expressionistic" and "unrelentingly" "grim" and "realistic." Most revealingly, faced with how to still into urban normality his ominously restrained depiction of Sikes's murder of Nancy, and after experiments (as his draft script reveals, still extant at the British Film Institute) with the touristic idea of a dawn shot of St. Paul's seen across the glittering Thames, Lean based one of the most quietly flamboyant sequences in the history of mainstream cinema on pure transcription of Dickens's original text: "The sun . . . burst upon the crowded city in clear and radiant glory. Through costly-colored glass and paper-mended window, through cathedral dome and rotten crevice, it shed its equal ray. It lighted up the room where the murdered woman lay. It did. He tried to shut it out, but it would stream in" (*OT* 48).

Where Lean relied heavily on Cruikshank instead of Dickens, it was with disastrous effect. The grotesquerie of Fagin's big-nosed make-up in the 1948 *Oliver Twist* may be (as Lean defensively claimed it was) directly ascribable to Cruikshank's nightmarish caricature of "the Jew" in the original illustrations. What is clear, however, is that in striving to reclaim a British text from its American usurpers, by all "authentic" means possible – including employing a convicted burglar as a research consultant – Lean committed an act of unthinking anti-Semitism, in the wake of the Holocaust, that was made particularly gross by an international context of unrest in Palestine, still under British rule. There, as in Berlin, *Oliver Twist* provoked riots; in America, the film was banned for two years before release with 12 offensive minutes cut out. Even Lean's home audience, however, might have revolted at the *Twist* he had really wanted to make. There is a character entirely missing from his draft script of 12 April 1947: Monks, the evil brother of Dickensian melodrama. His deletion turned Fagin unequivocally into the film's principal source of evil. Only intervention by the American Production Code Office derailed this explosive, if logical, streamlining of Dickens's story.

Yet where Cruikshank could not be ambiguous, Dickens could, and that too is reflected in Lean's controversial masterpiece. The "curious game" of pick-pocketing (9), that makes Oliver laugh "till the tears ran down his face" – as delightedly played by Alec Guinness, sometimes direct to camera, in the (later) style of the film musical, was evident inspiration for "the Jew's" transformation, in *Oliver!*, into an "only slightly bent scoutmaster" in a Pied Piper coat, at the hands of a musician and lyricist of Russian Jewish extraction, Lionel Bart.[22] As Dickens had written and innumerable stage Fagins had played it, the scene was also inspiration for Charlie Chaplin's indirect remake of *Oliver Twist*, in cinema's first full-length comic feature film, *The Kid* (1921).

Born in a "miserable garret" round the corner from the Marshalsea prison, consigned to the Workhouse at seven, orphaned by drink and madness, and obsessed all his life by food and city streets, Chaplin's filmic self-representation as a grown-up lost child was sanctified by identification with Dickens's Oliver and Artful Dodger: he "read and re-read" *Twist* "constantly";[23] its idiom and its mythic moments are the small change of his *Autobiography*. In *The Kid* he doubled his Tramp persona in the diminutive figure of child actor Jackie Coogan, while the film as a whole is structured (like *Twist*) by yearning for the lost mother, and even includes a highly cinematic chase sequence (reminiscent of Sikes's final flight) across the rooftops. Rescued from the refuse-strewn streets, the orphaned and outcast Kid is taught Charlie's crooked tricks with the gas-meter, plate-glass windows, etc. He is even glimpsed sitting up in bed – like Dickens's Dodger, and dressed in the same miniaturized mannish outfit (a neat reversal of Chaplin's signature under-sized jacket and giant pants) – to study the *Police Gazette*. (This Dickensian inheritance made for a Dickensian consequence: Coogan's next major role was in Frank Lloyd's fine silent version of *Oliver Twist* in 1922 [figure 15]. No less inevitably, he made innocent Oliver look a close cousin of Dodger.) Chaplin plays the Kid's volunteer father as a benign Fagin, his garret as an anarchic haven of all-male domesticity. In Dickens's *Twist* (we

15 Child star Jackie Coogan asks for more in Frank Lloyd's silent *Oliver Twist* (1922).

remember) it is Fagin who lays Oliver "gently" to rest for the first time in his life, and first feeds him to happy repletion (8). In the same spirit, Chaplin's Tramp heaps piles of food on the Kid's plate from a bucket, and improvises a baby-feeding system with a coffee pot and a length of rope. The investment Chaplin makes in Fagin is testament to the creative energy Dickens vested in the role; it helps us understand how "the Jew" could conclude his twentieth-century odyssey (in British independent television's version of 1999) as a (non-Jewish) magician from Prague.

Of the great directors who have been influenced by Dickens, besides Chaplin and Lean, Hitchcock never made a Dickens film, preferring the artistic license of adapting inferior works. But his macabre vision of the modern city, his interest in doubles and mirrors, his insistent sense of narrative style, his personal intrusion into his texts, and his cynical distrust of public institutions owe much to his boyhood soaking in Dickens: *Bleak House*, in particular, "seems to have engraved itself on [his] memory."[24]

Most important for film history, however, is D.W. Griffith, world-dominating pioneer of film "grammar" and the multi-reel feature film. He made only one Dickens film, a 1909 version of *The Cricket on the Hearth* that forwarded his use of close-ups, but he pays his debt to the favorite author he claimed publicly as formal inspiration (and justification) in every one of his major films: in the ride-to-the-rescue climax of *The Birth of a Nation* (1915), an epic of national identity fundamentally founded on a Dickensian threat to female chastity; in the conversion of sex to violence (as in Dickens's murder of Nancy), and the drive to infantilize his female characters, as when a brutish father takes an axe to the closet that hides his terrified daughter, in *Broken Blossoms* (1919); and in his development of the technique of parallel editing or "cross-cutting" from one line of action to another that made those sequences possible, a technique that structures even such mammoth works as Griffith's 1916 *Intolerance*. Through Griffith, a Dickensian moral vision made its way into the structure and the unconscious of modern film. And through Sergei Eisenstein, the great Soviet director and author of the seminal 1944 essay "Dickens, Griffith, and the Film Today," with its bravura formal reading of *Oliver Twist*, that vision began to make its way into theoretical and critical consciousness, though much work remains to be done. "Our cinema," as Eisenstein pronounced, "is not . . . without parents."[25] And the father of fathers was Dickens.

NOTES

1 Michael Pointer, *Charles Dickens on the Screen: The Film, Television, and Video Adaptations* (Scarecrow Press, 1996), p. 7.

2 The most up-to-date filmography of Dickens is given in Pointer, *Charles Dickens on the Screen*, 117–94.

3 Editing incorporates all means of joining shots together, whether by straight cuts, dissolves, fades, or wipes. Camerawork includes not only camera movement (tracking with the whole camera, on a moveable dolly; elevating the camera on a crane; tilting the lens up or down, moving it side to side in a panning shot, etc.) but composition within the frame. Design incorporates props, made sets, and found locations.

4 Charles Thomas Samuels, quoted in Brian MacFarlane, "A Literary Cinema?" in *All Our Yesterdays: 90 Years of British Cinema*, ed. Charles Barr (BFI, 1986), p. 137.

5 The rate of novel adaptation to film production stabilized at one third between 1946 and 1950, and has since averaged about one quarter (MacFarlane, "A Literary Cinema?" pp. 132, 126). On the "literary cinema" of 1921–56, also see Roy Armes, *A Critical History of British Cinema* (Oxford University Press, 1978), pp. 198–215.

6 *Bioscope*, 21 August 1913.

7 Cecil Hepworth, *Came the Dawn: Memories of a Film Pioneer* (Phoenix House, 1951), p. 111.

8 *Radio Times* preview of *Martin Chuzzlewit*, 5–11 November 1994.

9 On Dickens, urban tourism, and film, see my "Imagining Victorian London: An Entertainment and Itinerary (Chas. Dickens, Guide)," *Stanford Humanities Review* 3:1 (Winter 1993), 67–97.

10 Reviews of 15 and 11 January 1915, reprinted in *Barnaby Rudge* souvenir program. I am grateful to Fred Lake of Walton-on-Thames for a replica of this publication.

11 I am indebted for this insight to Kamilla Elliott of UC Berkeley.

12 *Daily Mail*, 11 December 1946.

13 Kevin Brownlow, *David Lean* (St. Martin's Press, 1996), p. 208.

14 Julian Moynahan, "Seeing the Book, Reading the Movie," in *The English Novel and the Movies*, ed. Michael Klein and Gillian Parker (Frederick Ungar, 1981), p. 147.

15 Cineguild press release by Stuart Chant for *Oliver Twist*, "Production Story" (BFI microfiche, 1948), p. 12.

16 Chant, "Production Story," n.p.

17 See interviews with John Box and Terence Marsh in Vincent Lobrutto, *By Design: Interviews with Film Production Designers* (Praeger, 1992).

18 Jack Harris, in Karel Reisz and Gavin Millar, *The Technique of Film Editing* (Communication Arts Books, 1968), p. 240.

19 Script as transcribed (with emendations) by Alain Silver, "The Untranquil Light: David Lean's *Great Expectations*," *Literature/Film Quarterly* 2 (Spring 1974), 146–49.

20 Stephen Watts, *Daily Express*, quoted in Brownlow, *David Lean*, p. 225.

21 Silver, "The Untranquil Light," p. 151.

22 Vincent Canby, *New York Times*, 6 December 1968.

23 Charles Chaplin, *My Autobiography* (Simon and Schuster, 1964), p. 12; David Robinson, *Chaplin: His Life and Art* (McGraw-Hill, 1985), p. 628.

24 Donald Spoto, *The Dark Side of Genius: The Life of Alfred Hitchcock* (Ballantine Books, 1984), p. 28.

25 Sergei Eisenstein, "Dickens, Griffith, and the Film Today," in *Film Form: Essays in Film Theory*, ed. and trans. Jay Leyda (Harcourt Brace, 1949), p. 232.

FURTHER READING

Altman, Rick. "Dickens, Griffith, and Film Theory Today." In *Silent Film*, edited by Richard Abel. Rutgers University Press, 1996.

Bolton, H. Philip. *Dickens Dramatized*. Mansell (UK) and G. K. Hall, 1987.

Brownlow, Kevin. *David Lean*. St. Martin's Press, 1996.

Davis, Paul. *The Lives and Times of Ebenezer Scrooge*. Yale University Press, 1990.

Eisenstein, Sergei. "Dickens, Griffith, and the Film Today." In *Film Form: Essays in Film Theory*, edited and translated by Jay Leyda. Harcourt Brace, 1949.

Marsh, Joss. "Inimitable Double Vision: Dickens, *Little Dorrit*, Photography, Film." *Dickens Studies Annual* 22 (1993), 239–82.

Moynahan, Julian. "Seeing the Book, Reading the Movie." In *The English Novel and the Movies*, edited by Michael Klein and Gillian Parker. Frederick Ungar, 1981.

Paroissien, David. "Dickens and the Cinema." *Dickens Studies Annual* 7 (1980), 68–80.

Petrie, Graham. "Dickens, Godard, and the Film Today." *Yale Review* 44 (1974), 185–201.

Pointer, Michael. *Charles Dickens on the Screen: The Film, Television, and Video Adaptations*. Scarecrow Press, 1996.

Poole, Mike. "Dickens and Film: 101 Uses of a Dead Author." In *The Changing World of Charles Dickens*, edited by Robert Giddings. Vision (UK) and Barnes and Noble, 1983.

Smith, Grahame. "Dickens and Adaptation: Imagery in Words and Pictures." In *Novel Images: Literature in Performance*, edited by Peter Reynolds. Routledge, 1993.

"Novel into Film: the Case of *Little Dorrit*." *Yearbook of English Studies* 20 (1990), 33–47.

Zambrano, Ana-Laura. *Dickens and Film*. Gordon, 1977.

SELECTED BIBLIOGRAPHY

The amount of scholarly work on Dickens is enormous. What follows is a necessarily incomplete listing of important primary sources and reference materials, as well as a selective list of critical studies, most of them published during the last two or three decades. Some older materials that have stood the test of time are included. Readers should also consult the recommended "Further Reading" section at the end of each chapter as well as the "Note on References and Editions" at the beginning of this volume.

Primary sources

Collins, Philip (ed.). *Charles Dickens: The Public Readings*. Clarendon Press, 1975.

Fielding, K. J. (ed.). *The Speeches of Charles Dickens*. Clarendon Press, 1960.

House, Madeline, Graham Storey, Kathleen Tillotson, et al. (eds.). *The Letters of Charles Dickens*. The Pilgrim Edition. Clarendon Press, 1965 to present.

Kaplan, Fred (ed.). *Charles Dickens's Book of Memoranda*. New York Public Library, 1981.

Slater, Michael (ed.). *"Sketches by Boz" and Other Early Papers, 1834–39*. The Dent Uniform Edition of Dickens' Journalism, vol. I. Ohio State University Press, 1994.

"The Amusements of the People" and Other Papers: Reports, Essays, and Reviews, 1834–51. The Dent Uniform Edition of Dickens' Journalism, vol. II. Ohio State University Press, 1996.

"Gone Astray" and Other Papers from "Household Words," 1851–59. The Dent Uniform Edition of Dickens' Journalism, vol. III. Ohio State University Press, 1998.

Stone, Harry (ed.). *Uncollected Writings from "Household Words," 1850–59*. 2 volumes. Indiana University Press, 1968.

Dickens's Working Notes for His Novels. University of Chicago Press, 1987.

Biography

Ackroyd, Peter. *Dickens*. HarperCollins, 1990.

Allen, Michael. *Charles Dickens' Childhood*. Macmillan, 1988.

Forster, John. *The Life of Charles Dickens*. Chapman and Hall, 1872–74.

Johnson, Edgar. *Charles Dickens: His Tragedy and Triumph*. 2 volumes. Simon and Schuster, 1952.

Kaplan, Fred. *Dickens: A Biography*. Avon, 1990.

Smith, Grahame. *Charles Dickens: A Literary Life*. Macmillan, 1996.

Tomalin, Claire. *The Invisible Woman: The Story of Nelly Ternan and Charles Dickens*. Viking, 1990.

Selected bibliography

Reference materials

Bentley, Nicolas, Michael Slater, and Nina Burgis (eds.). *The Dickens Index*. Oxford University Press, 1988.

Collins, Philip (ed.). *Dickens: The Critical Heritage*. Routledge and Barnes and Noble, 1971.

Lohrli, Anne. *"Household Words": A Weekly Journal 1850–1859. Conducted by Charles Dickens*. University of Toronto Press, 1973.

Newlin, George. *Everyone in Dickens*. 3 volumes. Greenwood Press, 1995.

Every Thing in Dickens. Greenwood Press, 1996.

Oppenlander, Ella Ann. *Dickens's "All the Year Round": Descriptive Index and Contributor List*. Whitston Publishing Company, 1975.

Page, Norman. *A Dickens Chronology*. Macmillan, 1988.

Schlicke, Paul (ed.). *Oxford Reader's Companion to Dickens*. Oxford University Press, 1999.

Readers may also wish to consult the useful series of Garland bibliographies on individual novels. Individual "Companions" are available for many of the novels in a valuable series published by Greenwood Press.

Periodicals

The Dickensian. London, 1905 to present.

Dickens Studies. Boston, MA: Emerson College, 1965–69. Continued as *Dickens Studies Annual: Essays on Victorian Fiction*. AMS Press, New York, 1970 to present. (Each volume of *DSA* contains a comprehensive review essay on the previous year's work in Dickens Studies.)

Dickens Studies Newsletter. Louisville, KY, 1970–1983. Continued as *Dickens Quarterly*. Amherst, MA, 1984 to present. (Each issue of *DQ* contains a checklist of recent work on Dickens, including new editions and scholarship.)

Collections of critical studies

Baumgarten, Murray and H. M. Daleski (eds.). *Homes and Homelessness in the Victorian Imagination*. AMS Press, 1998.

Bloom, Harold (ed.). *Charles Dickens*. Modern Critical Views. Chelsea House, 1987.

Christ, Carol T. and John O. Jordan (eds.). *Victorian Literature and the Victorian Visual Imagination*. University of California Press, 1995.

Connor, Steven (ed.). *Charles Dickens*. Longman Critical Readers. Longman, 1996.

Ford, George H. and Lauriat Lane, Jr. (eds.). *The Dickens Critics*. Cornell University Press, 1961.

Gross, John and Gabriel Pearson (eds.). *Dickens and the Twentieth Century*. Routledge and University of Toronto Press, 1962.

Hollington, Michael. *Charles Dickens: Critical Assessments*. 4 volumes. Helm, 1995.

Jordan, John O. and Robert L. Patten (eds.). *Literature in the Marketplace*. Cambridge University Press, 1995.

MacKay, Carol Hanbery (ed.). *Dramatic Dickens*. Macmillan, 1989.

Sadrin, Anny (ed.). *Dickens, Europe and the New Worlds*. Macmillan, 1999.

Schad, John (ed.). *Dickens Refigured: Bodies, Desires and Other Histories*. Manchester University Press, 1996.

Wall, Stephen (ed.). *Charles Dickens: A Critical Anthology*. Penguin, 1970.

General

Andrews, Malcolm. *Dickens and the Grown-Up Child*. University of Iowa Press, 1994.

Arac, Jonathan. *Commissioned Spirits: The Shaping of Social Motion in Dickens, Carlyle, Melville, and Hawthorne*. Rutgers University Press, 1979.

Axton, William. "'Keystone' Structure in Dickens' Serial Novels." *University of Toronto Quarterly* 37 (October, 1967), 31–50.

Baumgarten, Murray. "Calligraphy and Code: Writing in *Great Expectations*." *Dickens Studies Annual* 11 (1983), 61–72.

Bolton, H. Philip. *Dickens Dramatized*. G. K. Hall, 1987.

Bowen, John. *Other Dickens: Pickwick to Chuzzlewit*. Oxford University Press, 2000.

Brooks, Peter. "Repetition, Repression, and Return: the Plotting of *Great Expectations*," *Reading for the Plot: Design and Intention in Narrative*. Knopf, 1984.

Butt, John and Kathleen Tillotson. *Dickens at Work*. Methuen, 1957.

Carey, John. *The Violent Effigy: A Study of Dickens' Imagination*. Faber, 1973.

Chittick, Kathryn. *Dickens and the 1830s*. Cambridge University Press, 1990.

Cohen, Jane R. *Charles Dickens and His Original Illustrators*. Ohio State University Press, 1980.

Collins, Philip. *Dickens and Crime*. St. Martin's Press, 1962.

Dickens and Education. Macmillan, 1963.

Connor, Steven. *Charles Dickens*. Blackwell, 1985.

Daleski, H. M. *Dickens and the Art of Analogy*. Schocken, 1970.

Davis, Paul. *The Lives and Times of Ebenezer Scrooge*. Yale University Press, 1990.

Dever, Carolyn. *Death and the Mother from Dickens to Freud*. Cambridge University Press, 1998.

Duncan, Ian. *Modern Romance and Transformations of the Novel: The Gothic, Scott, and Dickens*. Cambridge University Press, 1990.

Eigner, Edwin. *The Dickens Pantomime*. University of California Press, 1989.

Eisenstein, Sergei. "Dickens, Griffith, and the Film Today." In *Film Form: Essays in Film Theory*, edited and translated by Jay Leyda. Harcourt Brace, 1949.

Flint, Kate. *Dickens*. Harvester, 1986.

Frank, Lawrence. *Charles Dickens and the Romantic Self*. University of Nebraska Press, 1984.

Frye, Northrop. "Dickens and the Comedy of Humors." In *Experience in the Novel*, Selected Papers from the English Institute, edited by Roy Harvey Pearce. Columbia University Press, 1968, pp. 49–81.

Gallagher, Catherine. "The Bio-Economics of *Our Mutual Friend*." In *Fragments for a History of the Human Body*, vol. III, edited by Michel Feher. Zone, 1989.

The Industrial Reformation of English Fiction: Social Discourse and Narrative Form, 1832–1867. University of Chicago Press, 1985.

Garis, Robert. *The Dickens Theatre.* Clarendon Press, 1965.

Glavin, John. *After Dickens: Reading, Adaptation, and Performance.* Cambridge University Press, 1999.

Hochman, Baruch and Ilja Wachs. *Dickens: The Orphan Condition.* Fairleigh Dickinson University Press, 1999.

House, Humphry. *The Dickens World.* Oxford University Press, 1941.

Ingham, Patricia. *Dickens, Women and Language.* Harvester/Wheatsheaf, 1992.

Jaffe, Audrey. "Spectacular Sympathy: Visuality and Ideology in Dickens's *A Christmas Carol.*" *PMLA* 109 (1994), 254–65.

Vanishing Points: Dickens, Narrative, and the Subject of Omniscience. University of California Press, 1991.

Jordan, John O. "The Purloined Handkerchief." *Dickens Studies Annual* 18 (1989), 1–17.

Kaplan, Fred. *Dickens and Mesmerism: The Hidden Springs of Fiction.* Princeton University Press, 1975.

Kincaid, James. *Dickens and the Rhetoric of Laughter.* Clarendon Press, 1971.

Kucich, John. "Dickens' Fantastic Rhetoric: Semantics of Reality and Unreality in *Our Mutual Friend.*" *Dickens Studies Annual* 14 (1985), 167–90.

Repression in Victorian Fiction: Charlotte Brontë, George Eliot, and Charles Dickens. University of California Press, 1987.

Langbauer, Laurie. "Dickens's Streetwalkers: Women and the Form of Romance." *ELH* 53 (1986), 411–31.

Larson, Janet L. *Dickens and the Broken Scripture.* University of Georgia Press, 1985.

Leavis, F. R. and Q. D. Leavis. *Dickens the Novelist.* Chatto and Windus, 1970.

Manning, Sylvia. *Dickens as Satirist.* Yale University Press, 1971.

Marcus, Steven. *Dickens: From Pickwick to Dombey.* Chatto and Windus, 1965.

"Language into Structure: *Pickwick* Revisited." *Daedalus* 101 (1972), 183–202.

Marsh, Joss. "Inimitable Double Vision: Dickens, *Little Dorrit*, Photography, Film." *Dickens Studies Annual* 22 (1993), 239–82.

Meckier, Jerome. *Hidden Rivalries in Victorian Fiction: Dickens, Realism, and Revaluation.* University Press of Kentucky, 1987.

Michie, Helena. "'Who Is This in Pain?': Scarring, Disfigurement, and Female Identity in *Bleak House* and *Our Mutual Friend.*" *Novel* 22 (1989), 199–212.

Miller, Andrew H. "Rearranging the Furniture of *Our Mutual Friend*," *Novels Behind Glass: Commodity, Culture, and Victorian Narrative.* Cambridge University Press, 1995.

Miller, D. A. *The Novel and the Police.* University of California Press, 1988.

Miller, J. Hillis. *Charles Dickens: The World of His Novels.* Harvard University Press, 1958.

"The Fiction of Realism: *Sketches by Boz, Oliver Twist*, and Cruikshank's Illustrations," *Charles Dickens and George Cruikshank.* W. A. Clark Memorial Library, University of California Press, 1971, pp. 1–69.

"Introduction" to *Bleak House*, edited by Norman Page. Penguin, 1971. Reprinted as "Interpretation in Dickens' *Bleak House*," *Victorian Subjects.* Duke University Press, 1991, pp. 179–99.

Moglen, Helene. "Theorizing Fiction/Fictionalizing Theory: the Case of *Dombey and Son.*" *Victorian Studies* 35 (1992), 159–84.

Morgentaler, Goldie. *Dickens and Heredity.* Macmillan, 2000.

Moynahan, Julian. "The Hero's Guilt: the Case of *Great Expectations.*" *Essays in Criticism* 10 (1960), 60–79.

Newsom, Robert. *Charles Dickens Revisited.* Twayne, 2000.

   Dickens on the Romantic Side of Familiar Things: Bleak House and the Novel Tradition. Columbia University Press, 1977.

   "The Hero's Shame." *Dickens Studies Annual* 11 (1983), 1–24.

Nunokawa, Jeff. *The Afterlife of Property: Domestic Security and the Victorian Novel.* Princeton University Press, 1994.

Orwell, George. "Charles Dickens." In *Dickens, Dali and Others: Studies in Popular Culture.* Reynal and Hitchcock, 1946.

Patten, Robert L. *Charles Dickens and His Publishers.* Clarendon Press, 1978.

   George Cruikshank's Life, Times, and Art. 2 volumes. Rutgers University Press, 1992–96.

Pointer, Michael. *Charles Dickens on the Screen: The Film, Television, and Video Adaptations.* Scarecrow Press, 1996.

Polhemus, Robert. *Comic Faith.* University of Chicago Press, 1980.

Poovey, Mary. "Reading History in Literature: Speculation and Virtue in *Our Mutual Friend.*" In *Historical Criticism and the Challenge of Theory*, edited by Janet Levarie Smarr. University of Illinois Press, 1993.

   Uneven Developments: The Ideological Work of Gender in Mid-Victorian England. University of Chicago Press, 1988.

Pope, Norris. *Dickens and Charity.* Columbia University Press, 1978.

Sadoff, Dianne F. *Monsters of Affection: Dickens, Eliot, and Brontë on Fatherhood.* Johns Hopkins University Press, 1982.

Sadrin, Anny. *Parentage and Inheritance in the Novels of Charles Dickens.* Cambridge University Press, 1994.

Sanders, Andrew. *Dickens and the Spirit of the Age.* Clarendon Press, 1999.

Schlicke, Paul. *Dickens and Popular Entertainment.* Allen and Unwin, 1985.

Schor, Hilary. *Dickens and the Daughter of the House.* Cambridge University Press, 1999.

Schwarzbach, F. S. *Dickens and the City.* Athlone Press, 1979.

Sedgwick, Eve Kosofsky. "Homophobia, Misogyny, and Capital: the Example of *Our Mutual Friend*," *Between Men.* Columbia University Press, 1985, pp. 161–79.

Slater, Michael. *Dickens and Women.* Stanford University Press, 1983.

Steig, Michael. *Dickens and Phiz.* Indiana University Press, 1978.

Stewart, Garrett. *Dickens and the Trials of Imagination.* Harvard University Press, 1974.

   Death Sentences: Styles of Dying in British Fiction. Harvard University Press, 1984.

Sutherland, John L. *Victorian Novelists and Publishers.* University of Chicago Press and Athlone Press, 1976.

Tambling, Jeremy. *Dickens, Violence, and the Modern State.* St. Martin's Press, 1995.

Tillotson, Kathleen. *Novels of the 1840s.* Oxford University Press, 1954.

Trilling, Lionel. "*Little Dorrit.*" *Kenyon Review* 15 (1953), 577–90. Reprinted as "Introduction," the New Oxford Illustrated edition of *Little Dorrit.* Oxford

University Press, 1953. And as "*Little Dorrit,*" *The Opposing Self*. Viking Press, 1955.

Vanden Bossche, Chris R. "Cookery, not Rookery: Family and Class in *David Copperfield.*" *Dickens Studies Annual* 15 (1986), 87–109.

Van Ghent, Dorothy. "The Dickens World: a View from Todgers's." *Sewanee Review* 58 (1950), 419–38.

Waters, Catherine. *Dickens and the Politics of the Family*. Cambridge University Press, 1997.

Watt, Ian. "Oral Dickens." *Dickens Studies Annual* 3 (1974), 165–81.

Welsh, Alexander. *The City of Dickens*. Clarendon Press, 1971.

From Copyright to Copperfield: The Identity of Dickens. Harvard University Press, 1987.

Wilson, Edmund. "Dickens: the Two Scrooges," *The Wound and the Bow*. Oxford University Press, 1941.

INDEX

Page numbers of illustrations are in italics. Discussion within chapter endnotes is indicated by "n" and the number of the note.

Index